Social Entrepreneurship

What motivates someone to become a social entrepreneur? What are the competencies needed to be effective social advocates and agents for change? This book answers these questions in an accessible and practical way, providing comprehensive guidelines, numerous examples, and sources of information and training for anyone who wants to start a community-based social advocacy and change initiative or for employees who want to start a corporate social responsibility initiative.

Features include the following:

- Examples of individuals and organizations who have learned from successes and failures in social entrepreneurship
- Self-assessments to help readers evaluate their own talents and proclivity to be social entrepreneurs
- Steps and strategies, competency-building activities, and assessments to evaluate and facilitate initiatives
- Resources available from foundations, government agencies, and other sources for the budding social entrepreneur.

Social Entrepreneurship

How to Start Successful Corporate
Social Responsibility and
Community-Based Initiatives for
Advocacy and Change

**Manuel London and
Richard G. Morfopoulos**

Routledge
Taylor & Francis Group

NEW YORK AND LONDON

First published 2010
by Routledge
270 Madison Avenue, New York, NY 10016

Simultaneously published in the UK
by Routledge
2 Park Square, Milton Park, Abingdon, Oxon OX14 4RN

Routledge is an imprint of the Taylor & Francis Group, an informa business

© 2010 Taylor & Francis

Typeset in Sabon by HWA Text and Data Management, London
Printed and bound in the United States of America on acid-free paper by
Sheridan Books, Inc.

Library of Congress Cataloging in Publication Data
London, Manuel.
   Social entrepreneurship: How to start successful corporate social
   responsibility and community-based initiatives for advocacy and change.
   Manuel London and Richard G. Morfopoulos.
       p. cm.
   Includes bibliographical references and index.
   1. Social entrepreneurship. 2. Social responsibility of business.
   I. Morfopoulos, Richard G. II. Title.
   HD60.L66 2009
   361.7068'1–dc22   2009025513

ISBN10: 0-415-80128-1 (hbk)
ISBN10: 0-415-80129-X (pbk)
ISBN10: 0-203-87814-0 (ebk)

ISBN13: 978-0-415-80128-7 (hbk)
ISBN13: 978-0-415-80129-4 (pbk)
ISBN13: 978-0-203-87814-9 (ebk)

For Marilyn, David, and Jared London; Melissa Vineski; and Charles, Frances, Mark, and Andrew Morfopoulos

Contents

Preface

This book is about skills and methods for social change. The focus is on social entrepreneurship—an umbrella term that covers social action initiatives that start in companies and communities. You may start a social action initiative as a corporate employee, elected government official, nonprofit agency leader, university student, and/or community activist. Effective social action requires motivation and skills that are important for any entrepreneurial endeavor. Social entrepreneurs are motivated by a passion to help others and themselves. They believe in their own ability to overcome barriers and accomplish good deeds. They have skills to motivate and influence others to volunteer, make contributions, or make decisions to bring about change. Social entrepreneurs see a problem and are motivated to do something about it, usually finding ways to involve those who stand to benefit from the advocacy process. Goals may focus on environmental cleanup and protection, health and wellness, poverty, or education. Social advocacy and change bring public attention to a social need, change opinions, obtain resources, perhaps by influencing legislation or collecting donations, and/or deliver services.

Social entrepreneurs may be people who encourage their companies to support a social cause. Corporate social responsibility initiatives may have spin-off benefits for both the company and the people the initiatives help. Social entrepreneurship may also occur in communities as people create initiatives to help others, seeking a variety of sources of support and in partnership with other organizations. Social entrepreneurs may form an organization, for instance a foundation, not-for-profit agency, or nongovernmental organization, thereby embedding the initiative in a sustainable enterprise. They may start a for-profit business that addresses a social problem. Concerned citizens may band together in an informal group to address a social need. The beneficiaries may be local (e.g., homeless in a local town) or global, as when individuals in one community or organizations in a Western country raise money to redress poverty in a village in Africa. Social initiatives may require partnerships of local citizens working with companies, governments, and nongovernmental organizations to address the need.

Social entrepreneurs go out of their way to do something they do not have to do. They see a problem and initiate action. They take it upon themselves to be responsible and accountable. They envision a solution and make it happen. This may be a one-time initiative or it may become a lasting organization. There are many well-known examples of such people and their initiatives. Some have national and, indeed, international reputations. Others are more local, becoming vital support enterprises in their communities.

This book is a multi-level approach to social entrepreneurship. That is, we cover individual and organizational perspectives. We consider what motivates someone to be a social entrepreneur and the competencies people need to be effective social advocates and change agents. We describe how to identify and elicit the support of stakeholders (including supporters and volunteers, decision makers, beneficiaries, and naysayers who can hinder an initiative), and how to evaluate, sustain, and develop these initiatives. We also examine corporate and organizational strategies and structures for social entrepreneurship.

The book is for people who want to be social entrepreneurs themselves and start organizations to promote a cause or solve a problem, engendering the support of their companies and/or communities. It is also for corporate managers and executives, local government officials, and managers of support agencies who want to encourage social change initiates at the grass roots level. The book will guide high school and university students who want to contribute community service and develop their leadership skills. In addition, the book will be of interest to faculty and organizational development consultants who facilitate service learning, leadership development, and organization change. As such, the book can be used by individuals who want to be social entrepreneurs. It can be used in college courses on service learning, organization behavior, entrepreneurship, and advocacy in departments of business, social welfare, psychology, and sociology. It can be used in community workshops, corporate social responsibility task forces, and university peer mentoring programs.

Special features of this book include examples of individuals and organizations who learn from successes and failures, self-assessments to help readers evaluate their own talents and proclivity to be social entrepreneurs, steps and strategies for implementation, competency building activities, assessment and facilitation methods to evaluate and facilitate initiatives, and resources available from foundations, the government, and other sources.

Overview

In Chapter 1, we give examples of different types of social entrepreneurship. We see how these efforts emerge from the insights and passion of individuals engaged in corporate social responsibility programs and community action groups. Some efforts support other activities, such as matching donors to beneficiaries, providing fellowships to people who initiate creative efforts for social change, and generating venture capital funds to invest in socially responsible for-profit firms.

The next two chapters are about understanding individual characteristics that motivate people to get involved in social entrepreneurship and the skills and competencies that they have, or develop, to help them succeed. The chapters help would-be social entrepreneurs evaluate their own motivation and abilities to give them self-insight, recognize their strengths and weaknesses, and develop activities to help them improve. In particular, Chapter 2 focuses on motivation. It describes components of what we call *social entrepreneurship orientation*. This is a combination of altruism, strength of conviction and beliefs, self-efficacy, resilience, and insight. Chapter 3 covers social entrepreneurship skills and competencies. Transactional skills include communicating, planning, organizing, directing, and controlling. Transformational skills include envisioning, communicating, engaging, empowering, networking, and coalition building. Competencies are combinations of skills and experiences that are needed to take effective action. Social entrepreneurship competencies include knowing how to build awareness, market social causes, influence public opinion and policies (corporate and government), collect resources (e.g., fund raising), form alliances and networks, conduct research to understand issues and reactions to them, establish and build an organization, recruit and retain volunteers, set and meet goals, deliver services, and sustain the initiative.

The next chapter moves the book from a focus on individuals to a focus on organizational methods. Chapter 4 describes the steps of social entrepreneurship as a cycle of envisioning, formulating, taking action, evaluating, and sustaining. Building on Chapters 2 and 3, Chapter 4 shows how to use individual competencies at each step of the social entrepreneurship process. The chapter covers key strategies for effective social entrepreneurship. Strategies vary depending on the leaders' assumptions, for instance, whether to change others' opinions and behaviors or build new systems and ways of taking action that don't depend on people who currently control resources. Other strategies depend on the social entrepreneur's assumptions about whether people respond to information and facts or emotions surrounding possible gains or losses and threats.

Chapter 5 is about how to develop high-performing teams of volunteers. This is often difficult because people get involved for different reasons, sometime for personal motives along with a desire to help. Also, people may disagree about goals and methods. The chapter covers ways teams evolve and learn to be more effective, sometimes transforming themselves and their organizations in new and different directions.

Chapter 6 is about overcoming barriers. This includes how to deal with wayward members who don't follow direction or seem to have selfish goals that do not serve the organization well. Other barriers are naysayers in the community, sometimes people who control needed votes, money, and other resources. The chapter covers how to maintain motivation in the face of barriers, where to find new resources, and how to seek advice and facilitation.

Chapter 7 covers how to track and evaluate the success of the initiative. Corporate social responsibility efforts are measured by indexes called corporate social performance. The chapter describes different criteria of outcome and process effectiveness. We give examples of methods to measures these criteria and how to collect measures over time to evaluate social change. This includes establishing evaluation worksheets and feedback mechanisms and working with stakeholders to seek continuous improvement.

The last chapter considers examples of excellence in social entrepreneurship, sources of information and training on social entrepreneurship, curricula for workshops and courses on social entrepreneurship, and challenges in implementing social entrepreneurship ideas.

Each chapter in the book ends with one or more exercises to help you develop ideas for social ventures as part of corporate social responsibility initiatives or as stand-alone for-profit or not-for-profit social entrepreneurship efforts. As you proceed through the exercises, you will develop the components you need for a comprehensive business plan.

Acknowledgements

We are grateful to our colleagues who supported our efforts to promote and learn about social entrepreneurship, specifically, at Stony Brook: Dr. Charles Robbins, faculty director of the Community Service Living Learning Center and Associate Dean of the School of Social Welfare; Jonathan Ragone, Residence Hall Quad Director for the Undergraduate College of Leadership and Service; Militta East and Candace O'Neill, both undergraduate advisors for the Undergraduate College of Leadership and Service; and Urszula Zalewski, director of Volunteers for Community Service; and at Briarcliffe College: Dr. Mitchell Laube and Catherine Tyrie.

About the Authors

Manuel London, PhD, is Professor of Management and Associate Dean of the College of Business at the State University of New York at Stony Brook. He is also Director of both the Undergraduate College of Leadership and Service, and the Center for Human Resource Management. He received his PhD in organizational psychology from the Ohio State University. His areas of research are performance management and work group development, 360-degree feedback, and advocacy processes. Recent books include *Continuous Learning* (with Valerie Sessa, 2006, Erlbaum) and *First Time Leaders of Small Groups* (with Marilyn London, 2007, Jossey-Bass).

Richard G. Morfopoulos is Associate Professor of Management at Briarcliffe College. He received his PhD in organizational studies from the State University of New York at Albany. His areas of research are social entrepreneurship, innovation, business ethics, and support for employees with disabilities. He has published in *Human Resource Management Review*, *Business Horizons*, and the *International Journal of Social Entrepreneurship*.

About the Author

1 An Introduction to Social Entrepreneurship

In this chapter, you will learn how to do the following:

1 Identify needs for social action locally and globally
2 Define social entrepreneurship and corporate social responsibility (CSR)
3 Give examples of competent, creative social entrepreneurs
4 Recognize the different structures for non-profit and for-profit social entrepreneurship
5 Cite the benefits of CSR initiatives to the companies and the recipients of their efforts
6 Use this book to improve your chances of success as a social entrepreneur in your company, developing CSR initiatives, or in your community, developing programs to help yourself and others

Introduction

If I am not for myself, who will be for me?
If I am only for myself, what am I?
If not now, when?

Hillel

One of the great liabilities of history is that all too many people fail to remain awake through great periods of social change. Every society has its protectors of status quo and its fraternities of the indifferent who are notorious for sleeping through revolutions. Today, our very survival depends on our ability to stay awake, to adjust to new ideas, to remain vigilant and to face the challenge of change.

Rev. Dr. Martin Luther King, Jr.
(King, 1967, p. 171)

Be grateful for social entrepreneurs. They are driven by an overarching desire to improve society, and they create for-profit or not-for-profit ventures to do so.

They identify problems and help solve them. They resolve injustices, feed the hungry, educate the illiterate, raise money for research to cure disease, and protect our environment. They are movers and shakers—people who are not satisfied with the status quo and are always trying to make things better. They care, and they are action-oriented. They act locally and globally. They work one-to-one, helping friends and strangers. They organize coalitions and institutions. They raise funds, influence decision makers, recruit volunteers, and organize resources (GSVC, 2007).

Entrepreneurship is "...the scholarly examination of how, by whom, and with what effect opportunities to create future goods and services are discovered, evaluated, and exploited" (Shane & Venkataram, 2000, p. 219). Entrepreneurs establish enterprises to implement innovations (Peredo & McClean, 2006). *Social entrepreneurs* recognize a social problem and organize, create, and manage a venture to make social change (Leadbeater, 1997).

Entrepreneurs recognize opportunities where others see chaos or confusion. They start enterprises, create jobs, support economic development, and improve quality of life (Kuratko & Hodgetts, 2004). Entrepreneurs are risk takers (Hisrich, Peters, & Shepard, 2005). Entrepreneurs discover market needs and then take necessary actions to meet those needs (Longenecker *et al.*, 2008). They are independent, creative, hard-working, and resilient. Social entrepreneurs possess these qualities, too. Social entrepreneurs are "hybrids": They seek profit that benefits other parties besides merely themselves. They apply approaches to social and environmental concerns that respect the bottom line (GSVC, 2007).

According to management guru Peter Drucker, entrepreneurs search for change, respond to it, and exploit it as an opportunity (Dees, 1998a, 1998b). Unlike business entrepreneurship for whom the primary purpose is wealth creation, the primary goal for the social entrepreneur is mission-related impact. Wealth may be a means to an end, not a way to measure value creation (Dees, 1998b).

The Schwab Foundation for Social Entrepreneurship Web site (http://www.scwabfound.org/whatis.htm, 2007) describes social entrepreneurship as follows: Social entrepreneurship is:

1   about applying practical, innovative, and sustainable approaches to benefit society in general, with an emphasis on those who are marginalized and poor.

2   a term that captures a unique approach to economic and social
    problems, an approach that cuts across sectors and disciplines.

3   grounded in certain values and processes that are common to
    each social entrepreneur, independent of whether his/her area
    of focus has been education, health, welfare reform, human
    rights, worker's rights, environment, economic development,
    agriculture, etc., or whether the organizations they set up are
    non-profit or for-profit entities.

4   marked by individuals who share an unwavering belief in the
    innate capacity of all people to contribute meaningfully to
    economic and social development.

(Schwab Foundation for Social Entrepreneurship, 2007)

Bill Drayton, who founded Ashoka, aspired to "make everyone
a change-maker." Ashoka has been dedicated to promoting the
philosophy of social entrepreneurship across the globe for the last
quarter century. Ashoka sponsors ventures that launch a big idea over
time, to create a lifetime of high-impact, independent change-making.
They demonstrate that there is nothing more powerful than a big
picture-changing idea if it is in the hands of a first-class entrepreneur
(www.ashoka.org, 2006).

> What is the most powerful force in the world? And I think you
> would agree that is a big idea if it is in the hands of an entrepreneur
> who is actually going to make the idea not only happen, but spread
> all across society. And we understand that in business but we have
> need for entrepreneurship just as much in education, human
> rights, health, and the environment as we do in hotels and steel.
>
> Bill Drayton (http://www.ashoka.org/node/1027)

Social entrepreneurship "...combines the passion of a social
mission with an image of business-like discipline, innovation, and
determination commonly associated with, for instance, the high-tech
pioneers of Silicon Valley" (Dees, 1998b, p. 1).

The term *social entrepreneurship* has been used in a variety of ways
(Dees, 1998a, b). Some apply the term to not-for-profit organizations
starting for-profit or earned-income ventures. Others apply it to any
not-for-profit organization. Another reference is to business owners
who integrate social responsibility into their organizations (what we
refer to as "corporate social responsibility").

This book is about the people who repair the world. They are
motivated to help others. They have pro-social and altruistic attitudes
and personalities. They use their entrepreneurial skills to create

organizations (big and small) to meet social needs—their own and others. It is about the individual characteristics that prompt people to start social ventures and the methods and strategies they use to implement, sustain, and evaluate these ventures.

Opportunities for Social Entrepreneurship

Consider the wide range of needs that are ripe for social entrepreneurship and examples of on-going initiatives to address them:

- Environmental protection and quality: Organizations such as the Sierra Club devote their energies to protecting the sanctity of the ecosystem (see http://www.sierraclub.org).
- Health care—fight and prevent disease: Consider the example of Thursday's Child of Long Island in Patchogue, New York. They assist people suffering from HIV-AIDS in the local community, including advocacy, referral, education, and outreach (see http://www.thursdayschildofli.org).
- Community safety and security: For instance, the Community Safety Network located in Jackson Hole, Wyoming, that provides shelter and support to individuals suffering from domestic violence (see http://www.communitysafetynetwork.org).
- Education: The Association on Higher Education and Disability (AHEAD) promotes the welfare of post-secondary students with disabilities (see http://www.ahead.org).
- Arts, culture, and humanities: Consider the Diversity & Multiculturalism Business Center (DMBC). The mission of the DMBC is to provide students and workers of all ages with information related to the business study of diversity and multiculturalism on a regional, national, and international level (see http://mdbaonthemove.com/).
- Social Justice (e.g., fight bias and adverse discrimination, support civil liberties, lobby for pay equity, and promote civic engagement): ERASE Racism, Long Island, New York, is dedicated to eliminating discrimination through advocacy and educational programs (see http://www.eraseracismny.org).
- Hunger and poverty—promote economic development, provide job training: Think about the Veteran's Administration providing vocational assistance to veterans. Another example is the Robin Hood Foundation. Its goal is to reduce poverty in New York City by finding and funding the best and most effective programs and partnering with them to maximize the results. Here's a bit more information about them: Founded in 1988 with on-going support

from major philanthropists and the general public, the foundation aims to apply sound investment principles to the organizations they help. They have a three-pronged strategy: (1) Attack root causes by preventing poverty through supporting programs in early childhood, youth, education, jobs/economic security, health care, hunger, housing, and domestic violence; they apply an extensive due-diligence process to ensure that the programs they support are generating results; (2) add value to their investment by providing expert management and technical assistance for strategic and financial planning, recruiting and legal needs, organizational issues, and capital needs; they rely on in-house experts and outside consultants who work pro bono; and (3) get results by evaluating outcomes and holding programs accountable for achieving specific, measurable goals (see http://www.robinhood.org).

Global Issues

Communities and countries suffering from economic decline are likely to need both economic and social regeneration (Thompson, Alvy, & Lees, 2000). Here are some examples of individuals and organizations that address global issues:

- The goal of the World of Good Development Organization is to eliminate poverty and structurally improve the quality of life for artisans in very-low-income craft-producing communities around the world. They achieve this by partnering with businesses and nonprofits to build a stronger fair trade crafts movement in the United States, promoting international standards for fair trade crafts and investing in economic and social development projects in craft producer communities (http://www.worldofgood.org, Emeryville, California).

- India's Foundation for Inclusion Growth was founded by Nachiket Mor to bring banking and business services to India's underserved. The foundation, part of Industrial Credit and Investment Corporation of India Limited, India's second largest bank, underwrites other nonprofit groups in their efforts to provide microloans, insurance, and other business and banking services to more than 600 million Indians living in poverty. The new model of microfinance that Mor proposes is that partners will now serve as intermediaries to direct efforts to provide microfinance in poor communities. The foundation mentors these partners, such as the Institute for Financial Management and Research (IFMR), which charges local savings branches 11 percent interest on savings that the IFMR pays 9 percent interest to receive. Mor's foundation also serves as an advisor to poor families, providing key information to help them take advantage of their situations. For instance, one project helped families establish bed-and-breakfast lodgings in the foothills of the Himalayas.

- Muhammad Yunus revolutionized economics by founding the Grameen Bank ("village bank") in Bangladesh in 1976 to offer "microloans" to help impoverished people attain economic self-sufficiency through self-employment, a model that has been replicated in 58 countries around the world.

- Seth Goldman founded Honest Tea in 1998. The company seeks to build communities and create an environmentally healthful product. Honest Tea is certified organic and kosher and the company works with fair-trade farms that practice sustainable farming and demonstrate respect to their workers (see http://www.honesttea. com).

- For more than 20 years, Synergos, headquartered in New York City, has addressed the underlying causes of poverty and inequity in Africa, Asia, and the Americas. The organization addresses a need in a particular region of the world by forming partnerships among governments, businesses, civil society organizations, and individual leaders and philanthropists. The process strengthens local leadership as it builds capacity and institutions to participate in those partnerships and help develop local solutions to overcome poverty and promote social justice (www.synergos.org).

- The Institute for Sustainable Communities, headquartered in Montpelier, Vermont, is in the business of "unleashing the power of people to transform their communities." Similar to Synergos, it ensures that solutions emerge from within the community rather than being imposed from the outside. Efforts combine technical expertise and leadership training with strategic investments in local organizations. Founded in 1991 by former Vermont Governor Madeleine M. Kunin, the Institute for Sustainable Communities has established efforts that support anticorruption, environmental protection, disability rights, economic policy, support for marginalized groups, HIV/AIDS, tobacco control, youth development, and energy sufficiency (www.iscvt.org).

- Ashoka was founded in 1981 by Bill Drayton in Washington, DC (now headquartered in Arlington, Virginia). Drayton was one of the early pioneers of social entrepreneurship as a field. Ashoka is a global organization that identifies and invests in leading social entrepreneurs who have innovative and practical ideas for solving challenging social problems (www.ashoka.org).

- Eddie Bergman founded Miracle Corners of the World, headquartered in New York City, to promote the motto: "Global Exchange for Local Change." The organization finds local communities around the world that need assistance—for instance, a new school, a well, an orphanage, a health clinic—and they work with local organizers to implement and sustain the effort (www.miraclecorners.org).
- Pattye Pece and her friends started the Sobornost (Russian for cooperation between multiple forces or togetherness) Foundation to operate a fair trade store in Hampton Bays, New York. The store is run by all volunteers. They sell only fair trade goods, products for which producers and growers in third world countries paid employees a fair wage. (For information about fair trade products, see http://www.fairtradefederation.org.) The Foundation gives all profits to orphanages in Kenya and Zambia (see www.fairtrademarket.org).

Toward a Deeper Understanding of Social Entrepreneurship

"Social entrepreneurs combine approaches of business and social welfare. They identify under-utilized resources—people, buildings, equipment—and find ways of putting them to use to satisfy unmet social needs" (Leadbeater, 1997, p. 2). They bridge gaps between social needs and current services. They apply entrepreneurship skills, going beyond the traditional role of the public sector, to innovate practices and structures to find solutions to pervasive social problems. Examples may be an AIDS care center, a drug treatment program, a tenants' cooperative, or a youth center (some of the examples described by Leadbeater, 1997). Social entrepreneurs, like business entrepreneurs, are driven, ambitious leaders. They are skilled in communicating their vision, inspiring the clients, staff, and volunteers, and often have ambitious goals. They establish organizations that are flexible, with flat, lean organizational structures, having strong cultures of creativity and openness, in contrast to rigid, bureaucratic structures of government agencies. They combine resources from several sources that are usually separate, corporate, government, and nonprofit. They strive for long-term relationships, creating a sense of identity and belonging on the part of their clients and volunteers. They create value by innovating new solutions to difficult if not intractable social problems, delivering services more efficiently than government. Also, they help establish complex, open, and dynamic networks and partnerships to bring together all kinds of resources, including education, health care, and employee training (Leadbeater, 1997). The social entrepreneur is at the heart of the organization, setting the tone for openness and innovation. This often leads to a wider mission than was initially intended, serving more clients, a larger geographical area, and/or a broader array of needs. The purpose of the venture may change over time as needs are redressed and the organization's capability is applied to emerging needs.

Social entrepreneurs are social activists, advocates for themselves and others, and developers of for-profit businesses and not-for-profit organizations that have a social mission. Their actions help others, directly by providing a social service or indirectly by raising money, lobbying policy makers, and conveying information that generates awareness of social issues and needs. "Social entrepreneurship encompasses the activities and processes undertaken to discover, define, and exploit opportunities in order to enhance social wealth by creating new ventures or managing existing organizations in an innovative manner" (Zahra *et al.*, 2008, p. 118). Social entrepreneurs are ordinary people who conceive innovative ideas, organize production, assume risk, and engage customers to accumulate wealth or address pressing social issues (Zahra *et al.*, 2008). They launch new organizations that serve a multitude of social needs and improve the quality of life and enhance human development around the world (Zahra *et al.* 2008). Social entrepreneurs are not easily discouraged and are not governed by the "status quo." We focus on why and how such entrepreneurs select particular social causes through the creation of new ventures.

The ingredients of successful social entrepreneurship are (1) characteristics of the social entrepreneur, (2) the nature of the organization they create, (3) the organization's interaction with its complex environment, which usually includes multiple stakeholders, and (4) the cycle of social capital (initial vision, network of contacts, generation of fiscal and physical resources, organization structure, recruitment and training of volunteers and staff, and service delivery) (Leadbeater, 1997).

Social entrepreneurship is a "...process involving the innovative use and combination of resources to pursue opportunities to catalyze social change and/or address social needs" (Mair & Martí, 2006, p. 37). There are three elements to this process: (1) creating value by combining resources in new ways, (2) exploration and exploitation of opportunities to stimulate social change or meet social needs, and (3) offering services and products and creating new organizations (Mair & Martí).

Social entrepreneurship differs from business entrepreneurship in giving relatively higher priority to promoting social value and development rather than increasing economic value (Mair & Mati, 2006). The principal focus is social value, with economic value creation needed to ensure financial viability. Of course, business organizations can have social performance goals. "Entrepreneurship is particularly productive from a social welfare perspective when, in the process of pursuing selfish ends, entrepreneurs also enhance social wealth by creating new markets, new industries, new technology, new institutional forms, new jobs, and net increases in real productivity" (Venkataraman, 1997, p. 133). In business entrepreneurship, social value is a by-product of the economic value that results but, in social entrepreneurship, the main focus is creating social value, not whether the organization is not-for-profit or for-profit.

The field of social entrepreneurship is blossoming. Organizations such as Ashoka are paving the way for aspiring entrepreneurs interested in profiting from socially responsive products and/or services. Ashoka supports "extraordinary individuals with unprecedented ideas for change in their communities. ... Ashoka's vision is that of a global society that is able to respond quickly and effectively to challenges everywhere (ashoka.org)."

Michael Kahn, senior officer of TIAA-CREF (2005), the pension fund for professionals in academic, medical, cultural and research fields, defines social entrepreneurship as "the process of doing well (making profits) while doing good (for the community) ..." This sentiment is echoed in cyberspace by journalists such as Laura D'Andrea Tyson who opens her article on social entrepreneurship (*Business Week Online*, 5/3/04) as "Good Works—With a Business Plan."

To show that you can prosper as you help others, the University of California at Berkeley's School of Business established the Global Social Venture Competition. Students submit proposals for the competition that project both a financial rate of return and a social rate of return. Such business models that simultaneously generate sound financial returns and demonstrable social returns are enticing to socially minded business school students and investors (Tyson, 2004).

Nonprofits are starting to take advantage of increased revenue, focus, and effectiveness that can come from adopting 'for profit' business approaches (Dees, 1998b). Bill Strickland was a pioneer of this hybrid approach of nonprofits seeking revenue-producing enterprises to achieve their social goals. He founded the Manchester Craftsmen's Guild in 1968 to improve the economic and social conditions of youth in inner-city Pittsburgh. The Guild offered ceramics classes and a small exhibition space. The program expanded quickly and led to the creation of the Bidwell Training Center, a vocational education program serving mostly displaced steel workers from the same community (see http://www.manchesterbidwell.org,; http://www.bill-strickland.org/; Terry, 2007).

A major goal affecting the support of nonprofits in recent times is the very survival of the organizations that financial backers support. According to Paul C. Light, a professor of public service at New York University, efforts should focus on supporting organizations that are strong enough to survive. Under such circumstances, the need for leaders of nonprofits to engage in advocacy efforts has arguably never been greater. Charities will be most affected by the loss of corporate donors from financial services and other suffering industries and by a decrease of funds from city and state taxes and available government grants.

The social entrepreneur as agent of change is an integral part of the community and social context. Social entrepreneurs who wish to bring the resources of their employers to bear on a social problem may not have smooth sailing. Being embedded in an organization helps gain access to resources and win legitimacy. However, such intentions may deviate from the company's current operations or threaten ongoing services and so may not gain support from existing stakeholders. As a result, it may be easier for individuals than existing corporate entities to establish new social ventures and radical social innovations with unspecified or defined social missions or business models (Zahra *et al.*, 2008). When social entrepreneurs are not embedded in organizations, they may be more likely to engage in social action that challenges rules and norms since they are not encumbered by an existing structure (Mair & Martí, 2006). In providing access to resources, embeddedness helps gain critical resources during start-up, development, and implementation steps; however, embeddedness may have a negative effect during the intention formation stage when the entrepreneur decides whether or not to embark on the challenge (Mair & Martí).

Structures for Social Entrepreneurship

In communities, social entrepreneurship happens when people take action to support social welfare. They may band together to form action groups to protect land, create a public park instead of another strip mall. They may open a homeless shelter or soup kitchen. They may organize a walk to raise money for scientific research to cure cancer, MS, or autism. Professionals act to help others. Dentists may volunteer to provide badly needed care to children in Madagascar, flying in with a team of students to deliver care in makeshift clinics. A college sorority may organize a book drive to help a one-room school in Peru. A high school may organize a car wash and bake sale to raise money to support rebuilding homes in New Orleans and then travel there on spring break to help build them.

There are a host of organizational structures for social entrepreneurship. Consider the following:

- CSR efforts, sometimes through foundations that are established by the company, to "give back" as part of their corporate mission. Examples are Ronald McDonald House, Starbuck's Fair Trade products, and community efforts of a company such as Henry Schein, the medical supplies distributor. These organizations may have profit and shareholder value as their primary mission, but they adopt social performance goals, recognizing that such goals are good for their financial bottom line, attracting customers and retaining valued employees.
- For-profit private enterprise established to devote profits to charity (e.g., Ben & Jerry's, Newman's Own). This is the so-called fourth sector of the economy or B corporations that mix profit and not-for-profit.
- For-profit, socially focused companies. These are for-profit companies that provide social benefit in such areas as health care, environment, and energy. *Business Week* asked readers to vote for the most promising social entrepreneurs who founded businesses that are trying to make money and bring about societal change (Leiber, 2009). Here are some examples:
  - Better World Books (the winner of the contest), a 200-person company based in Mishawaka, Indiana, sells donated books. The company donates profits to literacy programs and libraries, which in turn increases the demand. Currently, they sell about 10,000 books a day and anticipate $30 million in annual revenue (see http://www.betterworldbooks.com).
  - Big Belly Solar (coming in second in the *Business Week* popularity contest), a $4 million enterprise in Needham, Massachusetts, helps municipalities save time, money, and garbage truck usage by installing solar-powered trash compactors (see http://www.bigbellysolar.com).
  - Craft Network, founded by Christopher Benz in 2007 in New York and Bali, increases employment in poor communities by linking artist-producers with wholesale and retail customers (see http://www.craftnetowrk.com). The company employs 26 people, has exported goods from 1,355 artisans in 124 villages, and has annual revenue of more than $400,000.

- Pharma Jet in Golden, Colorado, intends to sell a needle-free injection device in third-world countries to prevent injury and disease (see http://www.pharmajet.com).
- Impact Makers of Richmond, Virginia, is a $300,000 annual revenue, nine-employee health care management and consulting company that develops disease management programs and performs IT work, systems consulting, and program audits. Its social goal is to provide free medication to the uninsured through its primary nonprofit partner RXpartnership.org (see http://www.impactmakers.org).
- Sam Goldman started D.light with the mission of marketing solar-powered lamps to replace millions of kerosene lamps now used in poor rural parts of the world (Alboher, 2009). This example shows that a social problem can be solved without creating a charity. Living in the Republic of Benin in Western Africa in the Peace Corp, Goldman discovered that kerosene is expensive, provides poor light, and is extremely dangerous. He believed that only a for-profit business, not a charity, could manufacture and sell enough lights to reach the large number of people who use kerosene as a primary source of light—and to do so quickly. His goal was to replace kerosene within the next 5 or 10 years, rather than the possibly 100 years it would take for charities to accomplish this goal. Goldman's company incorporated in 2007, raising $6.5M from a variety of investors. Wanting to be profitable does not require making decisions that diminish the quality of your program or limit your goals. Maximizing shareholder profit and public benefit can indeed be compatible. In the case of D.light, size produced economies of scale: the more units produced and sold, the cheaper the unit cost of the product (see http://dlightdesign.com/).
- Conchy Bretos, Florida's former secretary for aging and adult services. She formed MIA Consulting Group to address difficulties that older people face that force them to leave their homes and move into nursing homes (Alboher, 2009). Bretos's firm advises governments and private housing developers on how to bring assisted living services cost-effectively to low-income housing communities. A for-profit business model worked because the firm provided a service that no other firm was offering (see http://www.miaconsulting.com).
- Not-for-profit companies and institutions. Examples are Goodwill Industries, The Salvation Army, hospitals, hospices, and universities, often linked to the government through payment and

insurance plans. There are approximately 1.8 million registered nonprofit organizations, and nonprofit organizations generate annual revenue of more than $1 trillion and assets of more than $2 trillion and account for 5 percent to 10 percent of the United States's gross domestic product. Furthermore, more than 100 million adults do volunteer work (O'Neill, 2002).

- Not-for-profit companies that invest in or form for-profit enterprises. For example, a university that has an ownership stake in a business that grew from a faculty member's research.
- Social Service agencies, such as local nonprofit organizations that provide services for physically and mentally handicapped or mental health services often linked to the government through grants and fees for service.
- Non-governmental organizations (NGOs) providing lobbying and supporting initiatives around the world. Examples include the Acumen Fund designed to assist low-income people throughout the world.
- Charities and foundations: Heifer International, Habitat for Humanity, Ankizi Fund supporting education in Madagascar, American Cancer Foundation, and the March of Dimes).
- Religious organizations, student clubs in secondary schools and colleges, youth groups (e.g., Girl and Boy Scouts), and many other community organizations are involved in community service and help volunteers learn from their involvement (service learning). Religious organizations provide food pantries, help for the ill, and other forms of support for the needy. International community service clubs have a presence around the world to meet local community needs. Rotary International has more than 1.2 million members worldwide, many of whom assist organizations that provide a variety of services, such as helping the homeless or eradicating polio. The Rotary Club also helps socially responsible small businesses obtain funding to start and maintain their businesses, often providing the funding directly to these small businesses in the process (see http://www.Rotary.org). Lions Clubs is another business-based service organization with more than 45,000 clubs worldwide and 1.3 million members; it boasts the distinction as the world's largest service club organization. Examples of chapter activities include bringing 3,000 volunteers together to build a playground for children of all abilities in California, feeding 60,000 in a South African township, and sending a team of eye surgeons to Honduras to treat more than 100 adults and children. The organization's Web site provides

guidance about how to develop a successful service initiative (see http://www.Lionsclubs. org).

- Community organizations for economic development, urban renewal, low cost housing, mentors, tutors, and the like.
- Ad hoc community lobbying efforts: for instance, to encourage government or corporations to support initiatives, redress a perceived wrong, encourage involvement, educate, and/or raise money (e.g., a local walk to call attention to, and raise money for, breast cancer research and treatment, organ donation, or HIV/ AIDS in Africa).
- Social investors: for example, Acumen, a Google-supported funding agency that provides small loans to businesses in underdeveloped countries, and Good Capital, an investment firm focusing on social business (Alboheer, 2009). Good Capital, headquartered in San Francisco, invests in both for-profit and not-for-profit social enterprise, maintaining flexibility to fund the best of a growing number of organizations pursuing meaningful social and financial value (Alboher).

> Our mission is to accelerate the flow of capital to enterprises that create innovative, market-based solutions to inequality, poverty, and other social problems and in doing so amplify their total impact. ...Good Capital is actively building a community of people who are passionate about creating positive social change through market forces. We connect like-minded investors to one another and act as a conduit for capital—both human and financial—to flow to worthy social enterprises.
>
> (http://www.goodcap.net)

The company runs an annual Social Capital Markets Conference that brings together people with a deep passion to change the world through sustainable business (see http://www.socialcapitalmarkets. net).

- Web sites, blogs, worldwide television service, and easier travel internationally encourage founding social ventures, with individuals and corporations in developing countries forming, investing in, donating to, buying from, and partnering with organizations that socially benefit the developing world (Barendsen & Gardner, 2004; Zahra et al., 2008). Web sites help match individuals with needs to those who wish to give. Here are some examples:
  - David Girgenti, from Cherry Hill, NJ, started http://www. wishuponahero.com. Inspired by heroic acts of ordinary people after the 9/11 attacks and Hurricane Katrina, the

site gives donors a chance to help fulfill small and large wishes. The site matches donors directly to people in need, recognizing that people feel as good or better about giving as about receiving. It is run by volunteers, with ad revenues paying for costs of the Internet server. As of 2009, the site had granted more than 46,000 wishes since its founding in 2007 (Bruno, 2009). People place money in Paypal accounts of the beneficiaries. The site has security measures to avoid scammers. An example of a wish is a 26-year mother requesting $178 for wrap-around glasses for her 3-year-old son who lost his left ear in a dog attack. Her wish was granted after only 2 days of its posting. One donor has granted 830 wishes, from paying off someone's electric bill to providing a plane ticket to help a mother reconnect with the daughter she gave up for adoption (Bruno, 2009).

- James Stanford, a Silicon Valley executive founded Social Ventures Inc. to create, incubate, and acquire socially responsible companies that directly or indirectly benefit society. Moreover, it gives a percentage of its revenues to philanthropic organizations in the areas of health, education, and empowerment (see http://www.socialventuresinc.com).

- Kiva was founded by Matt Flannery, a computer programmer at TiVo, Inc., in 2004. The Web site (http://www.kiva. org) provides a way for people to provide small loans to entrepreneurs around the world. This microfinancing online service has given people a chance to loan small amounts of money to low-income entrepreneurs, creating economic development in impoverished areas.

- Volunteermatch.org uses the internet to make it easier for people and causes to connect (Holland, 2009). The site provides users with a host of volunteer opportunities in their area by typing in a city zip code and areas of interest (e.g., environment, mentoring, blind, animal rescue). Typing in "environment" and one of your author's zip codes yielded such volunteer "jobs" and organizations as cleanup director for "Planting Peace," volunteer for "Watch the Wild," leaders and side walkers for "Therapeutic Horseback Riding," and "the Prentice Ecologist Initative" and "Trash Cleanup for Youth." The online effort was founded in 1994 by four MBA graduates who wanted to launch an online nonprofit to promote community involvement. It is going strong today, with more than 3,000,000 matches. Its research study, *Great Expectations: Boomers and the Future of Volunteering* (July

16, 2007), examined attitudes about volunteering among people just entering their 60s.

- Consortia of private initiatives working with public entities to bring about change. Here's an example that shows positive action from government and private partnerships and the need for private social agencies and advocacy groups to lobby and propose solutions. The Blue Planet Foundation was founded by Henk Rogers, the Tetris software entrepreneur; it recognizes that Hawaii is an energy-hungry state that has no oil, natural gas, hydroelectric dams, or nuclear plants and depends on oil for its energy. However, it has an abundance of clean-energy sources, such as sun, wind, tides, and waves. In January 2008, Hawaii legislators approved a loan to reduce its reliance on foreign oil by 70 percent by 2030. Blue Planet wants to supercharge this effort, not by adding to the wind-farm relics that languish on Hawaiian hillsides but by pushing state government and energy companies to revamp the obsolete electrical system to increase its efficiency and allow customers with solar power to sell excess power back to the grid. ("Hawaii's Moon Shot" New York Times Editorial, Dec. 2, 2008; See also http://www. blueplanetfoundation.org). This requires a knowledge of energy systems and sustainability, the ability to frame and communicate the issues, and adeptness at lobbying.

Understanding Corporate Social Responsibility

Companies that are breaking the mold are moving beyond corporate social responsibility to social innovation. These companies are the vanguard of the new paradigm. They view community needs as opportunities to develop ideas and demonstrate business technologies, to find and serve new markets, and to solve longstanding business problems.

Rosabeth Moss Kanter, Harvard Business School
(Kanter, 1999, p. 122)

Our consumers are very sensitive to social and environmental issues... We have actively engaged with them on these issues in the last ten years, and they have become very aware as consumers. They especially ask for information on environmental policies, workers' rights and product safety.

Walter Dondi, Director of Co-op Adriatica
(Italy's largest retailer)
(http://www.interpraxis.com/quotes.htm)

Corporate social responsibility is a hard-edged business decision. Not because it is a nice thing to do or because people are forcing us to do it... because it is good for our business.

Niall Fitzerald, former CEO, Unilever
(http://www.interpraxis.com/quotes.htm)

Morally responsible corporate decisions and actions take place through the hand of the individual (e.g., Board members, the CEO, individual executives and managers throughout the organization) and government (legislators, jurists, and regulators at the Federal and State level). However, the idea that organizations have a moral responsibility as agents of society is debatable. One could argue that corporations do not have a moral responsibility to anyone except their shareholders. Conversely, one could argue that corporations indeed have a moral responsibility to the communities in which they reside. Extending this argument, transnational corporations have a moral responsibility to the countries in which they establish themselves, especially when they use their natural resources, pollute their environment, and pay the people substandard wages.

Bornstein (2004) offered several reasons for the increased attention corporations are giving to CSR initiatives: (1) Corporations are increasingly recognizing their social responsibilities locally and globally in a host of areas, including environmental protection, poverty, education, and health; (2) social support organizations are globally dispersed and diverse; (3) organizations are moving beyond stopgap solutions to systematic approaches and sustainable solutions to problems; (4) citizen (nongovernmental) organizations are emerging as critical sources of expertise and influence; (5) social institutions are developing partnerships with businesses, schools and universities, and governments; and (6) there is a natural and beneficial increase in competition, collaboration, and attention to corporate and social performance.

Employees often act as advocates for business issues, promoting their ideas to top management (cf. Dutton, Ashford, O'Neill, & Lawrence, 2001). Similarly, employees initiate corporate involvement in social welfare. They see needs locally or globally, link them to their corporation's interests, and convince the corporation's executives and fellow employees to act. They organize resources and service activities, perhaps in partnership with community and government organizations. A social entrepreneur is "called upon to channel energy and skill into helping...challenge institutional and social barriers that impede academic, career, or personal-social development" (Lee & Walz, 1998, p. 9, in Hof, Scofield, & Dinsmore, 2006). Corporate community involvement can have positive effects on human resource management outcomes such as employee motivation, morale, commitment, recruitment, retention, development and teamwork (Zappalà, 2004).

As one example of CSR (we provide more later), consider the American Honda Motor Company. Honda's Web site states,

> Honda's philanthropic endeavors are driven by our associates' commitment to being involved in their communities. Each year, Honda associates throughout the country volunteer thousands of hours to many organizations. Honda believes that volunteering shows the power of the human spirit and proves that by working together, we can build a better world.... Honda's Community Action Team (CAT) supplements Honda's Corporate Community Relations projects and helps to serve as the face of American Honda to the community.
>
> (http://corporate.honda.com/america/philanthropy. aspx?id=philanthropy_overview)

At Honda, volunteer hours are rewarded with "Dollars for Doers" grants of $100 to eligible nonprofit organizations. Employees have logged more than 198,000 volunteer hours, and organizations have received more than $400,000 in Dollars for Doers since 1995. Honda has national and local programs that support the environment, youth, and education.

Companies recognize their CSR in many ways. They may give a portion of their profits to charity (and advertise that they do so in hopes of increasing business). They may operate in ways that do not waste resources or spoil the environment. They may organize employees to volunteer to help local citizens in need. A business has social, legal, political, and ethical responsibilities to all external and internal groups that have a stake or interest in that business. Business decision makers balance and protect interests of stakeholders.

Companies work with governments, NGOs, and other companies to focus on issues of mutual interest (Zahra *et al.*, 2008). Social entrepreneurship is mainly focused on social, rather than economic, outcomes, so CSR should reflect both economic and non-economic goals (Mair & Martí, 2006; Zahra, Gedajlovic, Neubaum, & Shulman, in press).They find a basis for shared understanding of common needs, norms, and principles in common with other entities (Zahra *et al.*, 2008).

Companies are likely to tout their social involvement on their Web sites. Consider Mutual of Omaha's http://www.responsibility.com.

We cite this not to promote this company but as just one example of how a company gets involved and describes its initiatives to the public, relating their initiatives to the company's mission and goals. Here, they address the reasons for their CSR initiatives. They state, "As an insurance company, we like responsible people. Because people who believe in doing the right thing don't just make better people, they make better customers." In 2006, the company ran a television commercial about people doing things for strangers. They received thousands of positive e-mails and letters. So they took it a step further to create a series of short films and highlight the meaning of doing the right thing on their Web site. Their site lists some of the ways the company practices and encourages responsibility, for instance, community service and philanthropy such as bicycle safety fairs, child safety events, teen seatbelt safety, Students Against Drunk Driving seminars, fire safety education (e.g., "Where's the fire?"—an interactive experience located at INNOVENTIONS at Epcot in Walt Disney World Resort in Florida). Also, the company gives rewards such as the Firemark Award that annually recognizes firefighters throughout the country who best represent their communities through valor and selfless spirit, and the Chairman's Community Service Award that honors company employees who make significant and sustained volunteer contributions outside of company sponsored events. The company's Research Institute for Safety focuses on ways to improve occupational safety and health for workers improving workplace and highway safety and reducing work disability. The connection between these CSR initiatives and the company's insurance business are obvious.

Often, CSR is displayed by a company through its efforts to promote public works. An example is a project to encourage the education of girls in Babura, Jigawa State in Nigeria. The Oceanic Bank International Plc has rehabilitated the ancient Government Girls Arabic Secondary School and its hostels. Such actions are similar to the efforts of Levi Strauss in the past to educate young female workers who had not finished their schooling. Efforts by corporations that enhance educational opportunities in underdeveloped nations are prime examples of CSR.

Becoming Green: Another Direction for CSR

Companies provide better products and services and cut their costs by redesigning processes that reduce mistakes and lead to doing things right the first time. This increases competitive advantage and profit. This applies to implementing green technologies. Companies can go green and lower their costs at the same time (Robinson & Schroeder, 2009). Recycling and reducing waste can reduce costs and make the company more efficient. Subaru's Indiana plant is an example. They have reduced waste per vehicle, now put no garbage in landfills, and have reduced electricity consumption per car manufactured by 14 percent since 2000. Since the plant's inception 20 years ago, employees at every level of the plant look for ways to save energy, reduce waste, and make processes more efficient. The plant shows that profits come by increasing efficiency and reducing waste but not necessarily immediately. Some efforts had a quick and easy payoff, such as dimming assembly-line lights automatically when the workers took breaks or plugging leaks in compressed-air lines and recycling more materials. However, redesigning entire processes took effort, such as returning packaging materials to suppliers for reuse, which required significant changes in handling operations by both Subaru and its suppliers. Some efforts increased costs initially, such as the drive to achieve zero-landfill status. The company examined how it disposed of toxic solvents and instead of shipping them off-site, they now have an in-house distilling process to remove impurities and make the solvents reusable. Subaru estimates that it will take about 5 years for this process just to break even. Such goals are accomplished by ensuring that management's leadership is committed. This is key to setting goals and getting departments to cooperate. Also, frontline workers need to be engaged as they are ideally positioned to identify ways to reduce, reuse, and recycle. In cases wherein CSR and the bottom line conflict, are corporations still morally obliged to undertake CSR projects or refrain from anti-social, though profitable, behavior? And what is the extent of this responsibility? Ten percent of profits? Twenty percent. What do you think?

Not all stockholders of companies are enamored with the idea of their company participating in socially responsible behavior. Even though this type of behavior can arguably be beneficial to the bottom-line of a company, many stockholders see such behavior as a needless risk, with counterproductive results in relation to the bottom line. It is arguable that it is an even greater risk for a company to operate without a CSR strategy because many consumers view such practices favorably. According to Thompson, Strickland, and Gamble (2005, p. 306), it is in the enlightened self-interest of a company to act ethically as it enhances the reputation of the company.

Despite the recent economic downturn consumers are increasingly demanding that corporations be accountable for the socially responsible performance of their company (Brannen, 2008). In the wake of such visible scandals as Enron, companies are taking a renewed interest in protecting their reputations through visible CSR initiatives. Companies often select issues to work on that they can take ownership of to build the brand of their company. This is distinctive from pure philanthropy of a company whereby it does not seek to have its socially responsible activities visible in the market. We see no ethical dilemma in a company's claiming what we believe to be its rightful credit for socially responsible behavior. Arguably the public has the right to know that a company is practicing ethically sound behaviors as they, as consumers, select the brand(s) of their choice.

CSR can involve more than just charitable giving by the corporation. It has been more than 40 years since John F. Kennedy stated that we should "Ask not what our country can do for you, but what you can do for your country." Since that time, many companies have encouraged or even allowed on company time for their workers to donate time to a civic cause as representatives of the company. The added benefit of this practice is that it can provide hands-on assistance to the neighboring communities and build good will in the process. Community building is another prime example of CSR.

Many consultants emphasize the need for the strategic planning of CSR practices. According to Elizabeth A. Wall (2008), "In order for a firm to make a commitment to a CSR program, it must create a committee, discuss the drivers, set goals, formulate policies, source community partners, implement projects, and measure impact."

Sometimes CSR efforts include strategic alliances between a firm and a government. Such is the case with the pharmaceutical company Merk and the Chinese Ministry of Health (2008) in efforts to combat HIV/AIDS in China. Consumers in other countries often have strong feelings related to CSR as well. According to one survey, almost half (49 percent) of Canadian citizens say they refuse to buy a product that is accompanied by negative news from the media. In such countries, the negative impact of poor CSR practices by companies on the bottom line is obvious. Companies cannot afford to ignore the will of such a large proportion of consumers. Arguably, CSR is not just the right thing to do—it is big business as well.

CSR is the continuing commitment by business to behave ethically and contribute to economic development while improving the quality of life of their stakeholders and society at large (Ravindran, 2008). CSR is an organization's taking action to make a difference in the lives of its customers, employees, and the community. Business leaders choose social causes, design charity initiatives, gain employee support, and evaluate their efforts (Kotler & Lee, 2004). CSR and good corporate governance are indeed compatible (Alboher, 2009). For instance, Jonathan S. Storper, partner in the San Francisco law firm of Hanson

Bridgett, specialists in sustainable and socially responsible business, makes the point that modern culture demands that businesses be good stewards of the environment and society (Storper, 2008).

The idea that social entrepreneurs are motivated by altruism is problematic. People may be motivated by the glory and recognition of the work, the feelings they receive from the work, or the idea that they will be repaid in some way. Companies engage in acts of social responsibility *because* they get something out of it, not because they necessarily want to make a difference in the lives of people (Bakan, 2004). Corporations are especially likely to weigh the costs and benefits of everything they do so they can maximize their profit. If they do engage in social responsibility, it is more often than not because they will increase their profit. So we should not take organizational claims at face value. Although Honda (and any other corporation) may state that it adheres to an ideology and practice of corporate volunteerism, we may ask whether their social initiatives benefit the community and who benefits more—the community or the company. Starbucks engages in CSR through its limited use of fair trade products. Yet social entrepreneurs might argue that Starbucks has destroyed community-supported, privately owned coffee shops. So does Starbuck's use of fair trade products make up for the fact that they have put local coffee shops out of business and have contributed to what some may refer to as "the McDonaldization of society?" Or did they create a market for coffee that wasn't there previously? Walmart gives to communities, but is also cited for exploitation of employees and destroying local merchants and small town's Main Street. We say more later about this dilemma of self-benefit versus societal benefit when it comes to individual social entrepreneurship and CSR.

A key question is how do companies weigh costs and benefits of committing to social performance goals? Companies make decisions about involvement in social issues on the basis of the match between the opportunity to address a social need and the company's goals, resources, and skills (Zahra *et al.*, 2008). Companies' internal advantages include proprietary knowledge, access to networks, innovative business models, or useful assets, such as well-skilled staff and employees who have an entrepreneurial experience. CSR may contribute to an organization's profits by increasing reputation and standing in the community, attracting and retaining customers and talented employees. However, CSR has legal, ethical, philanthropic, and social pressure dimensions as well as economic (Doh & Guay, 2006; Zahra *et al.*, 2008). Some companies may see addressing social issues as increasing costs and depressing financial performance (Doh & Guay 2006). The multiple stakeholder approach recognizes that corporations have responsibility to multiple stakeholders, including those who are harmed or helped by the corporation in addition to those whose rights were affected by corporate actions or decisions. (Carroll & Buchholtz, 2007; Zahra *et al.*, 2008). Addressing these issues may increase corporate costs and depress financial performance in the short or possibly long run.

Clarkson (1995) argued that CSR can be evaluated by the organization's relationships with its stakeholders—"...persons or groups that have, or claim, ownership, rights, or interests in a corporation and its activities, past, present, or future" (Clarkson, p. 106). These include customers, suppliers, competitors, distributors, community members, investors, and employees. Public stakeholders include issues of health, safety, and protection; conservation of energy and material; public policy involvement (e.g., lobbying for the corporation's interests); social investment; and donation.

Companies should not be categorized as blanket "socially responsible" or not. For example, Walmart has engaged in a number of community service efforts while coming under fire for its policies for its treatment of workers. Social responsibility is fluid, and therefore a company may fluctuate in social performance. Also, many companies exhibit strong social performance when their financial performance is relatively strong, but may underperform socially when economic conditions are not as strong.

Milton Friedman's framework of effective CSR does not extend beyond the parameters of corporate profitability. This is the idea that corporations engage in CSR only if doing so will positively influence their profitability. This is a model that is rooted in the American version of the corporation, as opposed to the more collective vision of a corporation in such examples as the German or Japanese corporate model. Perhaps nowhere is the interference of greed on CSR more evident than in the bio-agriculture industry. Monsanto, a giant in that industry, has a long history of such questionable practices. For instance, Monsanto aborted an effort to assist smallholder farmers in the development of the farmers' crops for what only appears to be financially expedient motives (Glover, 2007). Monsanto has also been accused by others of developing mono-crops that threaten the biodiversity of many of the crops around the globe.

Monsanto's questionable activities are not an isolated phenomenon. Google has allowed its Internet searches to be monitored and censored by the Chinese government (Dizon, 2009). Tyson foods is accused of creating negligent working conditions that led to the death of one of its workers (Human Rights Watch, 2004). A most egregious example is that of the Unocal Corporation, which was sued by Burmese villagers after the company allegedly used the military from the Burmese government to rape and murder to clear the way for a pipeline. In essence, many corporations are called to task for alleged violations of human rights (Eviatar, 2005).

Some corporations manipulate the image of seemingly operating in a socially responsible manner for gain even when there may be no real benefit to the community from their doing so. An example of this is the tobacco companies' campaign to prevent smoking among Latin American teens even when there is no evidence that any number of these youths have actually decreased smoking (Landman, Ling, & Glantz, 2002).

Devinney (2009) argued that the idea of a socially responsible corporation is potentially an oxymoron because of the naturally conflicted nature of the corporation.

> ...CSR is no free lunch and that despite hopes to the contrary there is little if any logical or empirical evidence that more social activities on the part of corporations are likely to be socially enhancing, and that in fact they can be socially harmful. In other words, the holy grail of CSR—"doing well by doing good"—is an illusory goal that is noble in spirit but unachievable in practice... corporations, by their very nature, have conflicting virtues and vices that ensure that they will never be truly socially responsible.... Any position taken by a firm and its management, social ethical, or otherwise, has trade-offs that cannot be avoided.
>
> (Devinney, 2009, pp. 45–46)

Devinney cites L'Oréal, which engages in limited animal testing, and owns the Body Shop, which actively promotes its animal-friendly production.

So, according to Devinney, corporations are, in part, viable social entrepreneurs and an effective gauge of the social demands of conflicting constituencies. Corporations with more socially acceptable and beneficial practices are likely to have more satisfied customers, employees and, as a result, profits. They have the capacity to tailor their products and services to constituency demands (e.g., Toyota developing the hybrid vehicle recognizing a marketplace demand). Corporations understand the trade-offs, technologies, and societal trends and react more rapidly than governments. Furthermore, because they are free of transparency required of governments and social agencies, corporations can experiment with different social entrepreneurship ideas.

Devinney explains why not all corporations are "good." However, corporations are driven to generate economic returns, not solve societal problems. They skew societal standards to their own needs, for instance, in the ways they attempt to influence and respond to regulation. Corporations do not represent society at large, and they are likely to be naturally socially conservative, acting entrepreneurially when they see a possible profit. They attempt to influence regulation to their own benefit. Compared to government, they are less accountable and more subject to the whims of unelected decision makers.

For a CSR initiative to lead to a sustainable advantage for the company, it must be central to the firm's mission, provide firm-specific benefits, and be made visible to external audiences and ensure external defensibility by a firm's ability to assess its environment, manage its stakeholders, and deal with social issues (Sirsly and Lamertz, 2008). CSR must influence demand positively (more customers and/or higher willingness to pay), lower the firm's cost structure (e.g., lower turnover and absenteeism because employees are happier), or lengthen usage of assets through innovation, reduced risk from less interference from market fluctuations (Devinney, 2009). "Incorporating CSR into all strategic decisions is, arguably, one of the most difficult challenges a manager faces" (Bansal, 2006, p. 1, http://www.iveybusinessjournal. com). CSR is not merely an appendage of strategic decisions, something nice to think about and act on after financial and competitive issues are resolved. Rather, managers in successful organizations weave social issues into their strategic decision making. Bansal invited 19 firms known for their success as businesses and their CSR. The study identified the following best practices:

1   Include social issues in risk assessment analyses, meaning consider ethical, environmental, and social implications of possible decisions and actions.
2   Measure the cost or revenue effects of social issues that may result from the organization's decisions and actions.
3   Lengthen decision time horizons—do not make hasty decisions.
4   Take advantage of internal stakeholders' creativity; recognize the value of employees' ideas and interests.
5   Involve external stakeholders formally and informally— community members, suppliers, and customers.
6   Build social capital within the top management team; value and reward the social impact of their decisions and actions (e.g., their involvement in volunteer work on behalf of the organization; their decisions that protect the environment and contribute to the organization's good will in the community).

7 Show impassioned, not impersonal, leadership.
8 Apply values-based criteria to decisions.
9 Take the leap of faith that "doing the right thing" will pay off for the organization in many direct and indirect ways.

What You Will Learn From This Book

This book is about making a difference in the world. It's about what makes people take action when nobody else is doing so. It's about speaking out and taking risks to represent others who can't speak for themselves, resolve injustices, create safe environments, and improve the quality of life. It's about helping people in need whether you know them or not. It's about influence, impression management, and power. It's about caring and helping. It's about assessing and resolving needs. And it's about learning about ourselves and others. We will address:

- What motivates entrepreneurship for social good?
- What conditions stimulate social entrepreneurs to act?
- What strategies do entrepreneurs adopt?
- What beliefs about people do entrepreneurs hold?
- What skills do entrepreneurs need to be successful?
- What characteristics do entrepreneurs need to persist in the face of barriers?
- What outcomes do social entrepreneurs achieve?

You will learn how to do the following:

- Access your entrepreneurship orientation and recognize whether you have developed and can develop characteristics to be a successful social entrepreneur.
- Be a good social entrepreneur, organizing and applying resources to implement social programs.
- Use emotional, cognitive, and behavioral entrepreneurship strategies to change peoples' attitudes, affect their decisions, and take actions to benefit a cause.
- Implement these strategies successfully, including identifying decision makers, volunteers, and contributors.
- Be a transformational leader, expressing a clear vision and gathering support.
- Fine-tune goals, track outcomes and, when necessary, change to a more effective course of action.

Themes To Keep In Mind

We emphasize several themes in this book to help you understand social action in the context of CSR and community-based social entrepreneurship.

1   Entrepreneurship skills and abilities are needed for successful social action. We describe behaviors associated with each and suggest how they work jointly in this chapter.

2   Pro-social motivation is an important component for stimulating social entrepreneurship, and it is at the heart of entrepreneurship. Chapter 2 describes the elements of social action orientation indicating factors that drive people to be advocates for social causes and establish for-profit and not-for-profit entrepreneurial ventures to support them.

3   Motivation is not enough, of course. Successful social action requires skills and applying these skills to entrepreneurial competencies (behaviors and actions). This is the subject of Chapter 3.

4   People who start social action initiatives should recognize the process or steps of initiating and sustaining social entrepreneurship whether in the context of CSR or community social action. Social entrepreneurship strategies depend on the beliefs of the entrepreneur about how to bring about change and influence decisions. Chapter 4 describes steps and strategies for social entrepreneurship.

5   Social entrepreneurs do not work alone. They require committed volunteers and professional staff who have the same vision and emotional attachment to the purpose of the initiative. Chapter 5 focuses on how to attract and retain talented people, establish clear tasks, and ensure that the necessary time and resources are available. These are the foundation of a high-performing team.

6   Social action requires training and support to be successful and overcome barriers. Chapter 6 provides a range of training and education options, including readily available information and sources of support and techniques to facilitate social action initiatives.

7   Social entrepreneurs are concerned about bottom-line measures. These may be financial but, in the case of social action, they are also human, in terms of meeting needs, delivering services, and generally achieving positive social outcomes. Chapter 7 addresses evaluating outcomes.

8   Social action initiatives from within corporations or communities require the dynamic interaction of motivation, skills, competencies,

steps, strategies, and processes for overcoming barriers and measuring success. We conclude the book with resources including online tools and information sources and case examples.

By the way, keep in mind that volunteering and social action leadership can be valuable learning and developmental experiences and ways to help nonprofit organizations. With the spate of job losses in 2008 and 2009, talented and experienced managers who were downsized could start volunteering, helping nonprofits during this difficult economic period and maintaining their expertise and networks (Holland, 2009). Nonprofits are lean and often have insufficient resources to manage volunteers wisely. Volunteer Match.org connects nonprofits and skilled volunteers. For instance, a volunteer with technical expertise designed a Web site for Dress for Success, a New York nonprofit founded by Nancy Lublin to provide professional clothing to low-income women looking for jobs (Holland). Lublin is now the CEO of Do Something, a volunteer clearinghouse for teenagers.

Conclusion

Social entrepreneurship is taking action to support a social cause that helps a specific individual, group, community, or society at large. Social entrepreneurs are people who see a problem and resolve to do something about it by using entrepreneurial principles to organize, create, and manage a venture to make social change. CSR is an organization taking action to make a difference in the lives of its customers and employees and the community. Fortunately, there is no shortage of individuals who are concerned about taking social action to repair the world. Also, there is a growing array of support resources, much of it available on the Internet. The next chapter will help you understand whether you have what it takes to be an effective social entrepreneur in your company or community.

Questions for Reflection and Discussion

1   Identify a social action initiative in your community. Who started it? What motivated the individuals? Were the founders able to sustain the effort? Can you think of a social action initiative that failed? If so, why did it fail? To what extent did problems stem from the individuals involved in founding and leading the initiative?

2   Think about some examples of CSR. What motivated those involved? Did they involve many people in the organization?

In what ways was the initiative valuable to the company, its employees, and the community?

3 If you were to begin a social action initiative, what might it be? Think of one or two examples. What entrepreneurship actions would be needed at different stages of the effort?

4 Do you consider yourself a social entrepreneur? Why or why not?

5 What are the potential advantages and disadvantages of a company engaging in socially responsible behavior?

6 What are differences between an entrepreneur who starts a for-profit company and a social entrepreneur who starts a not-for-profit organization for social action effort?

Social Entrepreneurship Exercise

At the end of each chapter, we offer one or more exercises to help you develop a strategic plan for your own social venture.

Develop a project proposal plan that includes the following:

1 Goal: Articulate your mission. What do you want to do? Why is this cause worth promoting and/or aiding? What is the main purpose of your project? What are the defining features and benefits of this program/project?

2 Background and motivation: What is the setting-history behind the need for this project? What is the problem to be addressed? What are some current approaches?

3 List ways you could approach this project: for instance, sell a product or service to make money, which in turn can support the effort; raise funds to support the effort directly; convince one or more companies to help.

4 Describe the strengths and weaknesses that you and your proposed organization bring to the effort.

5 Describe the opportunities and threats that may influence your success.

6 Reference any documents or resources used in planning your program/project.

Need some help selecting a topic? Choose from the list below (or come up with your own):

- Global education (e.g., UNICEF)
- Hunger, homelessness
- Disaster relief

- Equal education opportunities
- Health care (Veterans' Home)
- Poverty (Habitat for Humanity)
- Domestic violence
- Autism research
- Animal rights
- Sustainability, Green Campaign (recycling and resource management)
- Sexual assault, HIV/AIDS
- Breast cancer, prostate cancer

If your goal is to produce a product or deliver a service that will support the initiative, you will need a business plan for the product or service and the social initiative. Be innovative, yet practical. You may be devising something that is transformational and valuable.

- Which product or service would you introduce?
- How will you ensure that your idea is practical?
- How will you ensure that you can produce the product at reasonable cost?
- How will you ensure that you can generate funds in a manner that is both lucrative for your organization and fair for the consumer?
- Why have you chosen this product or service? Whom will it benefit?
- How will you promote this product or service? What is your strategic plan? After all, the best product in the world that is not properly marketed will not necessarily be profitable—or help anyone.
- What are the three greatest challenges that would most plausibly confront the development of your venture and how will you overcome each of these challenges?
- Why should an angel investor invest funds in your project? Why is this proposed venture more than merely philanthropic? Is it potentially profitable as well? Explain.
- How does this venture capture your passion to change the world around you while benefitting you personally in the process?

2   What Motivates a
Social Entrepreneur

In this chapter, you will learn how to do the following:

1   Recognize the multiple sources of motivation
2   Define citizenship behavior and know how it relates to initiating and participating in community social action and corporate social responsibility
3   Understand elements of personality that predict and support social action involvement
4   Assess your motivation for social action and community service, including (1) the insight you have about yourself and the environment that sparks your involvement, (2) the extent to which you identify yourself as advocate for social justice, and (3) your resilience (self-esteem, self-efficacy, and feeling of internal control) that sustains your involvement, particularly in the face of barriers
5   Understand how proximity to social need (by personal contact or observing others) and potential to have an impact increase your social awareness and involvement
6   Define and assess your social entrepreneurship orientation— your readiness to start and participate in social responsibility initiatives in your company and/or the local or global community

Introduction

We begin this chapter with some examples.

Dan Schulman is a social activist and CEO of Virgin Wireless (reported by Patricia R. Olsen, *New York Times*, February 24, 2008). Family members were role models for social activism—his grandfather a union organizer in the garment industry and his mother a civil rights demonstrator. After graduating from Middlebury College, his first job was as account executive with AT&T. Several years after starting his career, his sister, who was just 20, passed away of a brain aneurysm.

Suddenly, career advancement did not seem so important to Dan. His work team helped get him through a major project at the time, and he learned the value of giving credit to his teammates, strengthening the team and their future success. Just 18 years later, at the age of 39, he became the youngest corporate officer in the operating group. Several years later, Richard Branson offered him the chance to start a new company using the Virgin brand to focus on wireless technology for the youth market. He started the company out of his house in 2001, growing the firm to 5 million customers in 7 years. One of his community service activities has been to contribute to StandUp for Kids. StandUp distributes survival kits and a hotline number to homeless teenagers. In the summer of 2007, he spent 24 hours on the street in New York with Rick Koca, who operates StandUp. Rick's idea was that Dan see first-hand how these kids live. Dan didn't shave for a week and wore dirty clothes. He had to beg money to eat. It took him 5 hours of begging to raise a dollar. His mind set changed.

> Time is usually my most valuable commodity, but for that 24 hours I had too much time. Forget Starbucks and a $4 latte — I walked two miles to find a 25-cent cup of coffee. We slept on concrete in an abandoned skate park. Being out on the street was a life-altering experience. If more people would get involved, we could all be a powerful force for change.
>
> (Olsen, 2008,
> http://www.nytimes.com/2008/02/24/jobs/24boss.html)

Dan Schulman shows how a successful executive extends himself to "give back" to society. Prompted by his upbringing and tragedy, he has the internal ethic and motivation to engage in social action.

Matthew R. Peters is another example of a social entrepreneur. Indeed, Matthew has made social action his life's calling. He spent most of the last 9 years in northern Guatemala teaching, educating villagers about the environment, planting trees, and building schools (Shelly, 2008). Now 33, Matthew directs Volunteer Petén, a nonprofit organization that works to improve the quality of life for local residents. (The Petén region is northern Guatemala.) A forestry major at Pennsylvania State University, Matthew began his work in Guatemala as a Peace Corps volunteer. Frustrated by the lack of progress, he realized that efforts needed to go beyond workshops and training to do the actual grunt work, like building and planting. He developed a plan to restore and replant the San Andrés town ecological park that had been neglected and deforested over the years. Acting on this life decision to stay in Guatemala, his foundation enlists the assistance of international volunteers who pay to travel to Guatemala, stay with local families, and work. They have built two schools and a library and run educational programs in addition to planting, repainting, and rebuilding. Volunteers work between 4 and 12 weeks, paying $120 a week for food and housing and for their own plane fare. Other volunteer groups that have worked in Petén include Builders without Borders, International Community of Youth, and Volunteer Latin America (see http://www.volunteerpeten.com).

Next, consider an international figure: Nelson Mandela. We all know his important contributions to South Africa, which has made him a role model as an advocate for freedom and justice. He was committed to the cause of freedom, motivated by the struggles he overcame, determined to make a difference for future generations, optimistic and counteracting negativity with positive actions, and forward-looking for the betterment of all people. Consider his history and legacy. Here is a short list of his central accomplishments from his bio (see http://www.anc.org.za/people/mandela.html):

- Joined African National Congress in 1942
- Helped to form the African National Congress Youth League (ANCYL) in 1944
- Elected President of the National Executive Committee in 1950
- Contributed to the creation of the Freedom Charter adopted by African Congress in 1955
- Charged with sabotage and sentenced to 27 years in prison in 1961
- Released from prison on February 11, 1990; ran for presidency and became the first black man appointed head of state in 1994
- During his 27 years of imprisonment, Nelson Mandela was given offers to shorten his sentence; he refused them all, stating that "Prisoners cannot enter contracts, and only free men can negotiate"
- Displayed his commitment to forward thinking and change for the future even though he was facing what seemed to be insurmountable obstacles

Dan Schulman, Matthew Peters, and Nelson Mandela are all examples of highly dedicated people who were motivated to improve the human condition. Surely you can think of many other examples, including yourself, perhaps. So consider the sources of their and your own motivation to repair the world. Where did the motivation come from and how did it develop?

We begin the chapter by exploring why people become social entrepreneurs working within their companies or as private citizens in their communities. We describe citizenship behavior within organizations and communities, examine characteristics of temperament and personality that underlie social service, consider external conditions that stimulate motivation (both personal experience and observation), and define the multidimensional concept of social entrepreneurship orientation—your desire and proclivity to create social action initiatives.

Foundations of Social Action Motivation

People's motivation to help others stems from many different sources. Consider the following possibilities:

- *Early education and experiences*: Following in the footsteps of parents and older siblings; participating as a youngster in esteem-building self-improvement and service clubs, such as Boy and Girl Scouts.
- *Religious foundation*: Religious fervor in practice of faith that emphasizes giving unto others; participation in service activities organized by religious institutions. Habitat for Humanity is a good example. It was founded by Millard Fuller. A self-made millionaire by age 29, health, integrity, and marriage crises caused him to reevaluate his values and priorities. He reconciled with his wife, renewed his Christian commitment, and founded a housing ministry.
- *Relation to career*: Corporations encouraging involvement, whether contributing to the company's United Way campaign or participating in company-sponsored community service programs during the holidays or throughout the year; demonstrating commitment to the company's service culture initiated by the firm's founders (e.g., working for a company that has a tradition of devoting resources and profits to community service).
- *Community service as a source of life satisfaction*: Developing habits of service as a central part of one's life; gleaning as much, if not more, fulfillment from social action as from one's job or career; and spending free time, involving one's families, friends, and coworkers (e.g., recruiting volunteers for a community food pantry). Some may do this because their jobs are not fulfilling or as a substitute for the career success they once desired but failed to achieve. Others, such as Dan Schulman, find that service goes hand-in-glove with a successful career; learning from both corporate achievement and community service—growing professionally and

spiritually as career success allows a person to do more for society and vice versa.

- *Relation to life stage*: Having the time to spend on community service (e.g., when children leave home or early retirement may be times to seek fulfillment by helping those in need). However, those who seem to have the busiest lives often find time for social service.
- *Friends and community*: Following peer role models; accepting friends' and neighbors' invitations to join clubs or organizations that promote civic pride; enjoying the social aspects of service.
- *Role models*: Observing and emulating others who are respected and recognized for their contributions to society. These may be people we know personally, know about in our community, or simply hear about through their publicized actions. We are inspired by their achievements and guided by their successful actions. In other words, they provide a path for us to follow so we don't have to reinvent the wheel. Also, they demonstrate that effort can indeed have positive benefits. We believe that, "If they can do it, so can we." Watching them enhances our feelings that we too can be effective if we try.
- *Major life hardships and challenges*: Hardships (e.g., illness in the family) motivating people to "do something" to help others in similar situations (e.g., other children stricken with a disease, other adults who have suffered similar disabilities). These social activists would never have known enough about the cause to invest their emotional energy on it otherwise.
- *Major life transitions*: Facing transitions (moving to a new community; changing jobs) as times of self-reflection and learning that prompt social involvement. Transitions open our eyes to problems and suggest that we can be effective in bringing about change.
- *Encountering hardship*: Traveling to new parts of the world may reveal others' hardships. Consider Debra A. Jones, director of Global Advocacy for Family Care International, an organization devoted to strengthening reproductive health programs in Africa, Latin America, and the Caribbean. On a visit to the Dominican Republic, she perceived the need for a medical clinic in a remote village. She returned to the United States to start a foundation to raise money and deliver medical services to the region, the Paraiso Assistance Program (for more on Debra and her role for Family Care International, see http://www.fci.expressiondev.com/en/about/22).
- *Opportunities for engagement*: Responding to unexpected opportunities that emerge, causing people to rise to the challenge.

For instance, a request from a friend to help with a clothing drive may spark one-time involvement or generate ongoing commitment.

- *College experiences*: Participating in community service as a college student. University campuses offer a range of programs. An example is the New York Publich Interest Research Group (NYPIRG). Through a number of activist endeavors, this organization serves as the hub for student organizing related to social action. NYPIRG is only one of many such student organizations that exist on college campuses. These organizations are significant for the spread of advocacy because they often have "captive audiences" in the form of students who live on campus and have a need to list civic activity on their resumes.

- *Internet activism*: Generating and responding to opportunities for civic activity on the Internet. Social entrepreneurs can learn to use the Internet effectively to communicate the purpose of their organization, raise money, solicit volunteers, and even deliver services (e.g., referral, counseling, and guidance). We cite such Web sites throughout the book.

Personality Characteristics of Social Entrepreneurs

Social entrepreneurs' motivation is fueled by their values, ideals, commitment, and hope (Ezell, 2000). They need to understand their personal motivation and commitment, particularly when facing barriers, such as failing to influence policy, disappointment at the number of volunteers turning out for an event, or other barriers and disappointments. Consider your own motivation for getting involved in social action. Are you hesitant? Your fears, doubts, and concerns can be obstacles (Ezell, 2000). Social entrepreneurs need to know how to analyze problems and issues to select effective advocacy strategies (Ezell, 2000). Moreover, they need to have the knowledge and ability to plan, coordinate, and implement these strategies.

Above all, social entrepreneurs need to be the visionaries of their organizations, acting as change makers who can visualize the big picture through their formation of attainable missions for an organization. Are you ready for the challenge? Take this short self-assessment.

Rate each of the following items on a scale from 1 to 5, wherein 1 = not at all, 2 = very little, 3 = somewhat, 4 = very much, and 5 = always.

    1 ___ I remain undaunted even when resources are scarce.

    2 ___ I am not afraid of failure.

3 ___ I remain true to my convictions even when it is not to my personal advantage to do so.

4 ___ I am a passionate person with boundless energy once I am motivated into action.

5 ___ I listen as well as I speak.

6 ___ I speak on behalf of the "underdog."

7 ___ I am not afraid to question authority.

8 ___ I am highly innovative.

9 ___ I am an extremely focused individual.

10 ___ I am extremely proactive.

Now add your ratings. If you received a score of more than 40 and you answered honestly and accurately, you have the makings of a successful entrepreneur. If you were a bit lower, consider items for which you rated yourself a 3 or below. These may be areas you need to develop. As you read this book, you will have a chance to examine your motivation and competencies more deeply and consider what you need to do to prepare yourself to be a successful social entrepreneur.

Successful entrepreneurs are not necessarily more confident, persistent, or knowledgeable than others who do not get involved in social activism, but they are the ones most determined to achieve a long-term social goal that was deeply meaningful to them. Social entrepreneurs are "driven, creative individuals who question the status quo, exploit new opportunities, and refuse to give up" (Bornstein, 2004, p. 233). They include J. B. Schramm, who helped thousands of low-income high school students get into college; Veronica Khosa, in South Africa, who developed a home-based care model for AIDS patients; Favio Rosa, in Brazil, who helped bring electricity to remote rural areas; and James Grant, who saved 25 million lives by leading and "marketing" a global campaign for immunization (Bornstein, 2004).

Ashoka (named for a peace-minded third century BC Indian emperor) is a network of entrepreneurs creating an entrepreneurial citizen sector (Hammonds, 2005). As noted in Chapter 1, Ashoka was founded by Bill Drayton in 1980. The network now supports more than 1,500 Fellows in 53 nations. Ashoka's guide, *Selecting Leading Social Entrepreneurs*, explains these qualities along with how fully to test for them (available at http://www.ashoka.org, as cited in Drayton, 2002). The site includes case studies of social entrepreneurs across the globe. Ashoka seeks social entrepreneurs with enormous ideas that can be tried and developed in one location and spread to others. Fellows receive a modest stipend and managerial support. The Fellows are selected according to five criteria: (1) the enormity of the idea—big enough to change society, (2) the person's creativity and quality of thinking, based on experiences early in life, (3) the individual's entrepreneurial ability to change a pattern across society, not just solve a specific, local problem, but constantly searching for the next advance, (4) the potential impact—a solution that will get traction elsewhere, and (5) the individual's ethical fiber (a good person you know you can trust). An example is J. B. Schramm, who launched a simple, low-cost approach to encouraging students who would not have been aiming for college but who could succeed with the right encouragement and attention. His College Summit program includes a visit to a local campus, meetings with role models about choices open to them, and help in writing college applications, along with follow-through with incentives for homeroom teachers to continue the encouragement, and work with the colleges. Eighty percent of J. B.'s students go to college and succeed. Over a decade, rolling out the program in cities across the United States, this could mean 1 million students attending college who would not otherwise do so (Drayton, 2002). Other examples cut the cost of rural electrification in Brazil by 70 percent to 80 percent, bringing power to thousands, and a 24-hour free telephone helpline for India's 48 million street children.

> Social entrepreneurs focus their entrepreneurial talent on solving social problems—why children are not learning, why technology is not accessed equally, why pollution is increasing, and so on. The essence, however, is the same. Both types of entrepreneurs [social and business] recognize when a part of society is stuck and provide new ways to get it unstuck. They envisage a systemic change, identifying the jujitsu points that will allow them to tip the whole society onto this new path, and then persist and persist until the job is done.
>
> (Drayton, 2002, p. 123)

Bornstein (2004) identified six qualities of successful social entrepreneurs: (1) willingness to self-correct when a strategy isn't working, (2) willingness to share credit, (3) willingness to break free of established organizational structures, (4) willingness to cross disciplinary boundaries to create social compounds of people with different ideas, backgrounds, and skills, (5) willingness to work quietly, spending considerable time (even years) to advance their ideas and develop a network of committed people and groups, and (6) strong ethical impetus—motivated not by profit but by belief. Dees (1998b) defined social entrepreneurs as people who are mission creators and sustainers: they do more than just promote private value; they are relentless identifiers of new opportunities for their mission; continuous innovators, adapters, and learners; and bold actors who are not restrained by existing resources.

Social entrepreneurs have positive psychological traits. These include confidence, hope, optimism, emotional intelligence, and resilience. Together, these characteristics form a core psychological factor of general positivity (Luthans, 2003; Luthans, Avolio, Walumbwa, & Li, 2005; Scheier & Carver, 1985; Seligman, 1998, 2002). Hope, optimism, and resilience are indicators of a higher-order psychological capital (Luthans *et al.*, 2005). They have a positive and inspirational view needed for transformation and entrepreneurship (Berson, Shamir, Avolio, & Popper, 2001). Optimistic people seek pleasant scenarios, ignore negative stimuli, and are less likely to have negative emotional states (cf., Segerstrom, Taylor, Kemeny, & Fahey, 1998). Hope includes two components: pathways and agency (Snyder, 1994, 2000). Pathways reflect people's perceptions of themselves as being capable of producing plausible routes to desired goals (similar to self-efficacy). Agency is the motivation that powers people along their imagined pathways to goal achievement. Pathways and agency work together and are both needed for goal attainment. They provide individuals with the means and motivation to accomplish their goals. People who lack hope believe that they don't have the ability to meet their goals and to overcome obstacles, and they don't have the motivation to continue driving toward their goals.

Emotions may blind the social entrepreneur and other participants to the stresses and likelihood of success. Here are some telltale signs that social entrepreneurs are not objective:

- When people tell them what they do not want to hear, they figure out how to rebut them rather than consider their viewpoint.
- They are attached to their vision in its original form and are not open to changing it.
- They move forward impulsively without considering the ramifications of their action(s).
- They act more quickly than their team can follow.

Social entrepreneurs are likely to have multiple motives for involvement. One or more motives may be primary, others secondary. Also, these motives may be overt (expressed) or covert (not expressed). Altruistic motives are likely to be at the center of social entrepreneurship. However, there may be secondary motives, such as status, visibility, and power. These may be viewed as self-centered, spin-off benefits that satisfy control, ego, social, and materialistic, and learning needs. Altruistic motives attract followers (volunteers). Transformational leadership requires that the social entrepreneur's primary motives be expressed and match those of stakeholders including volunteers, supporters in the corporation and community, shareholders, customers and, of course, beneficiaries of the initiative.

Feelings of sympathy, empathy, morality, altruism, and guilt are likely to affect the extent to which a person wants to help others. Some people may be more prone to these feelings than others. As a result, when they encounter social problems—whether on a personal, one-to-one level or an impersonal, distal level (e.g., hearing about starvation in a third-world country)—they are motivated to do something about it.

Prosocial Personality

Prosocial personality orientation is "an enduring tendency to think about the welfare and rights of other people, to feel concern and empathy for them, and to act in a way that benefits them" (Penner, Fritzsche, Craiger, & Freifeld, 1995, p. 147). It includes two dimensions: (1) other-oriented empathy—the tendency to experience empathy for, and to feel responsibility and concern about, the well-being of others; in other words, prosocial thoughts and feelings (e.g., "I often have tender, concerned feelings for people less fortunate than me.") and (2) helpfulness—a self-reported history of engaging in helpful actions, or prosocial behavior (e.g., "I have, before being asked, voluntarily looked after a neighbors pets or children without being paid for it."). Penner and Fritzsche (1993) found that people who volunteered at a service agency for homeless families were high on both dimensions, whereas non-volunteers were low. Moreover, the higher the scores of the volunteers, the longer they were likely to volunteer. (For more information about research related to prosocial motivation, see Dovidio, Piliavin, Schroeder, & Penner, 2006; Penner, Dovidio, Schroeder, & Piliavin, 2005; and Penner, 2004. See Batson & Powell, 2003; Piliavin & Charng, 1990; and Penner, Dovidio, & Piliavin, 2005, for reviews of the literature on personality correlates and predictors of prosocial behavior.)

Personality characteristics associated with prosocial behavior include high self-esteem, high competence, high internal locus of control, low need for approval, and high moral development, risk taking, attributing responsibility to oneself (low tendency to let others pay the cost of public goods—i.e., be a free-rider), and a basic trust and faith in people (cf. Rushton, 1981). As an example of research in this area, one study found that altruistic motives and prosocial personality characteristics predicted several of the volunteer behaviors of AIDS service organization volunteers (Penner & Finkelstein, 1998). In another study, helping behavior was positively related to personal norms, that is, a self-generated standard or the feeling of having a moral obligation to act (Schwartz & Howard, 1982a, 1982b). This may stem from the need to live up to a moral imperative or the desire to improve another's condition (Karylowski, 1982). Individual altruism may be increased by highlighting similarity to those in need, group identification, "mock kinship" (e.g., "we are all related"), or, when feelings cannot be aroused (as in the case of corporations), normative pressures to increase services no longer available in the public sector (Piliavin & Charng, 1990).

People who want to help others are likely to work for companies that take CSR seriously and indeed include these responsibilities in their mission statements (Brickson, 2007; Grant, 2008a; Margolis & Walsh, 2003; Perry & Hondeghem, 2008; Podolny, Khurana, & Hill-Popper, 2005). As employees, these individuals work hard, showing their commitment and dedication to the organization through their job performance (Besharov, 2008; Thompson & Budnerson, 2003). Even though they do not personally participate in social action initiatives in their company, they feel greater allegiance to their employer and perform at a higher level simply because they recognize that the company gives back to society. So firms can attract, retain, and motivate dedicated workers by having CSR initiatives, such as Target's donating 5 percent of profits to charities in the communities in which they operate. Seeing the benefits and having trust in the company and supervisors that such benefits are in fact delivered will help employees see how their own work for the company is helping others, even if indirectly. That is, this trust and clear communications about the organization's social role strengthen the link between their on-the-job performance and social outcomes, and this in turn motivates them to exert effort to perform even better (Grant & Sumanth, 2009). Moreover, the feeling that they are helping because they want to (intrinsic motivation) strengthens employees' motivation to help others by working for the company (Grant, 2007). Generally, socially responsible companies produce products or services that are beneficial to the health and the environment of the consumer (e.g., make life more meaningful and enjoyable for other people), create jobs in the community, and have a positive work climate (e.g., provide benefits such as health insurance, retirement plans, and vacation days; design jobs that employees find meaningful to themselves and society).

Grant, Dutton, and Russo (2008) studied prosocial sense-making and identity reinforcement. They noted that employee affective commitment (feelings of intrinsic satisfaction and self-determination) is associated with favorable outcomes for employees and organizations, including job performance, attendance, and low turnover, stress, and for work-family conflict (Meyer, Becker, & Vandenberghe, 2004). Grant *et al.* (2008) proposed that corporate giving to employees increases their affective commitment to the organization but also that employees' having a chance to give in return increases their commitment to the organization and their identities as prosocial, caring individuals. Maintaining a prosocial identity is an important motive that many people have, prompting them to get involved in volunteer efforts and making donations (Grant, 2007). For instance, when employees give to a company program that supports fellow employees (e.g., provides financial and other forms of support for employees who are facing illness or other personal problems), they interpret their and the company's actions as increasing their identities as caring, giving people and they are grateful to the company for reinforcing their personal prosocial identity (Grant *et al.*, 2008). Moreover, employees are attracted to, and take pride in, organizations that are doing good in their communities. This might reduce skepticism that employees might have about the organization's motives for community involvement. "Rather than pitting [an employee's or company's] self-interested and prosocial motives against each other, our findings suggest that giving can serve both sets of motives simultaneously" (Grant *et al.*, 2008, p. 914).

Citizenship Motivation

Citizenship refers to going beyond the call of duty to help others in the company, preventing work problems, making innovative suggestions for change, and generally supporting the organization. People who are high in citizenship behavior want to aid others, even if they are coworkers performing their jobs (not necessarily benefitting society; Borman, Penner, Allen, & Motowidlo, 2001; Smith, Organ, & Near, 1983; Whiting, Podsakoff, & Pierce, 2008). They are doing what the context requires, not just following their job description blindly. They are not the type to say "not my job" when asked to do something they wouldn't ordinarily do. Indeed, they wouldn't wait to be asked but would act on their own to help. They work hard to complete their own responsibilities, volunteer for work that is not part of their job, help and cooperate with others, follow organizational rules and procedures, and support the company's objectives (Borman & Motowidlo, 1997). In other words, they are good corporate citizens. They not only know how to do their jobs well but they have the skills, habits, and desire to help others, cooperate, be courteous, be loyal, take initiative, and overcome barriers (Motowidlo, Borman, & Schmit, 1997). People are more willing to help others when they know that people see them as willing to help others (Organ & Ryan, 1995).

Consider your own prosocial citizenship. People who are high in these characteristics are likely to have the following traits:

1   Believe that it is as important to be ethical as it is to make a profit
2   Try to be a mentor to younger colleagues
3   Believe they are goodwill ambassadors for their companies
4   Volunteer with other employees to take part in community activities
5   Behave ethically even when they are not being watched or monitored
6   Are willing to behave ethically even when it is not in their immediate best interests to do so
7   Are willing to confront suppliers, buyers, and colleagues who are not adhering to ethical standards

Altruism

Altruism is motivation to increase another person's welfare (Batson & Powell, 2003), the tendency to do something for others for purely self-less reasons, that is, for no personal benefit or at least personal benefit is not the primary driving force. Ben Cohen and Jerry Greenfield had altruistic motives when they established the ice cream company as a for-profit social entrepreneurial effort. Their corporate values were explicit in their mission statement:

> We have a progressive, nonpartisan social mission that seeks to meet human needs and eliminate injustices in our local, national and international communities by integrating these concerns into our day-to-day business activities. Our focus is on children and families, the environment and sustainable agriculture on family farms.
>
> (http://www.benjerry.com/our_company/our_mission/)

Although the tendency to be empathetic is a personality characteristic, feelings of empathy can be induced or enhanced by circumstances (Batson & Moran, 1999). For instance, it may be pointing out others' feelings and actions or showing and explaining the situations faced by people in trouble.

Volunteers cite altruistic reasons for becoming involved in social enterprises (e.g., feeling obligated to the community and wanting to help others). Self-oriented reasons are also common, such as interest in the activity, benefits to people the volunteers know, acquiring career-related experience, making social contacts, and improving social status (Pearce, 1983; Piliavin & Charng, 1990). Altruism is unselfishness and self-sacrifice:

> data from sociology, economics, political science, and social psychology are all at least compatible with the position that altruism is part of human nature. People do have "other-regarding sentiments," they do contribute to public goods from which they benefit little, they do sacrifice for their children and even for others to whom they are not related.
>
> (Piliavin & Charng, 1990, p. 29)

Altruistic behavior must benefit others, be voluntary, be intentional, and be performed without the expectation of reward (Bar-Tal, 1985–1986). An altruistic effort is likely to have a strong emotional foundation. This may be the key to creating a compelling vision. Such a vision may stem from the entrepreneur's demonstrating how the effort can increase the happiness or quality of life of those in need and conveying that "this is the right thing to do." The vision may rest on spiritual beliefs or religious values. There may also be an element of pulling at the heartstrings and/or creating guilt. Though affect is an important ingredient to creating a strong vision, the social entrepreneur and volunteers must also understand the requirements and challenges of acting the vision. Since there is no single bottom line, as there is in a for-profit enterprise, success or value is in the eye of the beholder.

Empathy

The tendency to act altruistically is closely tied to the tendency to feel empathy toward others. Empathy has three components: (1) an affective response to another person—sharing an emotional state, (2) a cognitive capacity to recognize another's needs, realize that "I could be in the same situation," and (3) a self-regulation or control of emotions and behavioral response to help (Decety & Jackson, 2006). Empathy may lead people to help others for no personal gain. Alternatively, empathy may cause others to realize the personal rewards that can be gained from helping others (e.g., being recognized, praised, honored in some way, or the feeling of pride). Empathy may also cause people to act out of guilt or shame, essentially avoiding negative feelings.

However, evidence suggests that people who feel empathetic toward others are more likely to help purely for altruistic reasons—that is, to benefit others in need—rather than the possibility of personal gain or because they want to alleviate their own negative feelings (Batson, Dyck, Brandt, Batson, & Powell, 1988).

Behavioral and cognitive studies and functional-imaging experiments have shown that empathy has a neurological component. That is, brain mechanisms produce feelings of empathy. These brain states in specific regions (the insula and anterior cingulate cortex, the right temporo-paretal region) allow us to monitor and regulate cognitive and emotional processes that allow us to distinguish ourselves from others, recognize the emotions that others are feeling, realize how we would feel under similar circumstances, and cause us to want to redress another person's hardships (Decety & Batson, 2007; Decety & Ickes, 2009; Decety & Jackson, 2006). Differences in brain processing may explain why some people are more likely to feel empathy than others and why some people are more likely to take initiative to help and act altruistically.

Proactive Personality

People who have a proactive personality are likely to take initiative to improve their own or others' current circumstances or create new conditions. They challenge the status quo rather than passively adapting to the current situation (Siebert, Kraimer & Crant, 2001). They don't just criticize. Rather they express the need for change, offer constructive ideas for improvement, and take actions to implement those ideas. They are likely to be high in conscientiousness and extraversion. The three other Big 5 personality characteristics — emotional stability, agreeableness, and openness—are also likely to be important for being proactive for social causes (Barrick & Mount, 1991; McCrae & Costa, 1990).

1 *Conscientiousness* is being self-disciplined, planful, and desirous of achievement. People who are conscientious prefer planned activities rather than being spontaneous. They are always prepared. They follow schedules and pay attention to detail (the psychological term for extreme forms of this behavior is *anal*). They don't procrastinate in starting and completing assignments. Generally, they like order. They don't shirk their duties, leave things out of place, or generate a state of confusion.

2 *Extraversion* (or extroversion) is being outgoing. People who are extroverted enjoy being with people. They are engaged with the

world around them. They are usually enthusiastic about taking action. They seek exciting events, and they like being the center of attention. They initiate conversations even with people they don't know. They are the opposite of shy, reserved, and quiet.

3   *Emotional stability* is not getting upset easily. People who are emotionally stable do not change their mood often. They are easy-going—not easily disturbed. They are relaxed most of the time. The opposite of emotional stability is neuroticism. This is the tendency to experience negative emotions, such as anger, depression, or anxiety. Such people have frequent mood swings and are often depressed. They worry a lot.

4   *Agreeableness* means being cooperative. People who are agreeable are likely to be compassionate. They value and support getting along with others. They are considerate, friendly, and helpful. They are generous with their time and effort. They are willing to put others' interests ahead of their own. They have a generally optimistic view of humanity. They are interested in other people. They care about how others feel, and they are empathetic and sympathetic. They don't ignore others, particularly those in trouble whether they know them or not.

5   *Openness to experience* is being intellectually curious, appreciative of unusual ideas, and open to a variety of experiences. People who are high in openness are full of excellent ideas and quick to understand things, have a vivid imagination, and spend time reflecting on what they see to find meaning.

According to Naffziger, Hornsby, and Kuratko's (1994) Model of Motivation for entrepreneurs, the interaction of several factors affects the motivation of the entrepreneur. According to their model, the entrepreneur's personal characteristics, personal environment, business environment, the entrepreneur's personal goals, and the level of viability of the business idea of the entrepreneur interact to form the basis of an entrepreneur's level of motivation in the business. The entrepreneur forms expectations that are compared to perceived or actual firm outcomes. These expectations in turn affect the level of motivation of the entrepreneur.

Kuratko and Hornsby (2009) identify six specific factors that positively motivate the entrepreneur.

1   *Independence:* Most aspiring entrepreneurs crave autonomy.
2   *Financial opportunities:* Most entrepreneurs believe they have the potential to earn more money as their own boss versus working for someone else.

3   *Community service:* Sometimes an aspiring entrepreneur will believe that there is an unfulfilled need for the product or service they intend to bring to market.

4   *Job security:* Entrepreneurs are their own bosses. They create their own opportunities and build their own safety net.

5   *Family employment:* Often family members can be provided with employment.

6   *Challenge:* Many new business owners are drawn by the excitement of a new challenge. They are not averse to reasonable levels of risk.

Components of Motivation

Motivation is a function of having a concrete, realistic goal: believing that effort will lead to accomplishing the goal and generating the desired positive outcomes in a reasonable time frame and that the outcomes are worth the effort. Stated in terms of personality dimensions, motivation requires insight, identity, and resilience (London & Noe, 1997). The three elements of motivation are made up of a number of different personality characteristics.

Insight is the spark that ignites motivation. It requires seeing oneself, others, and the environment accurately. Being self-objective means recognizing one's strengths and weaknesses. Being sensitive to the environment means seeing opportunities and challenges not just in terms of the need to adapt but in terms of creative, "out-of-the-box" ways to change things. Being interpersonally sensitive and "in tune" with others' feelings is perceiving others' abilities, recognizing their emotions, and understanding how others see themselves whether they see they have an inflated view of themselves, an unjustifiably modest view of themselves, or an accurate view of themselves. People who are high in these elements of insight are likely to have realistic yet optimistic views of what they can accomplish. Insight develops into strength of conviction. Characteristics associated with conviction to lead social causes are altruism, empathy, prosocial behavior, social exchange, and organizational citizenship (Kamdar, McAllistar, & Turban, 2006; McNeely & Meglino, 1994; Penner, 2002; Penner, Dovidio, Piliavin, & Schroeder, 2005) and altruism (Fehr & Fischbacher, 2003).

Identity is the direction of motivation. It is what you want to accomplish. Identity integrates the need for achievement with goal direction. People who are high in identity have clear and ambitious (yet realistic) goals and a high desire to achieve them. People who are high in career motivation want to become expert, be recognized as a leader, and in other ways advance in their profession. People who are high in social entrepreneurship want to take action and apply their skills and abilities to accomplish good in the world. Social entrepreneurship becomes part of their identity. For instance, they see themselves in terms of transformational change agents, advocates for justice, or stewards of social welfare. Characteristics associated with a transformational, leadership identity are agreeableness, emotional stability, openness, extroversion, passion for a compelling vision, and inspirational values (Bass, 1998; Keller, 2006).

Resilience is being able to overcome obstacles that are in the way of accomplishing your goals. People who are resilient do not get flustered when they are told "no." They have a can-do attitude, and they are not easily dissuaded. This requires have a high self-esteem: thinking highly of one's own abilities and self-worth and believing in one's own ability to be effective. Such people believe they can accomplish their goals. They feel they have control over their environment. They don't wait for others to give them permission, but rather they feel empowered to act. So they persist. They see difficulties such as inadequate resources, time, or agreement from others as challenges, not roadblocks. Resilience translates into self-confidence built on extroversion, conscientiousness, emotional stability, and self-efficacy to create change (Bandura, 1997; Eisenhardt, 1989).

Social Entrepreneurship Orientation

Prosocial motivation and proactive orientation are a productive combination. The tendency to be both prosocial and entrepreneurial are needed for effective social action. To demonstrate this point, Grant (2008b) considered the social psychological processes through which task significance affects employees' performance. People who are high in prosocial values but not conscientiousness are likely to work harder when they know that their efforts will benefit others (Grant, 2007; Zalesny & Ford, 1990). Stated another way, people work harder when tasks are made more significant in their value to others. For instance, in one field experiment, college fundraising callers heard two stories written by scholarship students about how the funds raised had made a difference in others' lives by helping to finance the student scholarships. Other callers heard stories written by former callers about how the job had made a difference in their own careers. Number of pledges and dollar donations improved more in the task significance condition than the personal benefit and control conditions in which no stories were heard. The callers who understood how needy students would benefit increased the perceived social worth of their actions. This is even higher for people who have prosocial attitudes, and they perceive that others appreciate their efforts. Knowing that others appreciate your work is important to people because they are motivated to pursue and value their own self worth (Baumeister & Leary, 1995; Grant, 2008b; Ryan & Deci, 2000). Feelings of self-worth and benefitting others allow employees to cope with difficult, unpleasant, or risky jobs (Grant, Christianson, & Price, 2007). Stated simply, highlighting a job's social value can increase employees' motivation and performance.

Prosocial motivation contributes to social entrepreneurship. Together, prosocial motivation and proactive personality combine to form a social entrepreneurship orientation. Prosocial motivation relates to what people want to achieve—to be altruistic, ensure fair treatment of others, and seek social change. They do so by being willing to take public action, express strong opinions, and promote self-interests, for others and for themselves.

Consider your own social entrepreneurship orientation. Think about the extent to which you have a tendency to engage in the following social action behaviors. Indicate Yes or No next to each of the following: Did you answer Yes to most of these items?

Be altruistic
    Stand up for the disenfranchized
    Champion the cause of people who can't speak for themselves
    Organize resources to help others
    Speak out when someone is treated unfairly
Ensure fair treatment of others
    Treat others' interests on a par with your own
    Treat others fairly and equitably
    Stand up for others' rights
    Give others a chance to voice their opinions
    Hold information in confidence when appropriate
Seek social change
    Are not satisfied with the status quo when a change is needed
    Upset the status quo; take people out of their comfort zone
    Are not satisfied with the status quo when a change is needed
    Do not take "no" for an answer
Take public action
    Stand up for what you believe is right
    Pursue a cause doggedly (do not give up easily in pursuing a cause)
    Campaign for causes
    Put your reputation on the line for a cause
    Participate in demonstrations to express your beliefs
    Let others know when they believe a change is needed
    Are not be afraid to be viewed as outspoken

Relish being a mover and shaker
Express strong opinions
State your opinions forcefully even when others disagree
Express a clear opinion on a controversial topic
Express your beliefs to others
Question others' beliefs that are different from your own
Try to get others to change their opinions
Promote self-interests for yourself and others
Argue to increase benefits for yourself and others
Promote what is in your and others' best interests
Stand up for what you or others are owed
Express your and others' rights

Conclusion

People who engage in social action have a background that predisposes them to be prosocially motivated and proactive. They have had hardships themselves or they have internalized social values that prompt them to care for the welfare of others. People who engage in social action are likely to be high in prosocial motivation and proactivity personality. Prosocial motivation encompasses characteristics such as altruism, empathy, and citizenship. People who are high in proactivity are likely to be high in conscientiousness and extraversion. Having strong emotional underpinnings and clear recognition of what is required to be successful may be a fruitful combination for a social enterprise. Emotional stability, agreeableness, and openness are likely to go along with proactivity and prosocial motivation. These characteristics can be combined to capture the concept of social entrepreneurship orientation. This is the tendency to be altruistic and concerned about fairness, to seek social change, to take public action, to express strong opinions, and to promote your own and others' self-interests. In the next chapter, we consider the skills people need to do this.

Questions for Reflection and Discussion

1   Did you engage in community service as a child, and did this become a life habit?
2   Did you have role models for what to do or did you have to discover this on your own?
3   Are you involved in a social action initiative now as a leader or volunteer? What spurred you to be involved?
4   What led you to believe that if you tried, you could be successful?

5   What could you do to create social action experiences that engage others?

6   Do you believe people are born altruists, or are they taught to be altruists? Explain your position.

7   Do you disagree with any of the theories of what motivates an individual to become a social entrepreneur that are presented in this chapter? Why or why not?

8   Which characteristic discussed in this chapter do you feel is the most important for a social activist to possess?

9   Think about people you know who are altruistic and concerned about others' rights. What personality characteristics do you observe in their behavior? Do you admire them? Are you likely to join them in accomplishing their goals?

10 What does social action mean to you? ...contributing money? ...volunteering? ...recruiting friends to help?...starting your own social action effort?

11 Are you prosocially motivated but not necessarily inclined to be proactive? If so, don't feel you are alone. Many people are like this. They care about others' welfare, whether people they know or don't know, but they don't take action to make a difference. Read the next two chapters to understand the skills you can develop and the tasks you can learn to be effective. This may increase your prosocial motivation and willingness to be proactive.

Social Entrepreneurship Exercise 1

1   Building on the initiative you started (or began to think about) at the end of Chapter 1, what is the source of your passion? Do you view your motivation as integral to the way you live your life? Do you see yourself working on this issue 5 years from now or longer? If not, is your objective to start something worthwhile now and see what happens, perhaps interesting others to continue the effort if it is successful?

2   Now that you have an understanding of your own motivation, consider steps you can take to identify others who share this passion or at least would be willing to volunteer for the initiative. List what you could do to identify others who have similar interests (e.g., put up flyers for a meeting, establish a Web site and/or blog, see whether there are efforts that already address the issue that you could join).

3   If you are staring a for-profit business to support a social goal, how much time and resources will you need to devote to the effort? How will you organize your time between developing

the business and working on your nonprofit objectives? Identify your competitors. Can you find people who would be good partners (silent partners who may invest money or active partners who share your goals and want to work along side you)? What resources are needed to get started?

Social Entrepreneurship Exercise 2

A focus group involves asking a group of approximately 5 to 12 individuals to consider, analyze, and discuss a number of interview questions collectively. Gather a focus group of aspiring business and social entrepreneurs and have them respond to the following questions:

1   How do you define acting in a socially responsible manner from a business owner's perspective?
2   What are the benefits and drawbacks of behaving in a socially responsible manner for a business owner?
3   What are the greatest challenges to acting in a socially responsible way in starting your own business? How can these challenges be overcome?
4   What motivates you to be social entrepreneur?
5   Tell us what you think are the personality characteristics of a successful social entrepreneur? What do you think motivates a social entrepreneur? What, if anything, discourages them?
6   What questions should I have asked the group as the moderator that I did not?

Social Entrepreneurship Exercise 3

This is an exercise in self-reflection. Choose the person who has been the greatest source of motivation to you in terms of your interest in becoming a social entrepreneur. Answer the following questions:

1   What is/was special about this individual?
2   What was the greatest lesson this person taught you? How has this lesson translated into affecting your vision as someone who wants to "do well while doing good"?
3   If there was one thing you could do differently in your relationship with this person, what would it be?
4   What was the greatest challenge this person had to overcome? What did the person do to overcome this challenge?
5   How do you attempt to emulate this individual?
6   What would you do differently than this person?
7   Who may have been/is influenced the same way by you as you have been influenced by this person? Why?

3 Competencies for Social Action

In this chapter, you will learn how to do the following:

1 Recognize key competencies for social entrepreneurship
2 Distinguish between transformational and transactional competencies
3 Establish ways to develop these competencies in yourself and others
4 Apply motivational and personality characteristics to competency development
5 Select competent people to assist with corporate social responsibility (CSR) and community social entrepreneurship initiatives
6 Be an effective social advocate

Introduction

The last chapter focused on motivational and personality characteristics that prompt a person to become a social entrepreneur. Let's assume you have the prosocial motivation and proactive personality to be a passionate, energetic social entrepreneur. Being effective requires more than motivation. You need to have the right skills and know how to use them (Mair & Martí, 2006). This chapter is about what a social entrepreneur does and the skills and knowledge you need to be a competent social entrepreneur.

Competencies are the key aspects of a task or role that a person needs to know to perform well. Competencies can be stated in terms of skills and knowledge. They can also be stated in terms of behaviors. We begin by showing that social entrepreneurs carry out a variety of tasks and roles. We use these tasks and roles to understand key transformational and transactional competencies for effective social entrepreneurship. We show how these are used in one particular role, social advocacy, as a principal component of social entrepreneurship.

Identifying Critical Social Entrepreneurship Skills: Some Examples

One way to identify competencies for social entrepreneurship is to analyze successful social entrepreneurs. Such an analysis will examine the critical task components and identify the skills required to perform each component well. Successful social entrepreneurs are role models or benchmarks of excellence. There are many examples of well-known people supporting important causes, such as Mia Farrow's work on human rights in Darfur; Al Franken's efforts to support our troops; Ashley Judd's contributions to empowering women; Jon Bon Jovi's investment in addressing homelessness and poverty; Elizabeth Edwards's speaking on cancer research and patient support; Magic Johnson's campaign to end Black AIDS; Sarah Brady's lobbying for gun control; Robert F. Kennedy Jr.'s initiatives to reduce America's carbon addiction; and Rosie O'Donnell's fight to aid disadvantaged children. (We recommend the book *Awearness: Inspiring Stories about How to Make Difference*, for essays by these and other notable social entrepreneurs. It was edited by fashion designer Kenneth Cole, 2008, who drew on his professional success for the eye-catching spelling of the title.)

We begin this chapter by highlighting the competencies of several social entrepreneurs. The first is a professional advocate—that is, an attorney—who has gone far beyond his practice to support a vital social concern: child welfare. His name is Don Keenan, and he practices law in Atlanta, Georgia. He established a foundation that supports a number of not-for-profit enterprises focused on child welfare in different ways. The credo of his efforts is evident in this statement from his foundation's Web site: "Children at-risk do not vote and have neither paid lobbyists nor high-powered public relations firms. Consequently, the interests of these children are often considered unimportant and are lost in the system" (http://www.keenanskidsfoundation.com/).

Here's what Keenan says on his Myspace page:

> My name is Don Keenan and I care about the safety of kids. My dream is that every child has a safe and happy environment in which to live. As a child advocate and attorney for catastrophically injured children, I have seen too many preventable deaths and injuries. I have drawn upon 30 years of experience to bring you a comprehensive list of dangers that most parents don't even realize exist. I then provide easy to follow, free or inexpensive to implement tips for safety and injury prevention. I believe this

book can save lives. I never want to represent another child who
has been burned by flammable clothes or injured by a toy.
(http://www.myspace.com/365waystokeepkidssafe)

Keenan engages in a host of charity efforts, including his Kids
Foundation, formed in 1993 to assist and advise these children both
directly and through the training of law students and practicing
lawyers so they are more aware of the needs of children at risk in the
legal system. His Kids Law Center is the first children's rights center
aimed at pro bono work to prosecute lawsuits on behalf of abused,
neglected, and at-risk children.

Keenan has been involved in a host of good works that stem from
his expertise and success as a child advocate. Instead of being content
with excellence in professional practice, he went much further to
support children in need and to prevent risk. His efforts build
awareness of issues, affect public policy, and engender support from
other professionals and parents, legislators, and concerned citizens.

Another example of social entrepreneurial competencies are two
people who use their professional skills to promote their passion for
environmental protection, public health, and quality of life. They
are Patti and Doug Wood, founders of the nonprofit organization
Grassroots in 2000. Patti is an educator, author, and environmental
advocate, and Doug is a composer, author, and documentary
filmmaker. Doug's compositions have been heard on television ("The
Cosby Show," "Saturday Night Live") and films (*The Bridge, Only You*).
He has served on the board of the ASCAP, the industry professional
association. He and Patti own a successful music publishing company.
They founded Grassroots to "educate the public about the links
between common environmental exposures and human health, and
to empower individuals to act as catalysts for change within their own
communities." They believe that broad-based public support through
education is the key to bringing about positive and lasting change.
Their programs are funded by private donations and grants. They
have used their expertise at organizing, communicating, and lobbying
to develop educational materials and programs to promote such goals
as preventing idling of school buses and eliminating toxic pesticide
on grounds of schools and parks. One cogent argument: How do we
know whether the 6-year-old child playing in the soccer field the day
after weed killer was administered developed lymphoma 15 or 20
years later?

One ambitious Grassroots initiative is "How Green Is My Town?"
It began with a simple question from one of the board members:
"How do I know if my town is really green?" The projects gets college

students and citizen groups involved in evaluating a town, school system, and business on such dimensions as energy use, green cleaning, land management, water conservation, recycling, environmental toxins, and contamination. Students learn about the environment, convincing people to take individual action for common good, how government works (who are the decision makers), effective lobbying, organizing, and how one person can make a difference. The Woods use their competencies to produce documentaries, ad campaigns, school curricula, a dynamic and informative Web site, and public speaking to convey their message and start local efforts to get more people involved throughout the United States. (For more information, see: http://www.grassrootsinfo.org and http://www.howgreenismytown. org.)

Another example of social entrepreneurship competence is Blake Mycoskie, founder of the One for One movement sponsored by TOMS Shoes. The company describes their purpose on their Web site as follows: "For every pair you purchase, TOMS will give a pair of shoes to a child in need. One for One. Using the purchasing power of individuals to benefit the greater good is what we're all about" (http:// www.tomsshoes.com). Traveling to Argentina in 2006, Blake observed that poor children had no shoes to protect their feet. He returned to Argentina with family, friends, and staff a year later and gave away 10,000 pairs of shoes. Since then, Toms has given away 140,000 pairs of shoes. The company was highlighted in a joint advertising campaign sponsored by AT&T Wireless. Why shoes? Shoes help keep children healthy and safe. Moreover, shoes are necessary to travel, work, and attend school. So the campaign helps reduce poverty and supports economic growth in the long run. The company recruits reps on college campuses as a way to get students involved in the movement and increase sales. Also, the company organizes young people in their Vagabond Tour as a way to harness the collective power of individuals to improve the lives of children in need. "TOMS Vagabonds spend three months traveling across the country engaging, educating and sharing the One for One movement." Blake had the insight to understand the link between shoes and child welfare around the world and the business acumen to create a firm that would market shoes people want to purchase and use the social need to attract sales, partner with other companies with more resources to expand awareness, and elicit the involvement of students and others.

Consider the skills that people such as Don Keenan, Patti and Doug Wood, and Blake Mycoskie needed to be successful in their social initiatives. Successful social entrepreneurs need to be adept at critical thinking, oral and written communications, interpersonal and cultural sensitivity, and emotional intelligence (Rose, 2007). To be self-confident, transformational entrepreneurs, they need to have transformational skills (envisioning, inspiring, innovating, self-regulating, sharing-participation-openness, innovating) and transactional leadership skills (organizing, planning, directing, controlling, delegating). To be successful learners, they need to be good at observing role models, engaging in trial-and-error efforts, requesting feedback, and volunteering for assignments that require new skills. Also, they need to recognize the value of having partners and senior volunteers who bring these skills to their initiatives.

Roles of Social Entrepreneurs

Exploring what social entrepreneurs do will help us understand the key competencies required to be an effective social entrepreneur. Entrepreneurship generally, whether business or social, involves three key elements: (1) a vision, (2) a leader to operationalize the vision (e.g., finding partners, engaging volunteers, dealing with setbacks), and (3) the will to build an initiative that will grow and endure (Thompson *et al.*, 2000). Social capital refers to peoples' ability to work together for common purposes in groups and organizations (Fukuyama, 1995). As change agents, social entrepreneurs bring together vision, resources, and values to address an unmet need that may be local or in another part of the world. Social entrepreneurs feel ownership of, and engagement with, the initiative to address a social need.

"Social entrepreneurs are driven, ambitious leaders, with great skill in communicating a mission and inspiring staff, users and partners... [They are] capable of creating impressive schemes with virtually no resources" (Leadbeater, 1997, p. iii). Social entrepreneurship entails value creation, innovation and change, pursuit of opportunity, and resourcefulness to create discipline and accountability in the social sector (Dees, 1998a, b). Social entrepreneurs are change agents. They adopt a mission to create and sustain social value, as opposed to enterprises limited to creating private value (Alvord, Brown, & Letts, 2004). They recognize and pursue the mission relentlessly. They engage in continuous innovation, adaptation, and learning. They act boldly and do not feel limited by resource constraints. They accept accountability to the constituencies they serve for the outcomes they create.

Social entrepreneurs are, by definition, *entrepreneurial*. They use resources in unique ways to meet unmet needs that are often intractable challenges (Dees, 1998a, b; Harding, 2004; Leadbeater, 1997). They are *innovative* in creating new ways of dealing with intransigent issues and problems that could not be addressed or solved by traditional means. Also, they are *transformational* in that they transform ways of doing things, sometimes taking moribund existing organizations and turning them into dynamic, creative enterprises or creating thriving organizations out of virtually nothing (Leadbeater, 1997). They build alliances. They are visionary opportunists who communicate compelling stories that motivate others. Bureaucracies are anathema to them. In the process, they "recognize when a part of society is stuck and provide new ways to get it unstuck" (Ashoka. org, cited in Harding, 2004).They face the challenges of holding themselves accountable and planning for their succession so that their passion and initiatives continue. They need to develop evaluative skills to analyze their impact, assess the barriers they face, and recognize their failures. They need to communicate clearly, be well-organized, and have a presence or demeanor that commands attention and respect (Rose, 2007).

Social entrepreneurship refers to good stewardship (Brinckerhoff, 2000). Good stewards try novel approaches and are life-long learners. As social entrepreneurs, these stewards:

- constantly seek to add value to existing services
- are open to taking on reasonable levels of risk in their attempts to meet and exceed their goals
- can discern between needs and wants
- understand that the mission of the organization involves more than just the bottom line
- do not lose sight of the need to generate funds.

Social entrepreneurs face the same challenges as traditional entrepreneurs: for instance, to recognize opportunities, find resources, and create the new enterprise. However, they have the additional problems of defining, generating support for, and achieving social outcomes (Tracey & Phillips, 2007). Their social and financial objectives create three challenges: (1) managing accountability (an expansive list of stakeholders including beneficiaries, community members, and governments), (2) managing a double bottom line (balancing social and commercial objectives that may create tensions, including the "costs" of the social mission), and (3) managing identity (combining the goals of the social side of the business with the commercial side (Tracey & Phillips, 2007).

Bornstein (2004) identified four practices of social entrepreneurs: They (1) institutionalize listening through systems, meetings, guidelines, and practices; (2) pay attention to the exceptional or unexpected (unexpected successes that overturn assumptions, such as people's paying back microloans; (3) design real solutions for real people—that are realistic about human behavior; and (4) focus on the human qualities (e.g., in hiring people, being as interested in whether the person demonstrates empathy, flexible thinking, and a "strong inner core," people who have an intrapreneurial quality, have a strong ethical fiber, and consider themselves to be innovators).

Consider how social entrepreneurs carry out change. According to Dees (1998a, b), social entrepreneurs bring about change in five ways: They (1) adopt a mission to create and sustain social value, not just private value, (2) recognize and pursue new ways to accomplish that mission, (3) engage in a process of continuous innovation, adaptation, and learning, (4) act boldly without feeling limited by lack of resources, and (5) feel accountability to the constituencies they serve for the outcomes they create.

Now, consider this list of activities for the social entrepreneurship role:

1   Step up to the plate to address problems.
2   Recognize the organization's role in corporate social responsibility, and be ready to use leadership skills to address the issue.
3   Find ways to create a compelling vision of the problem and potential solutions to attract others' attention and commitment.
4   Recognize a need or opportunity often through direct experience, seeing an issue close up and personal.
5   Use this experience to recognize stakeholders and generate sources of support.
6   Demonstrate characteristics of integrity, honesty, altruism, willingness to take risks and speak up, and knowledge of organizational change. They need the ability to communicate, understand others' situation and vested interests, and use political skills to influence opinions and decisions.
7   Formulate strategies by using the power of their position and their leadership and political skills.
8   Develop and coordinate support structures, recognize adversaries.
9   Make decisions, allocate resources, form coalitions, constrain others' behaviors.
10 Use commitment building and influence tactics, such as listening closely and giving others public voice to confirm their support.
11 Evaluate and learn from outcomes. They collect bottom line measures, for instance, showing that their efforts are actually a win-win situation (positive outcomes for beneficiaries, supporters, and the organization).

12 Report and celebrate results, acknowledge losses, and learn to improve structures and processes to be more effective.
13 Develop skills as they engage in social entrepreneurship.

Generally, innovators tend to be motivated by achievement, and achievement-focused people are results-driven. However, overachievers sometimes make poor leaders. They command rather than collaborate, take shortcuts, fail to communicate critical information, and are not sensitive to others' concerns (Spreier, Fontaine, & Mallow, 2006).

Social entrepreneurs need the innovative, achievement-oriented spirit along with personal qualities that garner others' support. They need to know when to be directive, visionary, affiliative, participatory, pacesetting, and supportive. They generate a climate in which people perceive the organization's and their own goals clearly, know what is expected of them, feel responsible for their actions and free to make decisions in areas for which they are accountable, feel there is flexibility, believe they will be rewarded for their accomplishments, and feel committed to the team (Spreier *et al.*, 2006). Some powerful leaders are narcissistic—arrogant, self-absorbed, and egocentric—with a grandiose belief system (Rosenthal & Pittinsky, 2006). Although a social entrepreneur may have a grandiose vision for change, he or she is not likely to be motivated by the need for power and admiration but rather by an empathetic concern for others. As educators and advocates, social entrepreneurs unfreeze opinions by exposing people to new ideas and encouraging them to express their commitment to these ideas publicly and take action to put these ideas into effect. Over time, opinions refreeze in line with the mission and values of the social initiative.

Leaders of social initiatives are often self-appointed. They decide on their own to take action to address a social problem. Their motivation rests in their foundational values, for instance, their religious commitment, public spirit, desire to help others, belief that their corporation should (and can afford to) "give back" to society, and/or desire to make a lasting contribution. Their power over others rests in social persuasion. As employees who start CSR efforts, they convince executives to support social initiatives, and they engage fellow employees as contributors and volunteers. Although they are leading an initiative, they do not have the same control over volunteers as they would if they were their supervisor on the job. As a consequence, they may have trouble holding fellow employees accountable for their volunteer behavior (cf. Farmer & Fedor, 1999; Freeman, 1997; Liao-troth, 2001; Pearce, 1983). The same holds true for leaders of community social initiatives who start volunteer organizations. Their influence depends on their power of persuasion and the compelling nature of the social purpose.

More specifically, though, as change agents, social entrepreneurs need to have strong transformational and transactional competencies. They formulate vision and goals for the transformation and take action and engage in transactions to achieve their goals.

Transformational Competencies

Transformational leaders are open to new ideas, are innovative, and have the goal of growing new and existing enterprises (Sessa & London, 2006). They develop and express a vision, inspiring others' involvement as partners in solidarity with a shared vision, not just as financial contributors and workers. Their goal is to make the vision a reality, thereby transforming a current problem or opportunity into novel, long-term solutions. We call these competencies *transformational leadership*, *rainmaking*, *recruiting*, *teambuilding*, and *change management*.

Social entrepreneurs, like corporate entrepreneurs, apply a combination of effective communication, impression management, and politics to create social pressures and gather adherents. Clearly, social entrepreneurs need strong basic interpersonal skills. After all, they need to express ideas clearly in writing and orally, listen patiently and accurately, interpret verbal and nonverbal cues accurately, express their own emotions, recognize emotions in others, respect others, and win others' confidence. Moreover, they need to understand and value how culture influences others' expectations and behaviors. Overall, they must develop respectful, friendly, and caring ties with partners, volunteers, donors, policy makers, and beneficiaries. They form alliances and bonds, collaborate, cooperate, build teams, and resolve conflicts. This requires more than effective interpersonal skills. It demands interpersonal sensitivity and emotional intelligence, cultural sensitivity, self-regulation, and emotional control. Essentially, they must be emotionally intelligent.

Emotional intelligence, an important part of transformational leadership, is an amalgam of abilities that center on a person's recognition of emotions in him or herself and others (Boyatzis, Goleman, & Rhee, 2000; Goleman, 1995). It includes the following characteristics:

1 Self-awareness: accurate self-assessment, emotional awareness and self-confidence

2   Self-regulation: innovation, adaptability, conscientiousness, trustworthiness, and self-control
3   Motivation: optimism, commitment, initiative, and achievement drive
4   Empathy: developing others, service orientation, political awareness, diversity, active listening, and understanding others
5   Social skills: communication, influence, conflict management, leadership, bond building, collaboration, cooperation, and team capabilities

Further, social entrepreneurs need to be generative learners. This can be considered another part of transformational leadership. Generative learners actively seek new information and skills, experiment with new ways of applying these skills and information, and then implement effective strategies, all the while educating and involving others in the learning and experimentation process (Sessa & London, 2006). Generative learners are open to new ideas, welcome input, and collaborate with others to generate, incubate, and implement novel (out-of-the-box) concepts.

Now review the following transformational competencies, associated skills, the importance of these competencies for social action, and opportunities for development:

Competencies

1   Transformational leadership

   a. Energizing, motivating
   b. Inspiration (instill passion)
   c. Catalyst for involvement
   d. Intellectual stimulation
   e. Consideration and support
   f. Empowerment

2   Rainmaking

   a. Resource generator
   b. Fund raiser (contributions, sponsorships, income in kind)
   c. Establishing connectedness (solidarity) between the organization and stakeholders

3   Teambuilding

   a. Creating and reinforcing a shared vision
   b. Facilitator building cohesion, consensus, and cooperation

4   Change management

    a. Identifying pockets of resistance

    b. Overcoming barriers (unfreezing, direction for change, refreezing)

    c. Maintaining resilience (self and organization) and remaining open to change

Skills Associated with Transformational Competencies
- Critical thinking
- Envisioning
- Influence
- Inspiring
- Innovating
- Self-regulation
- Sharing
- Engaging
- Empowering
- Generative learning

Importance of Transformational Competencies to Social Action
- Be Self-aware
- Recognize and evaluate opportunities
- Create opportunities
- Perceive emotion in oneself and others
- Manage one's own and others' emotions
- Self-regulation of one's own behaviors
- Motivate people to change

Sample Developmental Activities
- Write a motivational speech or short article. Use statements or phrases that are accurate and catch attention. Practice by speaking to a group and to individuals one-on-one.
- Convince others to join with you—attend meetings, join a board, committee, task force, project team, or club that is focused on the problem.
- Request commitments of time, money, or other resources (e.g., space for meetings, printing), gain involvement for specific tasks (e.g., flyer distribution).
- Work with others to develop consensus for statements of vision (what you hope to accomplish when successful), mission (what

you are working for; whose interests you are representing; what problem you are addressing), and objectives (specific decisions and resources you aim to achieve and a time table for achieving them).

- Hold team meetings; facilitate participation, control people who are argumentative or focus on their own selfish/vested interests at the expense of the group's goals. Play the role of evangelist for a cause. How would you do the following?
  - Sell your idea
  - Negotiate for resources
  - Influence decision makers
  - Persuade donors
  - Reflect on others' reactions
  - Track your success
  - Respond to rejection
  - Face uncertainty and ambiguity
  - Seek change
  - Avoid impulsive urges.

Transformational Leadership

Transformational leaders formulate and express a vision that captures others' imagination and inspires them to action. Their passion becomes contagious. They are persistent in communicating their ideas and engaging others to support them. They are catalysts for involvement, not looking for mere followers who do what they are told but seeking partnerships. They provide intellectual stimulation including clear ideas for discussion and directions for experimentation. Moreover, they show that they care about their partners and volunteers as individuals, recognizing and being respectful of their needs along with those of the intended beneficiaries. Transformational leaders of social action empower people, giving them avenues for actuating their commitment and the chance to innovate, improving chances for accomplishing their goals, and sometimes creating new goals and new initiatives that were initially unforeseen.

So, for instance, a transformational CEO who aims to integrate social responsibility in the company's values and decisions will express the vision, give employees the opportunity to discover avenues for CSR, guide initiatives in line with corporate goals, and provide the resources and reinforcement to make their ideas a reality and evolve programs for increasingly greater social benefit. The initial vision blossoms as the company grows, more employees and customers are involved, and new problem-solving opportunities arise. As a result, the early values are sustained and developed over time, going beyond the initial founders, and employees at all levels learn to be transformational leaders furthering the organization's social responsibility to the community, its customers, stockholders, suppliers, and other stakeholders.

Rainmaking

This is a colloquial term for identifying and increasing resources. Rainmakers find resources that others couldn't see. They discover new sources of funds and know how to obtain them, whether this involves engaging contributors who have deep pockets, applying for grants, or developing partnerships with resource-rich organizations and people, showing them the benefit of working together. The leader is creative, resourceful, and persistent, leaving no stone unturned. This is sometimes a matter of persistence. Other times, it is a matter of creative thinking to garner income in kind—contributions or barter for facilities, equipment, and services. The leader may seek sponsorships (e.g., advertising a company's involvement in exchange for resources from that company). The leader does this by emphasizing both the mutual benefit and developing commitment of the potential sponsor or volunteer to the shared vision to create true partnerships. Contributors come to feel connected in an integral way. They are not just writing checks but feel the passion, care about helping, are involved in decisions, and see the benefits of their efforts.

Transformational Teambuilding

Teambuilding for social transformation entails creating and reinforcing the shared vision. This vision will take shape, and the team will develop as volunteers and staff members realize their commitment and feel the same passion as the leader. To accomplish this, the leader must be open to others' involvement, which may mean compromising, altering the initial vision, and/or working on developing consensus. A leader who acts as if "It's my way or the highway" will probably not be a competent team builder. The leader needs to acquire facilitation skills. These include assessing how well people are working together, understanding the different perspectives (experiences and biases and knowledge and skills) that they bring to the effort. Facilitation then requires interventions that give people opportunities to express their viewpoints, use their talents, and make unique contributions. The leader seeks consensus and cooperation. Disagreements may arise and indeed be fostered. The facilitator does not let them fester or allow people to go away angry. Instead, the facilitator strengthens the team by engaging the members in reflection about what they learned about each other and their interaction and how they can use this awareness to improve their group performance.

Change Management

A competent change manager is able to diagnose the current situation and recognize what needs to change and what doesn't. This includes identifying pockets of resistance, whether subgroups of team members or employees or vested interests in the environment. This requires political insight—realizing what is important to different groups and individuals and how they are likely to respond to actions that may affect their self-interests. Generally, people (and organizations) resist change. Inertia is a powerful force, and the prospect of change is often feared as risky and threatening. Change management starts with unfreezing current views, perhaps by removing threats or risks or establishing trials that don't entail permanent change. Then it entails allowing people to experiment for themselves. They discover ways to solve problems that they may never have considered or thought possible. They invent new ways of acting and new models of organizing. They discover resources in themselves and others that promote excitement and enthusiasm. In the process, they forget why they were resistant in the first place. Then the leader needs to foster institutionalizing the change, creating processes and scripts for programs that can be repeated. These, too, need to be flexible for later transformation. This happens as people learn to be generative. They develop habits of interaction that promote generativity, for instance, learning to brainstorm, identify barriers, reflect on what worked well and didn't work well in their relationships, and suggest and test ideas for improvement.

Example of Transformational Leadership

Actor Brad Pitt has become a transformational social entrepreneur. The founder of Make It Right (http://www.makeitrightnola.org), he was motivated to take action after visiting the Lower Ninth Ward in New Orleans after Hurricane Katrina. Stunned by the devastation and inadequate government response, he attended a series of community meetings about the challenges, the cost of rebuilding, and the strain placed on the families and neighborhoods. Some officials argued against rebuilding in the wetlands, but Pitt, inspired by the hope and courage of families to rebuild, saw a chance to establish communities that would be better than what existed before. This was the only way to resurrect the unique culture of the Ninth Ward. One could say that rainmaking came easily to Pitt. Clearly his celebrity and personal wealth attracted talent and contributions. Still, he certainly didn't have to extend himself. Rebuilding a community is a mammoth task, one in which even someone with the goodwill and notoriety of Brad Pitt would have to work hard and long to garner needed resources. Resolving to do what he could to help, he solicited partners. Working with Global Green USA, an organization dedicated to "fostering a global value shift towards a sustainable and secure future" (http://www.globalgreen.org/), Make It Right sponsored an architecture competition to generate ideas about how to rebuild sustainably. Pitt then established a core team of local community leaders, experts from around the world, and a neighborhood-led coalition of not-for-profits to implement sustainable solutions. This required obtaining consensus around this new vision of a green community of innovative home designs, convincing power brokers, contributors large and small, and families that this was viable and that a new, thriving culture would emerge. Pitt and Make It Right partners have learned about community development and sustainable design for residences and infrastructure. This is a long-term effort that will become a model for cost-effective, sustainable communities elsewhere as the effort continues in New Orleans. Pitt's vision and ability to gather expertise and resources and foster local empowerment is a model of transformational leadership and creative, on-going change and development.

Transactional Management Competencies

As should be evident by now, social entrepreneurship requires attention to detail. This is the sweat and tears behind the lofty goals and expressions of passion and commitment. We address four competencies for growing effective initiatives and lasting organizations: the ability to (1) establish a high performing team, (2) form structures and processes that will sustain the effort over time, (3) supervise volunteers and paid staff, and (4) retain volunteers. These are outlined below along with associated skills, the importance of these competencies for social action, and opportunities for development.

Transactional Competencies

1   Establishing a high performing team

    a. Right talent
    b. Clear task structure
    c. Realistic time frame.

2   Sustain effort over long term

   a. Structure
   b. Rules
   c. Conservator of founding values.

3   Supervise volunteers and paid staff and manage performance in a systematic way

   a. Set performance expectations
   b. Establish joint goals
   c. Provide training
   d. Monitor performance
   e. Provide feedback and coaching
   f. Assume accountability for actions and outcomes.

4   Retain volunteers

   a. Reward and recognize.

Skills Associated with Transactional Competencies
- Sales and marketing
- Finance knowledge
- Time management
- Planning
- Organizing.

Importance of Transactional Competencies to Social Action
- Identification of opportunities
- Recognition of potential weaknesses of your idea
- Establish a time line
- Obtain start-up financing and implement an accounting system.

Sample Development Activities
- Identify the talent you need to help—the abilities and characteristics people should have to assist in the effort and ways to find people who have these talents (e.g., asking people to nominate others they know, observing people who were involved in similar efforts, interviewing people and asking about specific, verifiable experiences that demonstrate that they have these abilities and characteristics).
- Outline the tasks required to accomplish your goals (e.g., conduct a letter writing campaign, organize a fund raiser, set up a web site, take out newspaper ads, form a listserve for communicating information to interested people using emails and text messaging);

determine the resources needed and time frame for each activity; clarify how the activity will help achieve the goal (what matters, after all, is the goal, not the activity per se, and there are multiple ways to accomplish the same goal).

- Establish an organizational structure and set of processes (e.g., 501(c) (3) nonprofit entity).
- Formulate business-like processes for managing the performance of volunteers and paid staff. Recognize that volunteers can be held accountable just as paid staff members are, and that volunteers can be replaced. Write job descriptions, provide training for Board members about expectations and roles, review performance periodically, provide private feedback and discuss ways individuals can increase their efforts and improve their effectiveness, discuss with the group overall performance and reflect on how the group can do better. Recognize contributions with award ceremonies, publicize individual efforts and celebrate group accomplishments.
- Establish a welcoming, inclusive atmosphere in which people are appreciated (thanked), publically acknowledged, and invited to participate; applies to newcomers and to ongoing volunteers.
- Treat your idea as a business, and formulate a business plan that includes:
  - Communicating your idea to others to generate support
  - Creating initial activities
  - Assessing resource needs
  - Identifying available resources
  - Forming an organization structure
  - Setting goals
  - Tracking accomplishments
  - Analyzing barriers and failures

Establishing a High-Performing Team

A high-performing team requires a leader to form and structure the group. A high-performing team has three elements: talent, task, and time (Ericksen & Dyer, 2004). Finding and recruiting people with the talent required to do the job is the first step. Having people who don't have the knowledge, skills, experience, creativity, and other vital characteristics would be the downfall of the group, even if the people are motivated to help. Structuring the task and assigning team members to task elements that they can accomplish is key. Expecting people to do something that they don't have the capability of doing is the kiss of death. This may seem obvious, but it happens frequently in volunteer groups. Being sure that team members have sufficient time to complete their assignments is also important. (We provide more detail and advice about how to structure high-performing teams and manage poor-performing team members in Chapter 5.)

Sustaining the Effort

Group and organization structure, assignments, rules, and roles are important for continuity. This may include the usual components of an organization or club, such as having a constitution, officers, a board, and rules of order to follow at meetings. The nature of the organization's structure and roles will depend on the group's purpose. Small groups with short-term goals (e.g., an initiative to stop a company from building in an area and lobbying for a community park instead) may need less structure than institutions that are intended to be ongoing (e.g., an agency that will provide job training to the physically handicapped). Developing appropriate structures requires knowledge and experience and sometimes legal and organizational advice.

Supervision

The basic elements of supervision that apply in any work organization are also relevant to social service agencies, advocacy initiatives, and CSR task forces. Supervising volunteers adds issues that do not occur with paid employees. Rigorous selection is difficult as people are volunteering their free time. Having clear job descriptions and related performance expectations allows holding people accountable for the tasks to which they commit. The organization's constitution may spell out officer and committee chair responsibilities. Individuals should not be expected to commit to tasks for which they don't have the talent or time. If they do make such a commitment, let the "buyer beware." In other words, leaders should help to identify tasks that volunteers like and are good at doing. If you help them find their niche, everyone will be happier, and they will be likely to continue their involvement. Ask them about what they like to do, what they have done successfully in the past, and whether they are willing to spend the time learning, perhaps working with a partner who has had prior experience and success on a similar assignment.

In assigning tasks to volunteers and paid staff, discuss performance expectations. Set performance and time line goals jointly so you all agree. Offer training. Training materials are often available for free on the Internet or at the library. Run volunteer workshops, or simply explain the nature of the assignment and the outcomes you expect. Then monitor performance, asking for regular reports. Give feedback and coaching. The nature of coaching will depend on what the group requires at different stages of its life (Hackman & Wageman, 2005). At the outset of a team effort or when new members join the team, coaching should include motivating team members and structuring tasks so they know what they have to do to be successful. As the task gets underway, help the team improve its performance by monitoring performance, letting individuals and the group as a whole know how well they are doing and what they need to do better. Facilitate discussions about how they can improve their performance. After the team's goal is achieved, facilitate a discussion with the members about what they learned and what they might do differently next time. Then celebrate the team's accomplishments. Recognize individual merit and thank people for their efforts and productivity.

Transactional Leadership Examples

We offer two examples that demonstrate the importance of these organizational transactions and attention to detail.

The Wedge was a 17-acre piece of farmland that was left vacant after considerable building had occurred in a suburban community on Long Island, New York. Roads had been built on three sides of this triangular property, and the roads had become major thoroughfares providing access to housing developments and stores. During the rapid building days of 2003 to 2005, the property owners received an offer from a big-box hardware store to purchase the land. The proposal went before the zoning board. The announcement in the community led some residents to be up in arms. They felt that there were already sufficient stores not to mention enough traffic in the area. The tax dollars would be nice in an area that already had high property taxes to support the local schools, but quality of life was also an issue. Several residents who felt strongly about this started an initiative that they called, "Save the Wedge." The vision of a community park was inspirational and compelling. The question was how to formalize and provide structure for this grass-roots effort. The activists formed an ad hoc committee, held open meetings that were announced on flyers distributed in mail boxes throughout the town, started a campaign for residents to tie green ribbons around trees, circulated petitions, gained the attention of local newspapers and radios that produced stories on the effort, and attended zoning board and council meetings to be heard. These advocacy efforts required organizing skills and lobbying competencies. The committee members formed subcommittees to handle the numerous tasks that were needed, such as produce and distribute the flyer, arrange for meeting space, and investigate town government ordinances and decision processes. They commissioned and publicized an appealing design for a multi-use park with a track, ball fields, a playground, a building for cultural events and community meetings, and sufficient parking. A few residents volunteered to represent the group at town meetings. Rehearsals of testimony were held in living rooms to identify residents with the strongest communication skills. The effort succeeded. The town allocated funds to purchase the land and build the park, which is now a model community initiative in the region.

The next example is a company-sponsored Habitat for Humanity support group. Two secretaries who worked for the same company discovered Habitat for Humanity through their church. They participated in a bake sale to raise $2,000 for a local Habitat home that was under construction, and they participated with fellow parishioners to help build the house, working alongside the family members who were putting in their sweat equity. The experience was enriching and a good team builder for the congregants. The two employees wondered whether their company could participate in a similar way. As their company was a computer systems service firm, many of the workers were in the field and didn't know one another well. This would be a way to build camaraderie and company spirit. They suggested this to the owner, who saw that the initiative could be favorable for the firm, giving it some positive publicity while improving teamwork. The company had never done anything like this before. The owner asked the two secretaries to be part of a Habitat support committee. They would need to do this during their lunch breaks and after hours. The secretaries didn't mind. They enjoyed the prospect of going beyond their regular jobs to interface with other employees on an equal level— all benefiting Habitat. They sent a company-wide email announcing a formation meeting. At the meeting, they brainstormed fund-raising ideas. They came up with pot luck lunches, a bake sale in the company cafeteria, and a 50-50 raffle. The company owner agreed to match the amount raised. For every $2,000 they raised, they could send a group to help build a Habitat house. They raised a total of $75,000 in 6 months, enough to build a house entirely by company employees. This was terrific publicity for the firm, as the owner had hoped. Employees looked forward to the weekend building days. The effort strengthened employees' pride in the firm as it made a valuable contribution to the community. The company owner hoped to do this once every 2 years, and he recognized the two secretaries by creating a company "Team Leadership" award, which he gave to them at the company holiday party and announced in the company bulletin. The award was a $500 bonus each, which the secretaries promptly donated to the company's Habitat fund.

The effort was not without some discordance, however. At one of the first meetings, a sales manager stated that she felt that the group should be led by an executive, not secretaries. The owner quickly overrode this attempt to usurp responsibility and the limelight. The manager didn't give up easily and had her sales team run its own fund raiser. This didn't hurt, but it had the effect of conveying a "we-they" mentality, which the owner wanted to avoid. On another occasion, the planned bake sale was not announced to all departments, so there were few volunteers to bring in baked goods. For one of the building days, the temperature plunged, and too few employees showed up, despite having made commitments. The secretaries and other employees learned the hard way about the importance of organizing and monitoring events while at the same time giving people a chance to convey their own ideas for fund raising and volunteer for building days that fit their schedules and the building projects they enjoyed doing.

Competencies for Social Advocacy

Social advocacy is a principal role for a social entrepreneur (Sen, 2003). Advocacy is representing oneself, helping others to represent themselves, and speaking for others who cannot speak for themselves. Advocacy may be directed toward an individual, group, community, or society at large. For instance, the effort may focus on environmental cleanup and protection, health and wellness, poverty, or education.

As advocates, social entrepreneurs engage in a wide array of activities to accomplish individual and social change. They may do the following:

- Conduct research and disseminate information
- Educate the public
- Build coalitions with other like-minded individuals and groups
- Conduct policy analysis (i.e., analyze and try to influence legislation)
- Encourage citizen participation (civic engagement)
- Lobby decision makers, the public, and service providers to build awareness, change opinions, and influence resource allocation decisions

When we think of social advocates, we often think of health care professionals, social workers, or attorneys who act as advocates as part of their work (Bateman, 1995). An advocate is an individual who pleads, defends, recommends, or provides supports for others' benefit (Bateman). The goal may be to ensure others' rights, provide indigent people with essentials for living (food, clothing, housing), help people overcome a disaster in their lives, speak for others who do not have a voice, or add force to others who are in trouble and are working hard on their own behalf.

This book is about citizen advocacy, helping other people, whether they are individuals, groups, or communities. Social entrepreneurs have the vision to shape and reshape the mission underlying a social cause. Involving beneficiaries in advocacy initiatives or supporting beneficiaries as they advocate for themselves is important for the credibility of a social action. Activists find that including the beneficiaries for whom they are fighting is an important part of advocacy (see, for instance, social movement theory; Kaplan, 1997). Movements that are solely composed of constituents who are fighting "on behalf of" another group lose credibility (McCarthy & Zald, 1977). Community advocates work on their own behalf and on others' behalf as intercessors. For instance, many organizations in the Civil Rights movement were run by poor blacks in the South who were advocating for their own interests with their own voices. Many immigrant rights groups include immigrants, both documented and undocumented, who are advocating for their own interests... not the privileged conscience constituents acting on behalf of the underprivileged. There are many NIMBY ("not in my backyard") activists who speak for themselves and do not look to others to speak for them. Beneficiaries must be included in grassroots and nonprofit organizations to demonstrate relevance and importance of the effort on behalf of those who are most affected.

For example, Black activists criticized White middle-class students who occupied the leadership of various civil rights organizations (see McAdam's 1988 book, *Freedom Summer*). In 1964, in a campaign led by the Student Non Violent Coordinating Committee, more than 1,000 volunteers—mostly White, privileged, Northern college students—went to Mississippi to launch voter-registration drives, impromptu schools, and community outreach. Within 10 days, three participants had been murdered by local segregationists. McAdam (1988) dispelled myths surrounding Freedom Summer, showing that most of the participants were liberal reformers, not radicals, who acted upon idealistic values learned at homes, not rebelling against family. Many volunteers have since built their lives upon a progressive political base, joining the women's antinuclear, environmental, and other movements.

In the women's movement, White women were speaking on behalf of not just themselves but of women of color and poor women (see Rosen's 2000 book, *The World Split Open: How the Modern Women's Movement Changed America*). Jocylyn Frye, who founded the National Partnership for Women and Families, speaks, writes, and educates to increase awareness and teach peers, the public, and those who need the services the most to advocate on their own behalf (e.g., see Frye & Ju, 1999). She understands and involves the people they fight for.

Consumer advocacy refers to activities undertaken by individuals or organizations on behalf of the interests of the buying public. The period of the late 1960s marked an expansion of such practices in the United States. The U.S. Office of Consumer Affairs was created in 1971 to investigate and resolve consumer complaints. Consumer advocacy groups provide a public education function. A case in point is The Rosalynn Carter Institute for Care Giving. Its mission prominently includes educational initiatives. Efforts include sharing best practices and encouraging students to consider a career in care giving. Other common roles include providing direct services to their consumers. Sometimes, the consumers of advocacy groups are vulnerable and need protection. One such example is the Pueblo Child Advocacy Center, which is dedicated to the prevention, investigation, and treatment of child abuse.

Another example of advocacy organizations taking on the role of protecting the welfare of their vulnerable consumers is patient advocacy. Patient advocates may be former nurses or other health professionals, and they often play the role of coordinating the relationship between patients and their health care system needs. Patient advocates fill the gaps that confused patients in need of serious medical treatment may have in terms of making their way through the administrative maze that often stand as a barrier to their treatment.

Saul Alinsky, a community organizer, strategist, and tactician, provided impassioned counsel to young radials on how to effect constructive social change and know the difference between being a realistic radical and being a rhetorical one (Alinsky, 1971). Another example is César Chavez, the Mexican-American farm worker, labor leader, and civil rights activist who, with Dolores Huerta, co-founded the National Farm Workers Association, which later became the United Farm Workers and led to numerous improvements for labor movements (Ross, 1992).

Social entrepreneurs address needs of individuals, groups, or communities by alleviating a negative situation (fighting disease, reducing poverty, removing a hazard) or establishing a positive situation (providing education, increasing wellness, protecting the environment). Advocacy is a key part of social entrepreneurship. Advocates generate awareness about an issue, lobby for legislation, influence resource allocation, and try to influence or change corporate decisions. Social entrepreneurs need to become competent learners, stakeholder managers, marketers, and lobbyists.

Learning

Before jumping on a bandwagon (or creating one), would-be social advocates need to learn about the issue they wish to address. One simple way to learn is to talk to people—those affected directly, professionals who deliver services, and those who observe the problem. There are more systematic ways of collecting data, such as searching published research, locating government reports, and conducting surveys of service providers and target beneficiaries. Advocates should assess needs at the outset and periodically to track accomplishments and determine whether the nature of the needs has changed. So, for instance, a disease may require fund raising for vital research, but once it is controlled, if not eradicated, other pressing needs may emerge.

Identifying and Nurturing Stakeholders

In addition to learning more about the issue, determine who else cares about it. Identify government officials, community members, fellow employees, or professionals who work on the issue. You may find that few people are aware of the problem. Form a network or alliances for sharing information. Hold an organizing meeting. Invite opinion leaders and others whom you feel may have similar concerns or be sympathetic. Ask for their input and participation so they become part of the initiative. Be willing to allow others to lead. Compromise. Recognize that there are multiple ways to accomplish the same goal and that you can benefit from others' experiences and wisdom and their support (Sen, 2003).

In gathering a group of like-minded people, you may want to test whether your perception of their interest, ability, and willingness to help is accurate. Do not be disappointed if you discover that people you thought had concerns and perspectives similar to yours turn out to have different ideas and viewpoints. Spend some time getting to know them before you ask for their active participation. Begin by including them in correspondence and see their reaction.

Marketing

An important part of social entrepreneurship is influencing others to take action. This entails marketing to get the word out, change opinions, and effect behavior change. So you should be aware of the *4 Ps* of marketing: Product, Place, Promotion, and Price.

- *Product*: This can refer to something that is made, or it could relate to a service that is performed or delivered to a customer or beneficiary.
- *Place* This is where you are planning to offer this product and/or service. Location is a key consideration for virtually any sort of venture, keeping in mind that the place might be cyberspace (e.g., a Web-based referral service). Perhaps it is where you plan to raise funds, hold a rally to generate support, publish a message, or deliver help.
- *Promotion*: This involves methods for gaining people's attention and interest—enough for them to want to learn more. Start a marketing campaign through emails, print ads, the Web, and other means of communication.
- *Price*: Regardless of whether one is a for-profit or nonprofit organization, if there are services or products being purchased or produced and then sold or delivered, then the costs and prices must be in line with other means of providing the services, available resources, people's (or organization's) perception of value, other sources of the product or service (e.g., competitors), and willingness to pay. This applies to requests for volunteers and financial contributions—essentially, the price you want people to pay to help. Are you asking for something that is realistic, and do people perceive that their contributions will be valued and help accomplish the goal?

Lobbying

Lobbying is a form of marketing. It is about knowing the people you have to influence to accomplish your goals. You may want to build awareness of an issue, change people's opinions, raise money, or influence public policy decisions (laws and resource allocation). You might start by identifying different demographic groups (e.g., senior citizens or teens in the community) and determining their leaders, both formal leaders (e.g., elected, such as president of the senior citizens' club or president of the high school student body) and opinion leaders—people whose opinions are respected. Speak to people in the group and study actions they have taken in the past.

A lobbying campaign can have two elements: conveying information and/or evoking emotions. (See our discussion about strategies in Chapter 4.) For example, a campaign to encourage people to adopt stray pets might show pictures of cute, pathetic puppies and provide data on the numbers of stray animals in the vicinity and what happens to those that are not adopted.

The goal is to reach people whom you want to influence, those who make decisions, have financial resources, and/or the time to volunteer and the knowledge, skills, and abilities to help. Identify multiple ways to reach them. For instance, talk to individuals and groups about what you have in mind and who they think would care about the issue and be able to assist. Establish lists of contacts. Expand your contacts by calling, sending emails and snail-mail. Take initial action, such as holding organizing meetings, seeking signatures on a petition, writing emails and letters to policy makers (representatives in Congress or state legislatures), setting up an information Web site or blog, and the like.

An Example of Social Advocacy

Here's an example of a fledgling advocacy initiative. Collaborative Transitions Africa (CTAfrica) was founded by three graduates of the International Relations department at Tufts University: Jessica Anderson, Rachel Bergenfield, and Adam Levy. All three had strong interest and motivation that were supported by their individual field research projects in conflict-affected communities. They had an abiding belief that conflicts continue because sufficient efforts are not made to ensure justice for survivors, there is little or no accountability for crimes of war, root causes of the conflict are not addressed, and peaceful coexistence is not modeled and reinforced. The three organizers, recent college graduates, were learning and applying competencies of identifying needs, establishing alliances, communicating a clear vision, attracting contributors, involving stakeholders, and building on local traditions to create change. They formed a nongovernmental organization (NGO) to improve the efficacy of transitional initiatives that support innovative, local participation in establishing peace in war-torn African communities. Their motto was "sustainable peace comes from within."

Anderson, Bergenfield, and Levy applied for and won the Davis Foundation's 100 Projects for Peace grant of $10,000 to jumpstart their organization and their first endeavor, The Mato Oput Project in Northern Uganda. Mato Oput is the Ugandan term for a traditional ceremony of reconciliation and justice (Afako, 2002).

The goal of CTAfrica was to use field research and other tools to facilitate negotiation and dialogue, unlocking the power of academic tools to generate community members' participation in attaining mutual understanding and lasting peace after 22 years of civil war in Northern Uganda. They formed alliances with the Institute of Peace and Strategic Studies at Gulu University in Northern Uganda. CTAfrica's Web site (http://www.CTAfrica.org) provides information and public relations for the group, solicits contributions, and is linked to supporting organizations. Sponsors in Princeton, NJ, helped the group with further fund raising and opening a U.S. office.

The organization expanded its efforts to other creative peace advocacy projects. For instance, again working in partnership with local agencies and NGOs, CTAfrica helped to create a photo memory book that tells the story of the Barlonyo community, commemorates survivors' and victims' experiences, and contributes to collective memory and truth building in a community in which truth is highly contentious and uncertain. The Barlonyo Project was a way to transmit this valuable information to survivors of the massacre, in addition to supporting personal remembrance processes. The project included a detailed timeline of the massacre with several narratives, photographs showing how the community developed since the massacre, a section to address the current needs of the community, and a final tribute to the victims. Written in the local language, the book was distributed at a community memorial event.

Conclusion

Competencies are abilities to carry out elements of tasks well. Social entrepreneurs use transformational and transactional competencies to be effective. Entrepreneurship competencies include establishing a high-performing team, sustaining the effort, supervising staff, and retaining volunteers. They acquire knowledge, identify stakeholders, market their ideas, represent beneficiaries, and lobby. You can develop transformational skills by trying to be an evangelist for a cause you believe is important. See how difficult it is to communicate to others the critical nature of a cause and taking action. Learn transactional skills by treating your idea as a business. Formulate a business plan for organizing activities, recruiting volunteers, setting goals, delegating tasks, and tracking success.

Questions for Reflection and Discussion

1   How can social entrepreneurs build awareness of their cause within their communities?
2   Which is more important to an entrepreneurial venture, the ability to recruit members or the ability to train the members. (In most cases, both are needed.)
3   Which is more important to the socially entrepreneurial business, the advocate who frames the vision or the manager who maintains its execution? (Again the answer is both.)
4   Do you consider yourself a social visionary? Why or why not?
5   Select an example of a social action initiative in your community or an example of corporate social responsibility about which you have some knowledge. What entrepreneurship competencies did the leaders of this venture use? Was the venture successful? To what extent did the leaders' competencies contribute to the success of the venture (or lack of success)?
6   What entrepreneurship competencies have you practiced and applied in the past? Which ones would you like to work on the most?
7   What set of skills are your strong points (transformational, transactional, both)?
8   Make a list of everyone in your network (people you know socially and professionally). How can each member in your network conceivably provide you with resources and/or other support in your effort to be an effective social entrepreneur?
9   Do you consider yourself a transformational leader, or do you think you can become one? If so, how? If not, do you know someone who is? Why are they effective?

Social Entrepreneurship Exercises

Exercise 1: Competency Self-Assessment

Continuing the initiative you began at the end of Chapter 1 and the needed skills you identified after reading Chapter 2, consider the competencies you will require. Referring to our discussion in this chapter, which competencies would you need for your initiative? How can you develop these to become more expert?

Exercise 2: Acquire Marketing Competence

Use the following forms (adapted from Longenecker, Moore, Petty, & Palich, 2008, pp. 184–200) to develop your marketing plan for your social venture and in the process learn about marketing.

I   *Determining the need: A market analysis*
    Identify your target market: Who are your customers/beneficiaries?
    Profile of target market

    Age range_____
    Geography-locations of customer

    _____
    Average yearly earnings _____
    Male/female or both _____
    Other measurable characteristics

    _____

    Specify the benefit(s) of your product or service to your consumers/beneficiaries—that is, how you will improve the lives of your consumers/beneficiaries?

    1)_____
    2)_____
    3)_____

    Is there more than one target market? What differentiates each target market from the other(s)?

    Potential target markets:

    1)_____
    2)_____
    3)_____
    4)_____

    Differentiating factors:

    1)_____
    2)_____
    3)_____
    4)_____

II   *Competitive Analysis*

Summarize the relevant products/services of your main competitors or others who provide similar services, their unique attributes, and the challenges and barriers that each competitor/provider is likely to face during the next 5 years:

Competitors	Product/service	Unique attributes	Likely challenges and barriers for the next five years

III   *Marketing Strategy*

How will you make customers aware of the product or service? How will you persuade your potential customers/beneficiaries to buy/use your product or service?

IV   *Resources and Capabilities*

Given the stakeholders and skill requirements for each that you identified at the end of Chapter 2, what competencies do you expect from them? That is, what roles do you require from them?

Exercise 3: Skill Self-Assessment And Development Plan

Looking back at the skills described earlier in this chapter and considering the venture we asked you to think about at the end of Chapter 1, in the form below, circle the skills you will need most. For each, indicate whether it is a strength or weakness of yours. Again, for each of those you circled, indicate what you can do to improve—either enhancing a strength or overcoming a weakness.

Skills for Social Entrepreneurship	For each, indicate whether it is a strength or weakness. Underline those that are your three greatest strengths and three greatest weaknesses.	List opportunities you plan to seek to overcome your weaknesses and enhance your strengths
Social/interpersonal skills Oral and written communication Interpersonal sensitivity Cultural sensitivity Self-regulation and emotional control Forming alliances and bonds Collaboration Cooperation Teambuilding Conflict management		
Transformational skills Critical thinking Envisioning Influence Inspiring Innovating Self-regulation Sharing Engaging Empowering		
Transactional skills Sales and marketing Finance knowledge Time management Planning Organizing		
Elements of emotional intelligence Self-awareness Self-regulation Motivation Empathy Social skills		
Advocacy Creator/idea-oriented Visionary Craftsman Values-driven Change agent Architect		
Entrepreneur Innovator Pragmatist Executor Bottom-line Overseer Builder		

Exercise 4: Stakeholders and Talent Requirements

Again, thinking about the social initiative you began at the end of the first chapter, list the people or groups who are stakeholders in your enterprise. For each, draw on the preceding chart to indicate the skills you need/expect from them.

Stakeholders	*List names or types of people or groups*	*Indicate the skills you expect or need from each*
Potential partners		
Volunteers		
Paid professionals		
Paid staff		
Supporters		
Suppliers		
Customers/beneficiaries		

Exercise 5: Scenario Analysis (skills needed to meet unexpected events)

Consider two possible scenarios: (1) A philanthropist or foundation discovers your initiative, shares your passion, and wants to donate a large sum of money. What would you do with it to support your initiative? What challenges would this impose, and what skills would you need to meet these challenges? (2) Conversely, you lose a major source of funds or do not receive an expected donation or purchase. What challenges would this impose, and what skills would you need to overcome this barrier?

Exercise 6: Training Your Volunteers (this topic is covered more in depth in Chapter 8):

Start by focusing on the organizational analysis. In this section, you are responsible for the following:

I   *Organizational Focus*

What are the specific goals that the organization is trying to reach? Try to be as specific as possible with measurable criteria in your response.

State the reasons for the training program and explain the value of the trainee's position. This can be done by stating the specific reasons why the position is important and revealing what would motivate trainees to volunteer as contributing members of the organization and to participate with passion.

Which method(s) of training will you implement? Discuss the pros and cons of the method you choose. Methods include classroom training, case studies, simulation exercises, role plays, on-the-job training, coaching, and mentoring.

To what extent will the method of training you have chosen achieve the goals that the organization is trying to reach? Be as specific as possible.

Where should the training take place? Should the training take place at the organization or at a training center in another location?

How will you intrinsically (provide inner satisfaction) and extrinsically (reward through recognition, etc.) motivate your trainees?

How will you determine the degree that volunteers are ready, in terms of their skill level and attitude, to undergo the training?

II   *Task Focus*

Develop a description for the volunteer position.

III   *Person Focus*

What knowledge, skills, and other attributes are necessary for someone to complete this job?

What specific personality traits will you be looking for in your recruitment efforts?

How will you test your volunteers to ensure they have developed the competencies they need to perform their job?

4 Steps and Strategies for Social Entrepreneurship

In this chapter, you will learn how to do the following:

1 Know key steps for starting a social action initiative: envision, formulate, take action, evaluate, and sustain
2 Apply business planning methods to social entrepreneurship
3 Find available sources of support
4 Recognize the important ethical and fiduciary responsibilities of a board of directors
5 Distinguish between cognitive, emotional, and behavioral strategies for social entrepreneurship
6 Formulate strategies to conduct basic organizational functions (recruit volunteers, raise funds, build alliances, sell the message, and lobby)
7 Understand how social entrepreneurs' beliefs about people affect the advocacy strategies they adopt
8 Know the meaning of social capital and how it works to influence opinions and achieve advocacy goals
9 Integrate strategies of leadership, emotional appeal, and learning to effect social change

Introduction

People who have the spark of an idea and are motivated to take action for a social cause often do not know where to start or how to proceed. Those who are successful have been sufficiently persistent to keep their goals alive despite the frustrations of planning, organizing, and leading. They usually do not have training in social entrepreneurship competencies and methods. Starting any enterprise is a challenge, whether it is a for-profit or not-for-profit. It often requires learning skills and building competencies on the go, which means learning the hard way from mistakes and failures. This chapter outlines steps of starting and maintaining a community-based or corporate social responsibility

(CSR) initiative. We recommend that social entrepreneurs write a "business" plan, and we describe the components of such a plan, recognizing that elements of the plan will change as the effort evolves. We then offer a primer for establishing a nonprofit organization. We cover legal and organizational steps that are necessary to form and sustain a formal enterprise. Our goal is to help you avoid unnecessary errors and mistakes, reduce your frustration, and help make your effort a successful and satisfying experience.

Steps for Social Action

Social action follows a cycle of envisioning, formulating, taking action, evaluating, and sustaining. (For similar step models for starting a social entrepreneurial venture, see Avner, 2002; Barringer & Ireland, 2007; Brinckerhoff, 2000; Kaplan & Warren, 2007; Kawasaki, 2004; Leadbeater, 1997.) This is a cycle in that it is ongoing and repeats over time as new ideas emerge, learning takes place, needs are met, and new needs emerge. It applies to efforts with long-term goals that are meant to be sustained over time, such as starting an organization to shelter the homeless. It also applies to short-term or one-time initiatives, such as organizing a fund raising event to help a family with a sick child. Table 4.1 describes behaviors for transformational and transactional leadership in each of these steps (left column). The table considers what employees do in companies to start and lead corporate social responsibility efforts (middle column) and what social entrepreneurs in communities do to start and lead a social action effort (right column).

Envisioning entails identifying the problem and recognizing situational conditions that are challenges, pressures, and opportunities to solve the problem or meet a need. Envisioning requires innovative thinkers who are not satisfied or bound by the status quo (Kaplan & Warren, 2007). The visionary may not be the best person to actually execute the vision in later steps. An employee in a company who sees a social problem or need that the company can help meet begins talking about the vision to fellow employees and executives. The employee may have an idea for how the company can address the problem. Or the employee may raise the issue but not have a definite idea about what to do, other than that the company should devote resources and take action to solve the problem. Others in the firm need to share the vision and understand that the organization can and should help. They may view this as a responsibility (e.g., reduce waste) or act as a good citizen of the community (e.g., help the homeless). The community citizen who is trying to bring about change and social good begins expressing a vision to attract others'

Table 4.1 Steps of Social Entrepreneurship

Steps of Social Entrepreneurship	Initiating a Corporate Social Responsibility Initiative	Initiating Social Action in the Community
Envisioning Identify the problem(s) and need(s) Recognize situational conditions	Step up to the plate to address problems, recognize organization's role in corporate social responsibility, be ready to use leadership skills to address the issue Have direct experience with the problem, see an issue close-up and personal	Focus on ways to create a compelling vision of the problem and potential solutions to attract others' attention and commitment Recognize stakeholders Generate sources of support
Formulating Demonstrate personal characteristics that motivate advocacy Acquiring partners and financial resources Set mission and goals Formulate strategies	Demonstrate integrity, honest, altruism, willingness to take risks and speak up, knowledge of organizational change Meet organization's and personal goals while also addressing advocacy issues Use power of position and own leadership skills, draw on idiosyncrasy credits and call in favors	Ability to communicate, understanding others' situation and vested interests, political skills Focus on meeting the needs of beneficiaries Develop and coordinate support structures, recognize adversaries
Taking action Focus on decisions and tasks	Make decisions, allocate resources, form coalitions, constrain others' behaviors	Formalize support structures Use commitment building and influence tactics, such as listening closely and giving others public voice to confirm their support
Evaluating Learn from outcomes	Collect bottom line measures, show that this is a win-win situation (positive outcomes for beneficiaries, supporters, and the organization)	Report and celebrate results, acknowledge losses, learn and improve
Sustaining Develop advocacy and leadership skills Maintain organizational roles, transactions, and methods Adapt	Take risks, identify and communicate values, link corporate social responsibility to organizational goals, don't tolerate—and certainly don't contribute to—social injustice, indeed redress social injustices and promote fair treatment Establish organizational body for continuity (CSR Committee, for example), hold regular meetings, report and publicize decisions and actions, renew membership periodically Review and re-commit to change, refocus goals relative to changing needs (e.g., needs met, new needs identified), demonstrate executive support	Develop skills (communications, transformational and transactional leadership, openness to new ideas, teambuilding, continuous learning) Take charge, appoint others and delegate responsibilities, form and work with an oversight board or council, establish and implement bylaws and constitution for operation including procedures for officer election and roles for committee chairs and members Change constitution as needed, alter committee arrangements (establish new committees, sunset ones that are no longer needed), select chairs and elect officers based on skills and accomplishments

Source: Adapted from London, 2008. Used with permission from Elsevier.

attention and commitment. A start would be to hold informal meetings and eventually organize more formal town-hall type gatherings to discuss ways of addressing the issue, solicit resources and support, and form a plan of action. Concurrent actions would be to reach out to stakeholders in different constituencies who care about the issue (e.g., government officials, educators, clergy and lay leaders of religious organizations, directors and boards of existing social service agencies).

In the formulation step, the founder and lead activist demonstrates his or her motivation, skills, and competencies to work on the issue. He or she works with initial volunteers to formulate goals. Together, they become the first adopters—the principal emissaries who communicate the mission and are willing to be identified with it. They set initial action strategies to begin accomplishing their goals. Formulating requires a practical mind for such concrete tasks as analyzing need, determining situational conditions, writing a plan, and setting measurable goals. Within a company, the lead activists need to demonstrate to others that the company should get involved to help the cause. Knowing how to convince others and bring about change helps. This means knowing who controls resources, knowing what the executives of the company are interested in, and describing needs in a compelling way that others are willing to support. Within a community, citizen activists find or organize forums to get their ideas across. They may do this in PTA meetings in the schools, town council meetings, religious services, or simply gatherings of friends who have like interests and see the world similarly. They may begin to develop support structures to garner resources, address adversaries (e.g., residents who don't want a soup kitchen in their neighborhood), and implement solutions.

An important part of formulation is developing a mission statement. Innovative ideas need to be expressed concretely. Transformational leaders need to express their vision. They capture their vision in a mission statement for their social entrepreneurship venture. Consider the mission statement of an educational enterprise such as a university. Stony Brook University's mission statement is presented on its Web site as follows (http://www.sunysb.edu):

- To carry out research and intellectual endeavors of the highest international standards that advance theoretical knowledge and are of immediate and long-range practical significance.
- To provide leadership for economic growth, technology, and culture for neighboring communities and the wider geographic region.

- To provide state-of-the-art innovative health care, while serving as a resource to a regional health care network and to the traditionally underserved.
- To fulfill these objectives while celebrating diversity and positioning the University in the global community.

Another example of a strong mission-driven organization is The League of Women Voters. It has a long history and a fine-tuned organizational support structure. Founded in 1920, The League is a nonpartisan political organization that encourages informed and active participation in government, works to increase understanding of major public policy issues, and influences public policy through education and advocacy (http://www.lwv.org). There are more than 850 state and local Leagues through the United States. The League's goals are twofold: (1) to encourage Americans to learn about issues shaping our democracy and make an informed vote and (2) to advocate on behalf of Americans to bring about important change on issues that shape all our lives (Maggie Duncan, Communications Manager, League of Women Voters, personal communication, December 19, 2008).

There are so many key policy challenges facing Americans that one of the League's challenges is the selection of priority issues. They arrive at issues to address through an annual collaborative process that includes input from its grassroots network. Two issues now on the League's agenda are the transition to a clean-energy economy and providing affordable health care. They tackle these challenges in local communities and nationally, working with Congress and the Administration.

Taking action is making decisions, allocating resources, holding events, delivering services, and in other ways beginning to make a difference. For example, an action might be placing advertisements in local newspapers to inform others, develop sympathetic attitudes, and increase resources. Knowing how to build commitment, influence others' decisions, and establish organizational support structures are important competencies at this point.

Evaluation is an ongoing process. However, evaluating first efforts is critical to show that the goals can be accomplished. The first Habitat for Humanity houses showed community members that they could get together to provide low-cost housing for people in great need. This led people in other communities to see they could be effective as well, and the initiative spread quickly. The first efforts showed the challenges, costs, and mistakes (e.g., in the case of Habitat, possibly not having sufficient resources to complete a home or identifying a family who is in great need but who cannot maintain the home).

Table 4.2 Strategic Business Plan Components

	CSR Example: Holiday Toys for Tots Campaign	Community Social Action Example: Support Group for Parents with Autistic Children. Founded by One Couple.
Executive summary	Our company will help meet a community need during the holiday season. This plan outlines the mission, vision, and general goals for this effort. We expect to make this an ongoing campaign.	Parents with autistic children don't know where to turn for support and guidance. Once established, physicians will refer parents to this support group. Group members will help each other conveying their experiences, soliciting funds for research and children's education, and establishing a network of resources and referral agencies and services. Currently, severely autistic children need to go long distances for residential schools—we need to have more local support services.
Mission, vision, and goals (goals that are specific, measurable, actionable, realistic, and time bound—i.e, SMART)	Mission: Provide gifts so underprivileged children in our community can have a happy holiday. Vision: Our company employees will work together to purchase, collect, and distribute toys, food, and clothing at the Holiday time each year. Goals: Meet 50% of local need; work with other local corporations to meet 100% of need. (a) Implement communication/PR plan in the company by Nov. 15th, (b) Communicate what is needed and establish drop off points in company facilities, (c) Recruit and train area captains to communicate to their departments, increase gifts, make collections and deliveries to central point, (d) Hold competition for most gifts collected—winning department gets to play Santa and Elves at children's holiday party representing our company, (e) Communicate success in January edition of company employee newsletter.	Mission: Be a support parent support group, a knowledge base of resources, and a source of fundraising. Vision: Parents will bond together for self-help and link to professional social, psychological, and medical help. Goals: Establish the group immediately with announcement of formation meeting next month; interested parents meet with social service agencies about available support; hire or seek volunteer facilitator for the group; elect officers and board from the initial parents; hold events (information meetings); open an office, initially staffed by volunteers, to answer questions, collect data, identify high quality support resources.
SWOT analysis	Strengths: My desire to make a difference; skill in organizing others. Weaknesses: I don't know many wealthy people who could help; I'm shy; I don't know if others will help. Opportunities: People care about helping children. This is a win-win for the company and community—positive publicity for the company, also a teambuilding initiative; great need in tough economic times. Threats: We may start the initiative and not meet our commitment to the county agency, disappointing children and showing that our company does not come through for the community.	Strengths: My husband and I know what it feels like to be alone in this and not knowing where to turn; we now know other families and professionals in the community who can help and who will participate. Weaknesses: My husband and I don't have much free time—it's all we can do to cope with our own two autistic children and our older child who does not have autism but who needs our attention. Opportunities: There is a growing awareness of autism—what it is and how it affects children and their families; treatment possibilities and support needs are becoming clearer. Threats: Some parents don't want to reveal their problems to others, even other parents; children with autism vary in the severity and nature of their problems and parents have different situations, so they may not have as much in common as we think; parents are so busy coping that they don't have time to help others.

Market analysis	We know the need is high. The county will give us demographic details and ensure that the gifts go to needy children. Informal interviews with fellow employees suggest that lots of people like the idea and will be willing to help.	We need to work with the local county health department to identify the numbers of families affected and determine how we can communicate with them, perhaps through local physicians and schools. We need to determine the age range and types of needs, which may go beyond our own experiences.
Keys to success (what's needed to make this work)	Coordination of communication and drop off points; timely collection of gifts; people following directions about the gifts needed and how to prepare them (new toys in original packages unwrapped; nonperishable food; clean used clothing of type indicated by agency).	Some other committed families; possibly a start-up contribution from a local foundation or the United Way, a partner agency that delivers services to autistic children; ultimately, an office and staff support.
Resources (e.g., equipment, facilities, staff)	Materials for collection (boxes and space), volunteers to coordinate the effort ("area captains" by department and floor in all our buildings).	Initially we need few resources—just willingness of families to meet and discuss our needs and give each other support and guidance. This may blossom to be a source of direct support.
Support (e.g., training program)	Communication of need (PR flyers and posters, signs, decorated collection boxes); meetings of area captains.	We need training from professionals who facilitate support groups and who can inform us about needs beyond our own experiences.
Operations plan (logistics, PR)	Identify scope of need (numbers of children, ages, popular toys, clothing and food needs), establish six-week campaign between Thanksgiving and New Years, establish collection points, partner with county child welfare office for distribution.	We will start small and local—just a few families meeting to help each other. Briefings from local agencies and professionals can follow. We may identify a partner agency who can offer professional facilitation and the development of a data bank of information and support services for referral. We can determine if there are similar parent support groups and learn from them.
Financial plan (annual budget, anticipated revenue and expenses)	Company support for printing, meetings, snacks for meetings (not necessary but would be nice), company financial contribution to support the children's party at which gifts will be distributed; CEO must agree—can be invited to participate in party and gift-giving.	We will provide our own resources initially. We may apply for grants to (a) develop a communications plan about our efforts to identify other families in need and to raise money, (b) hire staff, (c) eventually (long-term vision) start a local school for children or agency to provide guidance and counseling for parents.
Evaluation and ongoing market review (goals for profitability for next 3–5 years)	Expand to other communities in which company has plants and operations; make our company known for this program. Perhaps expand further to other times during the year (e.g., raising money to send needy children to camp).	We meet other families with children with autism, share frustrations and strategies, identify needed resources. We initiate a PR campaign to build awareness in our region about this disease, lobby legislators to increase funding for research, and lobby local school districts to establish educational programs for our children. In five years, we obtain funds for a start-up not-for-profit private support agency involving health care professionals and educators.

Business Planning

Social entrepreneurs generally do not think of business plans as a way to begin their initiatives. Usually, they start by communicating their ideas, finding others who share their concerns, and begin developing ideas for action. They may have a vision in the back of their minds of what needs to be done and how they can help. Certainly the effort will evolve as it builds steam. Also, no one can anticipate precisely how the initiative will develop. Nevertheless, as transformational visionaries, social entrepreneurs have specific ideas and goals. A business plan is a way for them to express their vision, communicate it to others and, in the process, test its feasibility, recognizing that the plan will change as they obtain feedback, new ideas emerge, and the initiative builds. The plan should be strategic in that it not only expresses goals but indicates how they will be implemented and why this approach was taken.

The components of a strategic business plan are listed in Table 4.2 along with two examples. One example is a CSR initiative. The other is a community action initiative. The plans begin with an overview— an executive summary. The mission, vision, and goals statement expresses purpose and direction. The analysis of strengths, weaknesses, opportunities, and threats (referred to as a SWOT analysis in business plans) is a chance for the entrepreneur to reflect on his or her (or the group's) strengths and weaknesses and the external opportunities and threats that confront their efforts. The market analysis is a review of the current state of affairs, the extent of the need (who benefits), the likelihood of support from others, availability of resources, and the existence of stakeholders, whether they be suppliers, competing interests (other people with substantial needs), and people, groups, and regulations that would impose barriers. Keys to success indicate what the entrepreneur believes will be critical to achieve the intended goals—building a team with people who have the needed skills and competencies, motivating the team, structuring and delegating tasks, and evaluating outcomes. Other elements of the plan are to identify available resources and resource gaps, indicate levels of support, establish an operations plan (step-by-step, what tasks need to be completed), a financial plan, and a plan for reviewing and evaluating success, consider the need, and foresee possible directions for expanding and/or deepening the effort.

Legal Support

Some law firms specialize in helping social entrepreneurs create and implement organizational plans. An example is Adler and Colvin in San Francisco (see http://www.adlercolvin.com). The firm serves grant-providing foundations, nonprofit service providers, individual and corporate donors, nonprofit advocacy groups, and others. Their Web site states their approach: "Our lawyers and our staff are deeply gratified by our clients' contributions to a better world, and proud to provide them with legal services to support those contributions." Their Web site is a free source of information, such as:

1 How long does it take to set up a new charitable organization?
2 How long does it take for the IRS to classify our new charity as a Section 501(c)(3) organization?
3 How much does it cost to set up a new charity and obtain a favorable IRS determination for it?
4 What reporting obligations does a charitable organization have?
5 What reports must my organization file with the IRS?
6 What reports must my organization file on the state level?

They suggest a variety of other sources of information:

- The IRS Web site (www.irs.gov); see information governing charities.
- Search for your state attorney general's Web site and state laws governing charities.
- Tax exemption applications and annual returns of existing U.S. charitable organizations: www.guidestar.org and http://foundationcenter.org/findfunders/990finder/.
- Publications of grant-providing charities from the Council on Foundations at www.cof.org.
- Searchable database of sources of grants from the Council on Foundations: www.fdncenter.org.
- Overview of the basic legal rules; see *The Rules of the Road: A Guide to the Law of Charities in the United States, Second Edition* by Kelly Shipp Simone and Betsy Buchalter Adler (2008). This book may be ordered from the publisher at Council on Foundations (http://www.cof.org/store).
- Information on fiscal sponsorship; see *Fiscal Sponsorship: Six Ways To Do It Right*, by Gregory L. Colvin (Study Center Press, 1993, 2005). This book may be ordered from the publisher at http://www.studycenter.org.
- Information on advocacy and lobbying by charities and other nonprofits available from Alliance for Justice at http://www.afj.org.

Board Responsibilities

Given the public concern about ethical issues, boards of directors have a critical role to ensure the integrity and honesty of a charitable organization. Effective advocacy organizations stand to benefit from a strong board of directors that possesses key competencies. These include ethical, legal, and financial compliance; outcome evaluations; and agenda documentation management to promote transparency. Most notably, board members should have clearly defined and understood roles. Understanding board member obligations and establishing a board that follows these obligations, which are legal requirements after all, is critical. Consider the following duties and responsibilities of a charity's Board of Directors? (from Adler and Colvin; http://www.adlercolvin.com):

> The following are the general duties and responsibilities of nonprofit directors in California. Many states have similar provisions, although the specific laws of nonprofit corporate governance will differ from state to state:
>
> - The Board of Directors, as a group, is ultimately responsible for overseeing the corporation's affairs. Individual directors as such have no authority over the corporation or its staff.
> - The Board may delegate its responsibilities to others (staff, professional advisors, officers), but it retains the obligation to supervise those persons. Directors may rely on reports from officers and employees, reliable outside experts, or Board committees, so long as the director has no reason to believe that reliance is unwarranted.
> - Directors must act in good faith, in what they believe to be in the corporation's best interests (the duty of loyalty), with such care, including reasonable inquiry, as an ordinarily prudent person in a like position would use under the circumstances (the duty of care).
> - Board functions generally include strategic planning; hiring, firing, reviewing and compensating (if applicable) the Executive Director; approving the annual budget and annual financial statements; overseeing investments; fundraising (if necessary); ensuring legal compliance (including tax-exempt status) in administration and program operations. Boards should avoid micromanagement.
> - Both California corporate law and Federal tax law permit transactions with insiders, but impose additional procedural protections to ensure the transaction is beneficial to the

corporation. Those protective procedures include advance full disclosure of conflicts, reasonable investigation, findings of fairness, approval by disinterested directors, and proper documentation.

- Boards are required to ensure that assets are spent for the charitable purposes for which they were received by the corporation (the charitable trust doctrine), in accordance with the Articles of Incorporation, the bylaws, and the donor's intent. Deviation from these purposes may require court approval.

- The Board must ensure that assets held for investment are invested prudently.

- A director's breach of fiduciary duty that causes harm to the corporation will make the director personally liable to make the corporation whole. The Attorney General is responsible for enforcement.

Some Examples

Now consider cases of corporate social responsibility and community social entrepreneurship that create a compelling vision of problems, formulate strategies to address them, engage others' commitment and support, take action to make a difference, evaluate outcomes, and establish ongoing, yet continually evolving, efforts. The cases highlight two role models: an executive who promotes CSR in his company and a young man whose energy, motivation, and increasing competency have built an ongoing effort with a local and global focus. Perhaps not coincidentally, they are father and son (from London, 2008, pp. 314–315).

Stanley M. Bergman has been chairman and CEO of Henry Schein, Inc. since 1989. A CPA educated in South Africa, he is responsible for the firm's substantial growth and financial success and the continuation of a cutting-edge social mission that has been a hallmark of the firm since its founding in 1932. The company distributes health care products and services to office-based clinicians (dentists, dental labs, physicians, veterinarians, and government and other institutions) throughout North America, Europe, Australia, and New Zealand. Stanley Bergman started with the firm in the early 1980s and worked closely with its founder, Henry Schein, to grow the business and, with it, the company's tradition of social action. They forged a commitment to understand community problems and ways their resources could be used effectively to respond to current needs and prepare for emergencies. The company structures its social mission into categories that allow tracking and reporting of contributions and results. Bergman communicates his personal and corporate values through a history of action and social justice that is a legacy for the firm's future. The company has a global social responsibility program to support health care advocacy and education, increase access to care for underserved populations, prepare and respond to disasters, and generally strengthen community wellness programs. The company has donated millions of dollars in products, services, and cash. The firm's philosophy is to help people and groups at the grassroots level through a variety of local programs that often involve company personnel raising money and delivering services.

Edward J. Bergman co-founded Miracle Corners of the World, Inc. (MCW), a nonprofit organization that serves young people worldwide, primarily through programs of leadership training, community center and housing development, and health care outreach. The organization's motto is "Local Change Through Global Exchange." MCW focuses on Africa but has projects in the United States and China as well. Eddie traveled to Africa on missions when he was a high school student in the late 1990s. He continued his volunteer work as an undergraduate student in hotel and tourism management at New York University and a graduate student there, where he created an individualized study program in social entrepreneurship. Now in his mid-twenties, Eddie is director of the Africa Travel Association in addition to his leadership of MCW. He has a passion for service and creating initiatives that do good. Influenced by his father, Stan Bergman, and Team Schein as role models and sources of encouragement, Eddie is a passionate social entrepreneur with innovative ideas and a can-do attitude. MCW has helped develop community centers in Arusha and Songea, Tanzania, and Kissey, Sierra Leone. In Addis Ababa, Ethiopia, the MCW-built community center supports orphans and teaches community members about organic gardening, environmentalism, and health. MCW's annual Youth Leadership Retreat brings teens and young adults from underdeveloped countries to Burlington, Vermont, to learn about advocacy and social entrepreneurship. Eddie understands networking and fund raising. MCW's third annual gala in New York City in 2007 honored tennis legend Billie Jean King; World Team Tennis CEO and Commissioner Ilana Kloss; Cal Ramsey of the New York Knicks; and Baltimore Ravens linebacker and Super Bowl MVP Ray Lewis.

Reflection Exercise

Consider how the steps of social action applied to our examples of corporate social responsibility at Henry Schein and MCW. Select an initiative and imagine each step. Or select your own initiative. Then answer the following questions about envisioning, formulating, taking action, evaluating, sustaining the effort:

1 What are the problems/needs?
2 What situational conditions apply? Are they likely to help or hinder the effort?
3 What characteristics motivate the leaders (or your own) desire to get involved?
4 What goals were set? What strategies could be used to accomplish them?
5 What decisions need to be made? What tasks have to be carried out?
6 How will the effort be tracked and success measured?
7 What skills and competencies are participants likely to learn?
8 What elements of the organization of the effort will help sustain it over time?
9 What adaptations are likely ... adjustments to changing conditions?

Using Social Capital

Social entrepreneurs harness social capital for human good. Social entrepreneurs use social capital (relationships, networks, trust, and cooperation) as a core asset to provide access to physical and financial resources to those in need. "The development of relationships and a network of contacts (a typically entrepreneurial behavior) has brought trust, visibility, credibility and cooperation which has been used as an intellectual base from which the physical and financial capital required to generate social capital can be found" (Thompson *et al.*, 2000, p. 331). Social entrepreneurs need to learn how social capital and social exchange operate to engage volunteers, transform ideas into action, grow and sustain initiatives through effective leadership and management, and overcome barriers to goal accomplishment.

Social capital is the goodwill available to individuals or groups that bond people together through norms of reciprocity (Adler & Kwon, 2002; Dekker & Uslaner, 2001; Uslaner, 2001). It affects the flow of information, influence, and commitments people make toward each other. Social exchange theory (cf. Homans, 1961; Kelley & Thibaut, 1978) explains reciprocity processes, involving the balance between what people put into a relationship and what they get out of it, their beliefs about the kind of relationship they deserve, and/or their judgments about the chances of having a better relationship. They develop a comparison level against which they compare the give-take ratio. All relationships have give and take, although the balance of this exchange is not always equal. Their expectations for the comparison level will depend on setting. For instance, exchanges in the office or at home may be different from what they expect from strangers in the community (Cook & Whitmeyer, 1992).

Social exchange theory's fundamental premise is that human behavior is an exchange of rewards between actors (Zafirovski, 2005). It treats the exchange of benefits, notably giving others something more valuable to them than is costly to the giver, and vice versa (Homans, 1961, pp. 61–63). The exchange is assumed to be governed by reciprocal relationships that would not continue for long if the reciprocity were violated. Giving something more valuable to the receiver than it is to the giver creates imbalances that produce relationships of power, dependence, and cohesion. People enter into exchange relationships expecting mutual benefit (Blau, 1994). Corporate social entrepreneurship and volunteerism is such an exchange. The extrinsic value may be greater to the receiver than the giver, but the giver may receive a range of intrinsic (positive feelings) and extrinsic outcomes such as recognition and a more positive community environment (Wilson & Musick, 1997).

Social activists start with social capital, such as corporate resources and a network of contacts and supporters within their corporation. Social entrepreneurs recruit fellow employees, contact others outside the organization (e.g., beneficiaries, community support organizations, government agencies), and develop the structure, policies, and procedures to form an initiative. The development of the initiative entails (1) recognizing the need and envisioning an idea to address the need; (2) formulating a strategy that includes communicating the idea to others and finding partners and like-minded individuals who want to help; (3) taking action: formulating a partnership, seeking corporate resources, setting short- and long-term goals, taking action steps, such as recruiting volunteers and seeking donations; (4) tracking and evaluating outcomes; and (5) developing and implementing plans for continued operations and growth, including leadership succession.

The vision informs and attracts stakeholders who make commitments, refine the vision, and shape strategies and goals. Stakeholders' commitments are affected by the clarity of a vision and its tie to their underlying values, beliefs, and emotions. Generally, the social entrepreneur needs to apply principles of good management. The initiative needs a strong vision that matches corporate and other stakeholders' interests and expectations. By this, we mean that the vision needs to translate into operational goals that are specific, measurable, actionable, realistic, and time bound (Conzemius & O'Neill, 2005). These contribute to forming systems that impose accountability, recognize and resolve conflicts, and achieve and celebrate (reward) positive outcomes. This in turns leads to individual, group, and organizational learning about how CSR starts, is maintained, and produces valuable outcomes. In turn, learning is likely to affect the social entrepreneur's and other stakeholders' motivation. Social entrepreneurs who promote CSR within their employer organizations need to be adaptable to sustain and grow the initiative and, when necessary, redirect corporate energy to new areas in new ways as needs and situational conditions change.

The social entrepreneur needs the right team (people with the skills, motivation, and time; see Chapter 5). This is not necessarily simple, as volunteers self-select and leaders may have trouble turning away unqualified volunteers, especially if they are fellow employees. The social entrepreneur requires team members who share the same values, beliefs, interests, and concerns. The social entrepreneur must continuously inspire and motivate helpers and create a strong culture of engagement. Overall, the social entrepreneur establishes goals, provides strong leadership, aligns corporate and donated resources to match the goals, develops program plans that produce a measurable return, and inspires.

Within corporations, social entrepreneurs are likely to be accountable for their performance to a board of directors and executives. Social entrepreneurship initiatives are likely to be characterized by nurturing those served and those who serve, operating by consensus, and treating all volunteers with equal respect by avoiding status differences. The evolution of a social entrepreneurship initiative is likely to be a long-term process. Ongoing sources of pressure may be a variety of external factors (e.g., community needs and expectations, customer reactions and demands, corporate competition, the economy, globalization, government regulation). A social action effort can benefit from best practices of corporate performance management, such as goal setting, balanced scorecards, and dashboard measures to assess performance and track success (Paton, 2003). In short, social improvement efforts will change as the environment changes, imposing requirements and providing new methods, resources, and/or partners for success (Paton, 2003). The ongoing processes and outcomes of an initiative contribute to individual and organizational learning. The social entrepreneur and the volunteers individually and collectively learn to adapt, apply new knowledge and skills, and possibly change the vision goals and process. This enables everyone involved, especially the social entrepreneur, to recalibrate the vision for the enterprise and maintain inspirational leadership that keeps others interested and motivated. Indeed, such learning may have spin-off benefits for regular corporate operations, building teams, group efficacy, and pride in the organization.

By way of summary, the processes outlined earlier suggests the following:

- Situational pressures and opportunities drive the press for action.
- The social entrepreneur perceives the available social capital and possibility of exchange.
- The social entrepreneur's altruistic motivation, readiness to learn, and transformational leadership abilities contribute to a clear, engaging, and realistic vision.
- A clear, engaging, and realistic vision helps the social entrepreneur engage corporate support and create operational goals and strategies for success.
- A realistic, challenging, and exciting vision captures stakeholders' involvement and commitment, allows the social entrepreneur to recruit a team of fellow social entrepreneurs/volunteers and, in the process, strengthens the vision.
- Continued pressures increase the social entrepreneur's learning and provide direction and resources for accomplishing its objectives.
- Events and outcomes (whether positive or negative) strengthen the social entrepreneur's engagement and readiness to be flexible and learn.

Social Entrepreneurship Strategies

Social entrepreneurs use cognitive, emotional, and behavioral strategies to influence others' attitudes, behaviors, and/or decisions in support of their goals (Sharma, 1996; VeneKlasen, 1995). Table 4.3 describes entrepreneurship strategies for taking public action, ensuring fair treatment of others, and acting altruistically. Cognitive strategies involve providing information and facts. Emotional strategies warn of dangers or exude positive benefits of an action or decision. Behavioral strategies are actions to show support for a viewpoint, treat others fairly and organize resources to help others. (Note: These tables and this section of the chapter are from London, 2010).

These strategies rest on an understanding of interpersonal influence, impression management, and the social entrepreneur's beliefs about what strategies are likely to influence people the most. Social influence

Table 4.3 Examples of Social Entrepreneurship Actions and Strategies

What Social Entrepreneurs Do	How They Do It (Social Entrepreneurship Strategies)		
	Cognitive	Emotional	Behavioral
Take public action	Explain their viewpoint publicly Are not afraid to be viewed as outspoken	Pursue a cause doggedly (do not give up easily) Put their reputation on the line Warn targets about potential losses Do not take "no" for an answer	Stand up for what they believe is right Participate in demonstrations, boycotts, and other actions that constrain a target's behavior Upset the status quo; take people out of their comfort zone
Ensure fair treatment of others	Stand up for others' rights by expressing a clear opinion	Warn of the dangers of inequitable treatment	Treat others fairly and equitably Make fair decisions despite others' disagreement Give others a chance to voice their opinions
Act altruistically	Champion the cause of people who can't speak for themselves Provide information about others' hardships (for instance, data on numbers of people affected)	Express empathy and sympathy Show pictures of how others are suffering Express the dangers of the situation continuing	Organize resources to help others Deliver services

is the process of persuading others to comply and conform (Cialdini, 2001; Cialdini & Goldstein, 2004; Cialdini & Trost, 1998). This relies on self-identity and person perception processes. For instance, people infer their own attributes by observing the freely chosen actions of others with whom they feel a sense of merged identity, as if they see themselves performing the acts (Goldstein & Cialdini, 2007). Social influence theory concentrates on understanding a target's susceptibility to outside influence.

Table 4.4 summarizes how social entrepreneurs' beliefs about people are likely to affect the influence strategies they use to advocate for their cause.

Social Entrepreneurs' Beliefs About People

The strategies that social entrepreneurs adopt—for instance, whether to rely on emotional appeal, warnings, and/or rational/cognitive

Table 4.4 Social Entrepreneur's Beliefs About People and Associated Social Advocacy Strategies

Some Possible Beliefs about People	How Beliefs About People Affect Advocacy Strategies	Sample Actions
People are willing to change their attitudes and behavior, and they pay attention to inconsistent information (incremental theory) Alternatively, people do not change their attitudes and behavior easily, if at all, and they seek consistent information and ignore inconsistent information (entity theory) (Plaks, Stroessner, Dweck, & Sherman, 2001)	Cognitive strategy: Provide complete and accurate information believing that people will understand it even if it conflicts with their previous attitudes and behaviors "Once they know, they will do something about it." Acognitive strategy: Identify and recruit people whose attitudes and behaviors already conform to the goals of the advocacy initiative; if they don't, providing contrary information will not change their opinions "Work with true believers; seek other methods if decision makers are not already one of us."	Flyers, mailings, and ads with information (e.g., statistics on homelessness in the community or school drop out rates) Enlist those who already share the values and goals; work around those who don't or try other strategies (below)
People are motivated by expectancies—high probabilities of achieving valued outcomes. (Slovic, Fischhoff and Lichtenstein, 1977) (Behavioral decision theory; Slovic, Fischhoff, & Lichtenstein, 1977)	Expectancy theory: Cognitive-behavioral approach to inform people of probabilities of events and likely gains. Reward outcomes, withhold benefits for inaction. "Once they see the positive benefits for themselves or others, they will act."	Strengthen linkages between actions and outcomes (e.g., contributions go directly to people in need; support for research saves lives; renewable energy can be cost effective in x years)
People give more weight to the prospect of impending losses than impending gains and so are motivated by threats of loss. (Prospect theory, Kahneman & Tversky, 1979)	Emotional focus that concentrates on possible loss "Once they are aware of the threat, they will respond."	Arguments (talks, presentations, ads) with graphic depictions of dire consequences or suffering (e.g., showing hunger and poverty; beggars in the streets if we don't open a shelter; species extinction from rain forest depletion)
People copy others' lead and respond to peer pressure and the need to be accepted. (Social learning, social influence, commitment theories, Bandura, 1977, 2001; and advocacy coalition theory, Jenkins-Smith & Sabatier, 1994)	Use role models, pressure from people they emulate, form coalitions, and provide opportunities for voicing commitment "Once they realize there is a groundswell of opinion, they will join; once they express an opinion publicly, they will be consistent and demonstrate commitment."	Public demonstrations for or against an issue (e.g., the death penalty); endorsements from well-known people in the community; petitions with signatures published in the local newspaper
People judge how others are likely to act and they try to maximize their gains and minimize their losses relative to others' choices; viewing advocacy as a negotiation, competition, or opportunity for a win-win, consensus solution. (Game theory, Nash, 1950)	Negotiate with decision makers and adversaries; seek consensus; prepare for battle "Once they recognize we can both win, they will agree." "Once they reveal their intentions or limits, I can beat them." "Once they see that neither of us are getting anywhere, they will compromise." "Either we win, or they do."	Organize debates; establish trade-offs; facilitate give-and-take negotiations; compromise (e.g., establish marine protected area while allowing limited fishing rights); succeed or give up (e.g., "If the community doesn't do something to solve the homeless problem, we will move away.")

arguments—are likely to depend on their view of what motivates other people, in particular how and why people respond to different messages and influence attempts. Three social psychological processes center on the social entrepreneur's beliefs about people: (1) implicit theories about whether people are likely to change their attitudes and behavior—that is, whether they can be coached, developed, or convinced to change; (2) belief about whether people are sensitive to gains and losses and averse to risk (prospect theory); and (3) beliefs about the costs and benefits of action and outcomes, the probabilities that action will lead to the valued outcomes (producing gain or avoiding loss), and the immediacy and mutual, coalition-building benefits of the effects of these actions (motivation theory components).

Social entrepreneurs need to believe that people can be influenced and that they change their attitudes and behaviors as a result. They also need to have some idea about what motivates people to change. If social entrepreneurs believe that people do not change their attitudes or behavior readily, if at all, there is no point in trying to influence them. Social entrepreneurs who believe that people change their attitudes will provide them with information and in other ways work hard to alter their views. Social entrepreneurs who believe that people act for self-gain (i.e., they are selfish) are likely to try to change attitudes and behavior by focusing on potential gains. Social entrepreneurs who believe that people are altruistic are likely to focus on ways to help others. Social entrepreneurs who believe that people are risk averse are likely to give warnings about possible losses.

Consider several other interpersonal beliefs. Social entrepreneurs may believe that people respond primarily to emotional appeals, so they focus their advocacy on others' emotions. Social entrepreneurs may believe that people respond to cognitive appeals, so they offer information and appeal to reason. Social entrepreneurs may believe that attitudes follow behaviors, so they try to get people to act ("just try this") assuming that consistent attitudes will follow. Social entrepreneurs may believe that people only change when they have to, such as when the situation becomes dire. Social entrepreneurs may manipulate such situations (e.g., creating forums that essentially force decision makers into public expression of commitment). Other structural mechanisms may be creating interdependence with others who control positive outcomes, recognizing mutual benefit, or forming contracts that require a certain decision or action in return for personal benefit.

Social entrepreneurs' beliefs about how supporters and decision makers respond to potential losses and gains may determine the strategies they use to influence people. Social entrepreneurs may perceive others as responding to one of these two dispositions: the motivation to attain positive outcomes or avoid negative outcomes.

Consider how social entrepreneurs' perceptions of others' sensitivity to possible future gains or losses affect their choice of influence strategy. Social entrepreneurs who perceive that people give more weight to possible losses than they do to possible gains are likely to use verbal and nonverbal appeals, warnings, blame, promises of rewards, and/or social/peer pressures. Specifically, social entrepreneurs are likely to focus on such emotional strategies and emphasize losses when (1) information is not available, (2) outcome measures are not clear or available, (3) risks are high (i.e., valued outcomes are at stake), (4) risk aversion is high, and (5) conflicts are likely (e.g., there is competition for resources; self-interests differ). Social entrepreneurs may focus on losses that deal with individuals' dominant needs (e.g., for clean air, sustenance, and safety), and the warning may emphasize that severe negative outcomes will result, even though they are not immediate. Such social entrepreneurs may work outside the system, calling for others to join with them (e.g., to fight big business or top management).

Social entrepreneurs who believe that people respond to reason are likely to provide information and facts and engage in open and honest communication. Information about gains may highlight the value of the gains, and de-emphasize the low probability of occurrence and the long-time horizon for their emergence. Social entrepreneurs are likely to focus on cognitive levers that emphasize gains when (1) information is available, (2) outcome measures are clear and available, (3) risks are low, (4) risk aversion is low, and (5) conflicts are low. Such social entrepreneurs are likely to work within the system or at least feel comfortable as a boundary spanner, highlighting opportunities for mutual gain.

As a review, we make the following points:

- Social entrepreneurs' beliefs about how others respond and change affect the influence strategies they adopt to advocate for their cause.
- Social entrepreneurs' beliefs about what leads others to change determine whether they rely on strategies that provide information and rational arguments (a cognitive approach) and/or use warnings, playing on others' sympathy or feelings of guilt or promises of positive feelings (an emotional approach). Social entrepreneurs may use a combination of these techniques. Social entrepreneurs who believe that people change only when they have to are likely to use strategies that constrain behavior, ignore

conflicts of interest and other legalities, and possibly resort to force.

- Social entrepreneurs provide information about the values, probability, and immediacy of outcomes (cognitive/rational arguments) when they believe people respond to anticipated gains. Social entrepreneurs use emotional appeals when they believe people respond to anticipated losses.
- Higher potential gains and losses, more immediacy of effect, and greater controversy generate more attention and resources and motivate individuals to become advocates on their own or with others.

Long-term Impact of Emotional Appeals

People's affective responses weaken after one or more exposures to emotional events, especially those that are hard to explain or understand how this happened to them (Wilson & Gilbert, 2008). People attend to positive and negative emotional events that affect them, react emotionally, attempt to explain or reach an understanding of the events, and thereby adapt, paying less attention to them and having a weaker emotional reaction. Explanation hastens recovery from negative events. The people who are able to recover most quickly from traumas, such as the death of loved ones, are able to find meaning in the event, especially explanations that maintain their view of the world as a just place. As regards cultural differences: East Asian cultures have a holistic, dialectical reasoning process that allows them to explain contradictions that are harder for analytically oriented Westerners to comprehend. As a result, East Asians have are likely to have shorter and less-intense affective reactions to events than Westerners.

This adaptation process has implications for helping people deal with negative events. It also has implications for maintaining volunteers' and contributors' interests in social concerns. A recent bias crime produced contributions and expressions of support in a community. When an interfaith support event was organized several months later, however, participation was sparse. As such, social concerns need to be embedded in our decisions and actions, not rely on emotional appeal. The implications:

- Strike while the iron is hot (when events occur, raise money and recruit volunteers on the spot). Periodically remind people of the event and the attendant emotions.

- Focus on the confusion and uncertainty, not the explanation and resolution.
- Involve people in an active way so they can experience positive or negative emotions related to social issues; the closer they are to people who are affected, the more they are likely to act.
- Do not expect people to retain an affinity for a problem or issue if they have no tie or if the issue was in the past; memorials are ways to explain, resolve, and deal with emotions—they do not prompt more social action, at least not in major ways (e.g., the time to raise scholarship money in memory of someone is immediately after the person's demise, not years or even months later).

Spirituality

Graafland, Kaptein, and Mazereeuw (2007) discovered that socially responsible business conduct derived from economic, ethical and, to some extent, religious beliefs. They studied the relationship between the religious beliefs of corporate decision makers and socially responsible business conduct. On the basis of in-depth interviews with 20 Dutch executives from different religious backgrounds,they found that executives with a monotheistic conception of God had a higher propensity to engage in socially responsible business conduct than executives with a pantheistic conception of God (the idea that God equates to the natural forces and laws of the universe).

Practical Implications

Knowledge of interpersonal influence and impression management processes and associated cognitive, emotional, and behavioral strategies can have substantial practical value within organizations and communities. Organizations can train employees how to advocate constructively to promote CSR. Within communities, social entrepreneurship strategies can be incorporated into primary, secondary, and higher education and adult continuing education programs. These skills can be taught along with the value of civic engagement, community service, citizenship, and government. Teachers can be trained to incorporate social entrepreneurship in their curricula. Schools of business, government and public policy, social work and education, and environmental science can offer courses and workshops on social entrepreneurship. Nonprofit organizations often train social entrepreneurs. For instance, unions train organizers (see http://www.CampusActivism.org). Non-government organizations (NGOs) train recruits in political engagement (Sharma, 1996). Foundations provide workshops and information to support social entrepreneurs (e.g., University Network for Social Entrepreneurship and the Kaufman Foundation; see http://www. universitynetwork.org). The Institute for Sustainable Communities' Advocacy and Leadership Center offers programs, training, and tools that are readily available free online on such topics as fundamentals of social advocacy, strategic planning for social entrepreneurs, strategic project management, message strategy, building and leading coalitions, monitoring and evaluation, and advocacy life cycle issues (see http://www.iscvt.org).

Measures of social entrepreneurship behaviors, situations, and outcomes can be used for diagnosis and assessment. Situational measures can determine immediacy of impact, sensitivity of potential supporters and decision makers to gains/losses and costs–benefits, and probabilities of positive and negative effects. The results would indicate whether advocacy strategies should depend on the social entrepreneur's strength of personality, behavior-outcome contingencies, and/or rational argument and information. Also, as suggested, training can be developed to help potential and current social entrepreneurs understand themselves and the situation. This can be customized for different groups of social entrepreneurs, such as employee assistance counselors, professionals in ombudsman roles, union representatives, and social entrepreneurs.

Conclusion

This chapter outlined steps for establishing a new social action venture, whether in the community or as part of a corporation's social responsibility. Major steps include envisioning, formulating, taking action, evaluating, and sustaining the effort. Having a clear mission statement and detailed "business" plan are important for any social action initiative, whether it is meant to be an ongoing enterprise with an organizational structure or a one-time event or activity. For structured organizations, we emphasized the importance of board governance, particularly board members' ethical and fiduciary responsibilities.

Social entrepreneurs' implicit theories about human behavior, development, and attitude change affect the strategies they adopt. Social entrepreneurs are likely to use an influence strategy that provides information about the values, probability, and immediacy of outcomes (cognitive-rational arguments) when they believe people respond to anticipated gains. Social entrepreneurs are likely to use emotional appeals when they believe people respond to anticipated losses.

Questions for Reflection and Discussion

1   Which step of social entrepreneurship do you believe is the most important? Why?
2   What difficulties are you likely to encounter at various steps of starting a social action venture?
3   What is the greatest barrier to a company's operating in a socially responsible manner?
4   Can you think of some innovative social action ventures— innovative because of their goals and/or methods? What were the innovations? Do you know how they evolved? Investigate how they were developed and made successful.
5   Why is a mission statement important? How does it direct the initiative?
6   Why develop a "business plan" for a not-for-profit venture?
7   Which is more important for a social entrepreneur: the ability to plan a strategy in advance or the ability to adapt to situations as they arise and change? Why?
8   How can social entrepreneurs advance their agenda without initially possessing the needed resources to do so? What resources would they need to acquire, and how would they acquire these resources?
9   How can your organization be guided by reason as opposed to the emotions of its members when forming a strategic plan?
10   What is the greatest opportunity and threat to the advocacy organization of your choice?
11   Which actions do you believe are the most important for an advocacy organization to take as it continues to expand? Why?

Social Venture Exercises

Exercise 1: Mission Building

Think about a not-for-profit, social entrepreneurial or CSR venture with which you are familiar. Write down what you think its mission statement is. Then go to the organization's Web site or other material to compare your perception to the organization's actual mission. Was there overlap? Did you have an accurate view of the purpose of the organization? If so, the organization has done a good job of communicating its mission to the public. If not, the public may be confused about the organization's mission, and this may hinder its ability to raise funds and recruit volunteers. Or perhaps this lack of concordance between your perceptions and the organization's mission suggests that you were not sufficiently aware of the organization's purpose and that if you are interested in volunteering or contributing, you need to go beyond common perceptions or your minimal knowledge and investigate the organization more deeply.

Exercise 2: Actions

Take the next step to develop the social venture you have been thinking about at the end of each chapter. Explain the steps and strategies you might use to accomplish your goals. Indicate whether you would rely on cognitive, emotional, and/or behavioral strategies or a combination of both.

Exercise 3: Formulating Strategies and Recognizing Underlying Beliefs About People

Drawing on Table 4.4, explain actions you might take to recruit volunteers, raise funds, form alliances (and with whom), and influence decision makers and other stakeholders. For each action, indicate your underlying belief—whether the strategies and associated actions are based on your beliefs that (1) people are willing to change their attitudes and behaviors; (2) people are motivated by expectancies—high probabilities of achieving valued outcomes; (3) people respond to peer pressure and the need to be accepted; (4) people try to maximize their gains and minimize their losses relative to others' choices viewing advocacy as a negotiation, competition, or opportunity for a win-win, consensus solution; or (5) a combination of all.

Exercise 4: Building Image

Design a logo that readily identifies your venture and its purpose. How does the logo convey information, generate emotion, and/or call to action?

Suggest mechanisms for a lobbying campaign using an Internet site (to convey information), a blog (to allow people to exchange ideas online), a wiki (to allow people to share information online), message boards (to post notices and announcements), videos, town hall meetings, demonstrations, letter writing, and so on. How will you use these methods to (1) educate, (2) motivate, and (3) change behavior? Will you have different communication strategies for different constituencies and demographic groups (community members, merchants, students, senior citizens)?

Exercise 5: Financial Strategy Exercise

Regardless of whether you are an independent social entrepreneur or a socially responsible corporate executive, in order to strategically plan you must take into account the prospective revenues and expenses associated with your venture. To do this, you need to "know your way around" a basic EXCEL spreadsheet. This exercise asks you to identify and explain the revenues and expenses that you believe your venture will incur during the next 3 years.

Consider the following potential revenue streams and answer the associated questions, providing a summarized analysis of the relevance of each stream while also identifying and analyzing several new revenue streams of your own:

1   Advertising: Does your Web site and/or "brick-and-mortar" location serve as a means for sponsors to advertise their goods and services?
2   Webcasts and Webinars: Does your social venture offer workshops, lectures, or conferences that others might pay to attend?
3   Does your social venture provide an affordable product or service that is readily available to the consumer?
4   Does your social venture provide membership privileges for a fee?
5   Is your social venture eligible for any grants or government contracts?
6   Does your social venture market related electronic journals, reports, data, texts, or articles for a fee?
7   Does your social venture provide consulting to other corporations, small businesses, or educational institutions?
8   Does your social venture perform subcontracted work on behalf of other organizations?
9   What other potentially viable funding streams can you associate with the operation of your venture?

Now that you have started to develop your social venture, it is time to expand its scope. You may be developing a plan for both a money-making enterprise that will generate funds that you will donate to a cause and/or a not-for-profit enterprise that delivers services or raises funds for those in need. If you are developing a for-profit business with a CSR component, consider the following:

•   How will you use of the Internet? Choose a domain name for your venture. Use an established Web service such as http://www.

GoDaddy.com to determine whether the domain name has been chosen.

- Determine the e-commerce strategy of your top three competitors.
- Determine the strengths and weaknesses of your competitor's e-commerce strategies.
- On the basis of your analysis of your competitors' e-commerce strategies, design your company's e-commerce strategy.
- Discuss opportunities for increased sales and profits to your company on the basis of your new or improved strategy.

Prepare a SWOT analysis of your product or services of your social venture by answering the following questions (adapted from Thompson *et al.*, 2005, p. 85).

Strengths

1   Compare how your proposed strategy is superior to the strategy of your competitors.
2   Tell us how your product or service is differentiated from your rivals. How is it better?
3   Explain how you have adequate financial resources to fund your product or service.
4   Explain how you would attract a strong customer base.
5   Explain whether you can obtain economies of scale and/or a superior learning curve.
6   How does your technology give you a competitive advantage?
7   How are your advertising and promotion a distinct competitive advantage?
8   Describe your customer service plan as a sustainable competitive advantage.
9   How is your organization an "innovative learning organization?"
10 How does your geographic coverage provide you with a competitive advantage?
11 What valuable alliances with other organizations have you formed? What specific benefits will you obtain from these alliances?

Weaknesses

How do you plan on overcoming the following:

1   An unclear strategic direction
2   Inadequate resources

3   Inadequate or unmanageable capabilities
4   An undeveloped core competency
5   Unproven innovation capabilities
6   Product features that are either inferior or the same as your rivals
7   Weak brand image or reputation
8   Lack of management depth
9   Lack of funding

Opportunities

1   How can you win market share from your rivals?
2   How can the demand for your product be enhanced?
3   How can you serve additional customer groups or markets?
4   How can you expand into different geographic regions?
5   How can you utilize existing skills or technology to develop new products?
6   How can you benefit from online markets?
7   How could you vertically integrate backward and/or forward? (e.g., buying a supplier or distributor)?
8   How can you acquire rival firms?
9   How can you enter into competitive alliances?
10 What new technologies and/or capabilities can you acquire?
11 Which potential investors can you attract?

Threats

1   How do you plan for your present rivals' becoming more competitive?
2   How do you plan for additional rivals to compete with?
3   What will you do if the market takes a downturn?
4   What will you do if there is a shortage of key labor?
5   What substitute products could compete with you?
6   What if there is a shift in buyer preferences and tastes away from your product?
7   What if foreign governments place a tariff on your goods?
8   What if there are costly new regulatory requirements?
9   What if there is a new innovation that makes your product obsolete in its present form?
10 What if there is a scandal related to the ethical actions of some of your employees?

Exercise 6: Roles

Consider the roles you need to play for the social venture you have been thinking about starting. What will you do to create a vision, formulate strategies, take action, sustain your initiative, and evaluate your operational processes and outcomes? (See Table 4.1.)

Exercise 7: Drafting Your Business Plan

Outline each element of a business plan. Include a section on each of the following:

- Executive summary
- Mission, vision, and goals (goals that are specific, measureable, actionable, realistic, and time-bound—i.e., SMART)
- SWOT analysis
- Market analysis
- Keys to success (What's needed to make this work)
- Resources (e.g., equipment, facilities, staff)
- Support (e.g., training program)
- Operations plan (logistics, public relations)
- Financial plan (annual budget, anticipated revenue and expenses)
- Evaluation and ongoing market review (goals for profitability for the next 3–5 years)

5 Developing High-Performing Social Action Teams

In this chapter, you will learn how to do the following:

1 Apply the components of a high-performing team (talent, task, and time) to social entrepreneurship
2 Facilitate adaptive, generative, and transformative team learning
3 Recognize situational pressures and opportunities that promote team learning
4 Assess the leadership challenge to accomplish social entrepreneurship goals
5 Balance three continua: recognizing volunteers' vested interests versus emphasizing shared goals; being authoritative versus empowering volunteers; taking action versus taking time for reflection
6 Manage volunteers and paid staff
7 Deal with wayward volunteers

Introduction

Michael J. Brown, executive director of the Jewish Organizing Initiative and author of the 2007 book, *Building Powerful Community Organizations: A Personal Guide to Creating Groups That Can Solve Problems and Change the World*, describes community organizing as building the power of a group to change the world. This chapter is about creating effective teams of volunteers and partners in social entrepreneurship. Volunteer groups are especially difficult to lead and manage. Here we address the components of a high-performing volunteer team, leadership challenges, and ways of dealing with difficult people.

Components of a High-Performing Volunteer Team

A high-performing team is one in which all members are working together cooperatively to achieve shared goals. They communicate clearly and as often as necessary, coordinate activities, recognize and respect one another's talents, know how each person can contribute to the group, evaluate group progress, give one another feedback, and achieve their objectives. The tasks the team produces require that members work in synchronization. They have specific roles and task requirements, are aware of their obligations to the group, and exert effort to meet expectations. Volunteers may have different reasons for being involved in a social entrepreneurship effort but, as team members, they need to operate in a coordinated way, responding to the social entrepreneur's leadership cues and performing their tasks in tight formation even though they are not paid.

Three components are critical to a high-performing team: talent, task, and time (Ericksen & Dyer, 2004).

- Talent is having people with the skills, knowledge, and experience needed to perform the group's tasks.
- Task refers to the structure of the roles that each member is expected to perform. The more tasks are clearly delineated, the more likely the members will know what to do to accomplish the team's goals.
- Time refers to the willingness of the members to devote sufficient time and attention to the task and the leader's setting a time frame for goal accomplishment that is realistic.

High-performing teams also need leadership and coaching in relation to the stage of group process. For instance, teams need to be motivated when they begin. They need task structure as the work gets underway. They need time to reflect and process feedback about their behavior and results as individuals and a team once the task is completed (Hackman & Wageman, 2005).

Most work groups, however, do not have highly prescribed roles for their members. This is especially true of volunteer groups whose leaders, although perhaps elected, are also volunteers. Volunteers, by definition, are invited or self-selected. They may be given information about the task requirements (or maybe not), and they make commitments, which they may or may not keep. The challenge of leading a social enterprise staffed by volunteers is guiding members into roles that match their experience, expertise, and interest and changing assignments depending on results. We say more later about the challenges of managing volunteers, particularly when the team lacks adequate talent, task structure, and time.

Interpersonal Congruence and Transactive Knowledge

Teams are more effective when they start by acquainting members with one another (London, Polzer, & Omergerie, 2005; Polzer, Milton, & Swan, 2002). Simply introducing all the members and having them describe the task-relevant experiences they have had and the knowledge they possess will help members see one another accurately and agree about who is best at what tasks. Interpersonal congruence occurs when members see one another similarly. This helps them call on one another to perform elements of a task when the need arises. One member may be best at asking potential contributors for money. Another may be best at managing budgets or ordering supplies. Still others may be good at producing advertising flyers. Still others may have the technical knowledge to develop and deliver the services that are key to goal accomplishment.

Transactive knowledge develops as the members work with one another and establish operating routines for transactions among members (Lewis, 2003; Wegner, 1986). They invoke these routines time and again, developing team-level expertise. The group becomes adept at performing certain tasks. For instance, this might be an annual corporate task force to raise money for underprivileged children and families at Thanksgiving. The company has done this year after year. The same employees participate each year, adding new employees to the corporate social responsibility (CSR) task force over the years. The team goes into "automatic pilot" mode. They follow routines that may even be scripted with notes about tasks that are needed, time frames, what can go wrong, and how to avoid problems.

Routines about how to work together effectively help when circumstances change and unexpected events occur. Emergencies and opportunities are chances for a group to go into overdrive, drawing on their knowledge of one another's talents and work habits and implementing them to accomplish new tasks. They may make minor adaptations along the way, but basically, they adopt the processes that worked well in the past. This is fine as long as the processes continue to work. However, new circumstances may demand different talents, tasks, and time frames.

Adaptive, Generative, and Transformative Learning

Sessa and London (2006) articulated three types of learning.

1   *Adaptive learning* is making small changes in patterns of interaction in response to changing conditions. This happens with little thought. For instance, if someone doesn't come to a meeting or an event, others take over or their work is skipped with little effect on final outcomes. The group has adapted before. It has learned how to do so and will adapt again if necessary.

2   *Generative learning* is recognizing that what worked in the past may not work in the future. Teams that learn to be generative have members who acquire new skills and knowledge, teach these skills and knowledge to other group members, and experiment with different ways to apply the skills and knowledge. As they do so, they develop new interaction patterns. Moreover, they strengthen their ability to be generative in the future. They don't wait for circumstances to change. They change the circumstances to fit their goals. They may also change their goals to match changing circumstances. Generative teams are continuous learners, always on the lookout for new ways to do things better. Pressures and opportunities in the environment can stimulate generative learning. So can members' openness to new ideas and knowledge and readiness to learn.

3   *Transformative learning* is generative learning squared. That is, as the group engages in generative activity, it sometimes transforms itself into new enterprises, taking on new tasks and goals and reshaping its purpose and structure. Examples would be NGOs that expand their field of operations to new countries and new social services, or charities that broaden their goals or assume new challenges (e.g., new diseases to conquer).

Assessing Leadership Challenges

Table 5.1 lists 10 elements of a team that may pose leadership challenges. Teams vary in purpose, member motivation, number of members, their diversity, and the extent to which they turn over, with some members leaving and others coming in (the typically fluid membership of many volunteer organizations). Also, teams vary in the clarity of their goals, the time frame, and the extent to which work processes are structured. Moreover, the leader's role varies. Some leaders are controlling, others more facilitating and transforming; some leaders have high power to control goals, assignments, and time frames, and others have very little power to do so. Use Table 5.1 to evaluate the leadership challenges

Table 5.1 Evaluating the Leadership Challenge

		A	B
1.	Purpose	Uncertain	Certain
2.	Motivation	Low	High
3.	Size	Large	Small
4.	Diversity	Diverse	Homogeneous
5.	Turnover	High	Low
6.	Goal clarity	Ambiguous	Clear
7.	Time frame pressure	Limited time, tight deadline	Ongoing or no deadline
8.	Process	Unstructured	Structured
9.	Leader's role	Facilitating transforming	Controlling
10.	Leader's power	Low	High
	Total:	_____	_____

Source: London & London (2007). Used with permission from John Wiley & Sons, Inc.

of a team you know. Circle the adjective in column A or B that best describes your group. Column A lists the more difficult team leadership characteristics. The more adjectives you circled in column A, the more challenging the team will be to lead.

Leadership as a Balancing Act

Team leaders need to balance three continua with opposing ends.

1   Recognize that volunteer members have vested interests that they bring to the team and its developing shared goals. People volunteer for social entrepreneurship for different reasons. Some may be ego-involved, wanting the recognition that comes with more responsible volunteer roles (e.g., being elected president of a community organization). Others join for more (or purely) altruistic reasons, yet they may not have the same vision about the purpose and goals of the organization. A different vision may or may not be in conflict with the leader's vision and goals. The leader needs to balance individual viewpoints and interests with developing a single, shared vision and set of goals for the enterprise.

2   Leaders need to balance authoritative control with empowering members. Some volunteer leaders enjoy the "power trip" of

being in control. They may believe that tight control is necessary because volunteer members can't be counted on to meet their commitments. Other leaders may believe that empowering members to take responsibility for their roles and conduct tasks their way is a better approach as long as they are held accountable for the outcomes they produce. Chances are, some control and some empowerment are valuable and needed, and this requires the leader to balance these two elements.

3   Leaders and teams need to balance a bias for action with taking time for feedback and reflection. Teams can engage in continuous, generative learning by considering what worked well and what didn't and implementing improvements. As they move through their work, the group needs to focus attention on the goal and the process. Both are important. As the team works on the task, members should remember what they are trying to accomplish and why. Simultaneously, they must carry out each element of the task. Sometimes task elements seem to become ends in themselves. People devote time and attention to elements of the task and feel they have accomplished something important when the task is completed. However, this doesn't mean that the group's goals were achieved. For example, considerable effort may be expended in holding a fund-raising gala. The elements of the gala may be planned and carried out to the minutest detail. However, if the event fails to raise sufficient funds to support the organization's mission, the effort will have been of little value.

Managing Paid Staff and Volunteers

One of the most difficult aspects of a nonprofit organization is the management of people. Some organizations run totally on volunteers. Others have a mix of paid and unpaid staff. Paid staff may include professionals (e.g., social workers, clergy, managing directors, accountants, information technology experts), clerical employees, and skilled and unskilled workers. Some organizations have structures with volunteer boards who have fiduciary responsibility as overseers of the organization, especially its financial solvency and performance outcomes. The staff has a parallel structure, with professionals managing other workers, including volunteers. Consider an organization such as regional offices of Habitat for Humanity (see http://www.habitat.org/local/). There is generally a regional board of directors consisting of volunteers who assume officer responsibilities and chair committees (e.g., fund raising, selecting beneficiary families), and paid staff who support the effort (including fund raising and skilled construction workers). Following direction from the organization's international headquarters, the regional offices follow organizational structures to accomplish its goals. Other organizations that are less established have to formulate their own organizational structures and operational policies. They may write and adopt a constitution, by-laws, job descriptions, and performance review processes to systematize their efforts. Otherwise, the enterprise would be ripe for anarchy or at least pressures from vocal participants who have different views of the group's goals and/or how the group should proceed.

Nonprofit organizations can institute systematic processes for selecting volunteers for higher levels of responsibility. An annual nominating committee might review people who want officer positions; then the membership would vote for each position or a slate of officers and board members. The president and other officers may be able to appoint people to roles and committees. Volunteers who don't meet expectations can be reassigned or asked to step down. Of course, this is often difficult, particularly in a membership organization that relies on volunteers and their financial contributions. Saying "no" to a member who pays dues or makes substantial financial contributions is not easy. Indeed, the toughest part of a leadership role in a volunteer organization may be managing the politics and dealing with people who are disagreeable and/or not well matched to the roles they undertake.

Managing Dominant, Emotional, and Change-Resistant People[1]

Consider three types of misbehavior: domineering/aggressive, actions, emotional influence appeals, and resistance to change. Such behaviors are probably most likely in groups of volunteers, especially when the purpose and/or methods are ambiguous or when the leader does not exert sufficient authority to maintain control. We present examples of these behaviors, show how they emerge at different stages of group process, and offer research-based ideas to help group leaders and members foster more cooperative, fact-centered, learning-oriented behaviors.

Most of us have struggled with trying to control or at least bear unruly group members. These are people who are domineering, use emotions to influence fellow group members, and/or are resistant to change. Such behaviors disrupt group process and prevent progress. This can happen especially when the group is self-initiated, composed of volunteers, and lacking task structure and members don't have the talent, knowledge, and motivation needed to get the job done.

---

1 Portions of this section were published in London & Morfopoulos, 2009.

This creates an opportunity for dysfunctional behavior. Consider what happens when the leader or one or more group members is dominant, emotional, and resistant to change. The challenge for the leader, members, or facilitator is to foster a cooperative, fact-centered, learning-driven team.

As we discussed earlier, high-performing teams require time, task structure, and the right talent. The leader or others who commission the team invite members and structure the goals and tasks so that the team has the ingredients for high performance. However, in volunteer groups, members self-select on the basis of their interests in the group's mission. At other times, group members are recruited to represent a function or unit or just because they were available but not because they have the right skills, time, motivation, or task understanding.

Task and time frame are often unclear at different stages of a group's life. In such cases, the leader must generate member commitment, identify talents in the group, and try to match tasks to talent as much as possible while establishing systems, structures, and time frames. Members need to be engaged to invest energy, feel involved, and believe in their efficacy. This article is about leadership strategies for creating high-performing, continuous learning teams from initially unfocused, ill-formed groups of volunteers and recruits who have varying levels of motivation and skill.

An ill-formed group can occur in a variety of organizations and situations. Consider the following possibilities:

- A committee in a professional society organizing a conference or developing a new strategy for the organization to increase membership and involvement
- A task force organizing a merger with representatives of the merged organizations, attorneys, and financial institutions as members of the task force
- A hospital quality improvement team with members representing diverse departments and functions volunteering to participate
- A task force of volunteers who want to improve community safety
- An NGO-sponsored partnership in a third-world country bringing together grassroots organizers, government representatives, and foreign experts and facilitators
- A volunteer social entrepreneurship initiative to stop urban sprawl
- An elected board of a charity—elected because of their prior volunteer efforts, contributions, popularity, and/or connections

In some cases, these groups are one-time initiatives. In other cases, they are ongoing groups or work teams. However, the goal and nature of the task may be ambiguous, and members may have different conceptualizations of what needs to be done. Members may come and go over time as the initiative develops, with the group sometimes taking new forms and directions in response to challenges and opportunities in the environment. The leadership challenge in such cases is to coalesce a motley crew into a focused, visionary team that produces high quality outcomes (Morgeson, 2005).

Leading such an ill-formed group and making the group into a continuous learning team requires motivating members. Members need to feel a sense of urgency and excitement about working on a common vision. Members share the same vision, see it clearly, and understand they have the same primary goal, whatever their individual secondary motives for being in the group happen to be. Members understand what tasks are required to achieve the vision, their individual roles and assignments, and the extent to which they are held accountable as individuals and a team for carrying out these roles. So the leader needs a plan to motivate members, structure the work recognizing how members depend on one another, and evaluate the process and outcomes. The leader needs to build consensus around the common vision, integrated tasks, and measures of accomplishment for feedback and improvement. Members need to understand that they can do more if they work together.

Consider three ways in which leaders and members interact in groups and exert influence on one another. They rely on their force of personality, method of influencing fellow-members, and willingness to learn and change.

Leaders use a variety of personality characteristics to make their presence known, communicate their ideas, and reward (or coerce) members (Bass, 1998). Unfortunately, some leaders are dominant. They are forceful, loud, outspoken, and hard to ignore. Members may be dominant, too, voicing their opinions and influence whenever there is a void in the group process. Others may prefer a participative environment. They listen and learn from their fellow members. Leaders who favor a participative environment are more likely to empower other group members by sharing the leadership role with them during the group decision-making process. Naturally, participative environments are more conducive to the acceptance of diverse views and can benefit from the synergies that result from the integration of these views.

Leaders and members can also vary in how they try to influence their fellow group members. Some rely on emotional appeals, emphasizing potential gains or losses. Often, these individuals are charismatic and yield influence through the force of their dynamic personalities. Alternatively, they may rely on cognitive and rational appeals, presenting objective information and facts to support a position.

Some leaders and members are resistant to change. They become naysayers in the group, adapting only grudgingly when necessary and making only the slightest adjustments. These group members often exhibit passive-aggressive resistance to change when they are prevented from openly presenting their views. Other leaders seek new knowledge and information and enjoy trying new ways of working together.

Patterns of Leader-Member Characteristics

Now consider two possible patterns that represent opposite extremes. (Of course, other combinations are possible too.)

Dominant, Emotional, Change-Resistant

A forceful leader may concentrate on warnings about possible losses (dire consequences from not acting) or gains (the benefits they can achieve). This leader may adapt the message and strategies only when challenged in some way, for instance, when insufficient resources require delaying a goal. Other forceful members of the group may exert their influence, creating discord and preventing progress. Members who are conscientious yet cooperative may cow-tow to authority, join factions that create conflict and split the group, be passive-aggressive (appear to accept decisions but not act on them), and/or feel frustrated and cynical. Such a group develops patterns of interaction that follow the leader's authority or result in stagnation and intransigence. Often, this results in the dynamics of the group suffering from groupthink, whereby the followers blindly follow the leader with confidence even when it is dangerous or even disastrous to do so.

Participative, Fact-Centered, Learning-Oriented

A participative leader may concentrate on providing factual information and remain open to involvement of others, engaging them in the process of conceptualizing and clarifying the vision, sharing ideas, collecting information (facts and figures), educating one another, trying different strategies, and building an effort that members feel is as much their own as the leader's. Other cooperative members of the group are respectful of one another and are open to divergent views. Dominant members of the group may try to usurp the leadership role or create conflict. The group develops and practices patterns of interaction that allow them to learn continuously from one another ready to experiment, shift goals in new directions, and try new tactics. The participative leader is especially adept at encouraging effective brainstorming as he or she is nonjudgmental and open to new ideas during group discussions.

Evolving Team Patterns

Consider how these three patterns emerge and develop at three general stages of group evolution: inception (when the idea is first conceptualized and communicated), formulation (when volunteers are recruited and organized), and sustained action (when the group engages in the task and, in some cases, becomes an ongoing entity). Table 5.2 summarizes how different patterns of leadership occur during each stage.

Inception is a time for envisioning and engaging members and stakeholders. The leader clarifies the need for the team, shares the initial vision, and recruits members. The dominant, emotional, change-resistant leader warns of dangers. The leader rewards like-minded individuals who respond to authority and structure. The team alters its vision, strategies, or behaviors only in minor ways when influenced by more powerful forces or constrained by resources.

In contrast to the dominant leader, the participative, fact-centered, change-oriented leader creates a compelling statement of the vision accompanied by facts that demonstrate the need. This leader seeks input from others, is open to new ideas, aligns forces with other groups, and/or generally recognizes and welcomes divergent views. Unlike the dominant leader, the participative leader is a facilitator. Decision making is collaborative within the group directed by the participative leader as opposed to the more autocratic style of leadership displayed in the decision-making process of the group directed by a dominant leader.

Formulation is a time for strategizing and engineering. The leader and the team formulate goals and tactics, obtain resources, and establish task structures and job descriptions for team members. The dominant, emotional, change-resistant leader makes assignments autocratically. The leader's viewpoint is "It's my way or the highway." Members accept assignments or leave the group. Some may become passive-aggressive, meaning that they appear to accept conditions but get little done. The participative, fact-centered, change-oriented leader, conversely, shares responsibilities, engages the team in joint

Table 5.2 Developmental Group Processes and Patterns of Leadership

Developmental Processes and Actions	Dominant, Emotional, Change-Resistant Leadership Pattern	Participative, Fact-Centered, Change-Oriented Leadership Pattern
Inception: Time for envisioning and engaging Clarifying and expressing the need, identifying beneficiaries, sharing the vision Identifying stakeholders (possible contributors, volunteers, decision makers), recruiting, motivating	Vocal warnings of danger, or visions of positive outcomes from desired actions (donate money, volunteer, being aware); rewards like-minded individuals who respond to authority and structure; alters vision, strategies, or behaviors only in minor ways when forced by more powerful forces or constrained by resources	Compelling statements of vision accompanied by facts that demonstrate the need; seeking input from others, joining forces, open to new ideas, recognizing and welcoming divergent views, coalitions
Formulation: Time for strategizing and engineering Formulating goals and tactics, obtaining resources, establishing structures	Autocratic, one way ("my way or the highway"); makes assignments, members need to accept them or leave (may be passive aggressive so that little gets done)	Sharing responsibilities, joint decision making, structuring assignments with team members, suggesting alternatives
Sustaining: Time for taking action, assessing Advocating (speaking out, building awareness, influencing decision makers) Tracking actions and outcomes, experimenting	Directing actions, risk offending others, possibly ignoring unfavorable reactions, withdrawing if results aren't consonant with initial goals, seeking different decision makers and venues for activities, not taking no for an answer Leads to member burnout: exhaustion, cynicism, inefficacy	Trying different approaches, tracking data, seeking feedback, revising strategies, and tactics, possibly reshaping vision Leads to member engagement: energy, involvement, and efficacy

decision making, structures and integrates assignments with team members, forms coalitions with other teams, and explores alternative goals and courses of action.

Sustaining is a time for taking action, assessing process and outcomes, and making improvements. The leader and the team advocate for their beliefs. They track their actions and outcomes, experiment, and seek feedback. There is a greater need for the team to act in an efficient manner and execute operations with precision. The dominant, emotional, change-resistant leader directs actions, risks offending others, ignores errors and unfavorable reactions and, if results are not consonant with goals, withdraws, seeks different decision makers and venues for activities, or persists. This leads to member burnout (exhaustion, cynicism, and inefficacy) and group discord. In contrast, the participative, fact-centered, change-oriented leader tries different approaches, tracks results, seeks feedback, learns from errors, revises strategies and tactics, and possibly reshapes the vision. This leads to member engagement (energy, involvement, and efficacy) and group harmony.

Of course, patterns of leadership and members' use of personality, influence strategy, and learning-orientation are not as cut and dried as these descriptions. The ability of the leader to create a high-performing team will depend on the composition of the group. A leader is likely to be more effective at creating a vision, structuring tasks, and tracking outcomes if members have a common background, share prior experiences, and hold values that are aligned with the group's goals. In such cases, the members may respond more positively to the leader regardless, or in spite of, the leader's style. Alternatively, if the members don't have a common background, prior shared experiences, and aligned values, they are likely to be more critical of the leader and less responsive to one another. In the case wherein members do not have a common background yet their relationship is marked by specialization, credibility, and cooperation, the transactive memory of the team will be enhanced, resulting in what is likely to be a highly effective team.

Some Case Examples

Consider the following examples:

1 *Dominant leader, dominant members*: The president of the executive board of a not-for-profit organization that runs youth centers is a volunteer elected by organization's board for a 2-year term. She likes to dominate meetings, set agendas, and control

discussion and decisions. She is not a good listener. As soon as someone suggests an idea or makes a point, she is quick to evaluate, often refuting the point in some way, explaining why something can't be done or that it's been tried before and doesn't work. Board members respect her dedication to the cause. No one can compete with her in her commitment of time and energy. Now though, leading the board meetings, she raises the hackles of other members, especially several who are just as domineering and opinionated and who often disagree with her. Board meetings degenerate into free-for-all shouting matches. She warns of dire consequences of not following her prescriptions for programming and staff hiring. Sometimes, the board is forced to deal with external constraints, such as a shortfall in funds or a costly repair to one of their buildings. This requires minor adaptations to the ongoing stream of events but no major changes. Some board members would like to see the center make a major shift in direction to stave off the steady decline in funding and reliance on eroding government funding. Some board members feel that they should hire a new, more dynamic professional director who would be adept at fund raising and running the organization. Yet, the board seems to be filled of nay-sayers. Any idea that is raised is shot down by the president or the other domineering people on the board. The board sustains the status quo while the center seems to be in a slow and sometimes painful downward spiral. Board members who want change are exhausted by the ranker and feel ineffectual.

2   *Participative leader, dominant members:* The chairperson of an academic department in a large, public research university believes that faculty collaboration is the key to a vibrant department. His philosophy of leadership is that, unlike a business, an academic department should not be run by fiat or emotion but by a team approach that includes carefully collecting information, hearing all ideas, taking time for deliberation, and making joint decisions by majority rule. His predecessor was an autocrat who rarely consulted others, so the faculty members were relieved when the dean appointed the new department chair. However, the previous chair is still a member of the faculty, and several other faculty members are her friends and allies. The chairperson tries to run democratic department meetings. For any issue, his strategy is to ask for ideas on how to deal with the issue, record all possibilities, then review each one carefully, sometimes asking a staff member to gather some data so that the faculty can better understand what's going on. For instance, he may ask the director of the

department's office of student services to collect enrollment data for specific courses or evaluate numbers of students at various stages of the major to predict course demand. The faculty members then meet to review the data, discuss the implications, and initiate change (e.g., directions for new courses or programs). The chairperson welcomes new ideas, invites guests to provide outside perspectives, and seeks examples from other academic departments at this university and from the same discipline at other universities. Also, the chair is willing to invest department resources to experiment with new programs. However, on several occasions, the former chair and her compatriots lobbied other faculty outside of meetings to influence or overturn a decision. In the chair's first meetings at the start of the semester, they didn't hesitate to disrupt the meeting by filibustering, arguing forcefully for an issue, and preventing a vote. This domineering faction is likely to decry wasting resources on new ideas they label frivolous and unsound, whereas the chairperson and others who are more open to new ideas welcome change in the spirit of intellectual growth and helping students succeed. Under the new chairperson's leadership, the department has embarked on a series of new initiatives but not without argument and emotional pain getting there.

3   *Dominant leader, participative members*: The leading heart surgeon in a tertiary-care teaching hospital formed a team to transition from open-heart bypass and valve replacement surgery to less-invasive laparoscopic, minimally invasive surgery. During open-heart surgery, the chief surgeon coordinates the complex operating room procedure. Expert nurses, anesthesiologists, and technicians follow directions coordinated by the surgeon. In laparoscopic surgery, the team must be in synchronization in a delicate, meshed balance. The patient is off-pump, meaning that a heart-lung machine is not used, and the patient's heart is beating throughout the operation. One difference in the surgical team is that in using the new procedure, the team members must know their roles and how they are coordinated and timed. The surgeon operates delicate instruments remotely, requiring focused attention on the scopes and micro-processors. To learn the new procedure, the team attended several away meetings with other teams learning the procedures. In addition, the team met weekly to review progress. Early in the process, the facilitator led the team through a discussion of how members would work together. They agreed to the principle that all members of the team would treat one another as equals regardless of role or

position. This was not what the chief surgeon was used to. He was new to the hospital, so he didn't know the staff well, and he had a dominating style. He dominated the meetings, trying to intimidate the technicians and RNs. He was frequently late for meetings, took calls during meetings, and rarely let others finish what they were saying before interrupting. After the first retreat and several weeks of meetings, the group was making little progress. They were nowhere near ready to start test-runs. Several nurses and resident MDs spoke to the facilitator and said they were considering leaving the team. The facilitator spoke to the lead surgeon, who blamed the staff for not appreciating his central role and that he, not they, was in charge and accountable. Angry, he threatened to leave the hospital if the group members didn't become more "cooperative"—meaning follow his direction. The entire project was in jeopardy. The lead surgeon spoke to the hospital CEO and asked that a new team be formed. The CEO said she would think it over. Fortunately, the surgeon received a better offer elsewhere and decided to leave the hospital. Instead of hiring a new surgeon, the CEO invited two other cardiac surgeons on the staff to learn the process. They visited several hospitals elsewhere to observe the procedure in action and then returned to work closely with the team. The hospital was able to offer the new procedure within the next six months.

4   *Participative leader, participative members*: Two leading charities that operated soup kitchens and homeless shelters in a large city were considering a merger. The officers (president, executive vice president, and treasurer) of each organization met as a team to work out the details. Finances were a key concern, but the group also had to determine how they would merge their fund raising and operations. For instance, what name would they keep, or would they merge their names? Would they consolidate branches? How could they integrate computer systems, especially two quite different online banking systems? How could they reduce personnel costs? Everyone on the team recognized that downsizing would be needed at all levels, including some of the team members. The founder and director of one of the charities was ready to retire, and the director of the second charity was leading the merger and was motivated to assume the leadership of the merged bank. A social worker by training, she had worked for the other charity earlier in her career, so she understood its culture and knew its operations quite well. Her current organization had a reputation of being lean and efficient. The

other charity had a reputation of being an outstanding agency that hired and retained competent people in the fields of fund raising and social welfare. Despite the differences in corporate culture, the planning team recognized that the merger was in the best interests of both charities, and they wanted to cooperate to effectuate the merge and make it a success. This might not be a merger of equals exactly—a merger never is, and everyone knew that the leaner charity was more cost effective. Still, the group members wanted to make this work. They knew this was what their respective boards expected.

Implications for Practice

The components of a high-performing team (talent, task structure, and time) are often not under the control of the group leader. As a result, the challenge of turning an ill-formed group into a high-performing team (the proverbial turning of a sow's ear into a silk purse) depends on how leaders and members use their personal characteristics, leadership style, communication strategy, and learning behavior. Personal characteristics include the elusive concept of charisma—a force of personality that compels others to act. Leadership style may be authoritarian-directive or participative, inviting group members to contribute ideas and influence decisions and actions. Communication strategies may draw on emotions, facts, and data or a combination to influence opinions. Learning is openness to new knowledge and ideas and being willing to try new things. We suggest that leaders are likely to engage members' commitment and create a continuous learning team when they are open to new ideas and direction from group members, deliver forceful, and possibly emotional, messages but messages based on data and fact, and experiment with new ways of interacting and new programs and services. Leaders are less likely to generate membership commitment and learning when they dominate, use emotional messages without facts, and seek knowledge that reinforces what they know (or think they know) already. Of course, leaders are not all one or the other. Not all participative leaders rely on facts, and some may depend more on emotional appeals.

Here are some steps that leaders, group facilitators, and members can take to create a high-performing team, by developing a shared vision, making task assignments, and evaluating progress in a way that is participative, fact-centered, and change-oriented.

- Understand not only the nature of the mission as it currently is set forth but how this mission may currently be in need of transformation in the future
- View problems from different perspectives
- Identify the current strengths and weaknesses of individual group members and the team as a unit
- Recruit talent from outside the group to complement and improve the effectiveness of the initially ill-formed group
- Make task assignments in relation to group members' interests and abilities
- Coach and teach the members to develop the skills and/or other characteristics needed by the group; design jobs or roles to give members experiences that will help the group later
- Engage the leader and members in self-reflection to recognize how they use persona, convey messages, and learn
- Identify and emulate benchmark examples of other continuous learning teams
- Clarify expectations (those of executives and other stakeholders, the team leader, and members), and clarify available resources
- Energize, structure, and track group activity through participation, fact finding and analysis, and generativity. A leader who relies on a dominant persona, emotional messages, and change-resistant learning will probably have a difficult time retaining members and making process in the long run.
- Use "the devil's advocate" approach in a manner that encourages a culture wherein civil disagreement is encouraged while dysfunctional and needless conflict is not
- Be willing to delegate aspects of the decision-making process to members who specialize in the subject matter. In the process, the transactive memory of the group will be enhanced.
- Encourage imaginative thinking through the introduction of scenarios and "what if" exercises into group discussions
- Ensure that members with complementary yet divergent skill sets do not compete when they can be integrating their talents
- Provide challenging yet clearly obtainable goals for the group
- Ensure that critical feedback is not personal and is constructive and efficacy-building
- Recognize and reward accomplishments of members who may not otherwise possess a great deal of stature within the group
- Champion innovative ideas by providing necessary support and resources

Conclusion

This chapter focused on how to form and manage a group of volunteers and create a high-performing team—one with the talent, task structure, and time frame to support its goals. We reviewed how groups establish routine patterns of interaction and how a group can be facilitated by acquainting members with one another's capabilities early in the group's life. We reviewed challenges for leading volunteer teams. At the early stage of a group, members need to be motivated. Later, as the group gets underway, it needs structure. As goals are accomplished, the group members and the group as a whole need feedback and time to reflect on how they can improve. Leaders balance members' vested interests with shared goals, achieve a balance of control and empowerment, and focus on getting things done while reflecting on process and outcomes.

Many volunteer organizations have trouble controlling who leads or joins the group. In such cases, the group leader's and members' personality characteristics are likely to influence process and outcomes. Group members and leaders face the problem of what to do about people who are dominant, emotional, and change-resistant. Leaders and members who are cooperative, fact-focused, and open to learning can take action to reduce the influence of dominant, emotional, and change-resistant members in the group. By proactively addressing the need to harness the energies of all group members through assertive, cooperative leadership, the participative leader can transform an ill-formed group into a highly productive, dynamic team.

Questions for Reflection and Discussion

1   What are the most important characteristics of a high-performing team? Why?
2   What is the difference between a group and a team? Define teamwork in your own words.
3   In your personal experience, what is the greatest barrier to forming a high-performing team?
4   Consider a team that was not effective that you were either part of or witnessed. What caused it to be dysfunctional? How would you have improved its development?
5   What are the greatest advantages to being part of a high-performing team?
6   What are the most important characteristics of an effective team leader? Why?

Social Venture Exercises

Exercise 1: Recognizing Differences Between Members'
Perspectives

Volunteers bring different expectations and goals to a social entrepreneurship effort. Try this exercise with four friends to see the effects of member differences in expectations and goals. You be group leader and assign the others different roles. Spend 15 minutes developing the group's mission statement.

Friends of the Hobbs Farm: The Hobbs Farm is an 11-acre site in a suburban neighborhood of single family homes. It has been vacant land for the last 20 years. Twenty years ago, the last descendant of James Hobbs died and left the property to a local Church. The property had been farmed by the Hobbs family for three generations. This is unique because of the long time it was a farm and the fact that the Hobbs family was African-American. This is the oldest African-American farm in the region. Now, a group of Church members and community citizens have formed the "Friends of the Hobbs Farm" to make better use of the property. They need to determine how to use the property and then raise the money they need to bring their vision to reality. You are a subgroup of the "Friends" charged with setting a goal and writing a mission statement for the group.

- Role A: You are passionate about reclaiming the farmland and starting an organic farm on the property to grow vegetables that will be sold locally, with profits going to the church. You would demolish the dilapidated farmhouse to make more land for farming.
- Role B: You want to renovate the farmhouse and barn and make it into a cultural center. You would make a park on the land.
- Role C: You want to sell the property to a housing developer and use the money from the sale to build a museum on church property to celebrate and educate the community about its African-American heritage.
- Role D: You want to create a small museum in the farmhouse to house pictures and the history of the African-American family who farmed the land for three generations and about the African-American culture in the area. You would farm small portions of the land so that children can learn about local agriculture.

After the discussion, review the following reflection questions with the group:

1   Did a pattern of interaction emerge that influenced who spoke when and for how long?
2   Were some people more dominant than others?
3   Did the group members reveal their perspectives at the start of the discussion? If not, would doing so have helped the discussion?
4   What challenges did the leader face in arriving at a mission statement all group members could accept?
5   Did the leader structure the group process?
6   Did the group spend time planning how it would proceed?
7   Did group members feel free to express their views?

Exercise 2: Assessing the Leadership Challenge

In the social venture you are considering, use Table 5.1 in this chapter to evaluate the leadership challenge at least as you perceive it today. You will know more, of course, if you go about actually starting the venture. Recognizing the potential areas of challenge, what can you do to improve your chances of success? For instance, how would you do the following?

1   Clarify the *purpose*
2   *Motivate* volunteers, donors, and employees
3   Build the organization to a *size* you can manage (enough people to make an impact but not so many that you lose control or focus). What would that size be for you?
4   Seek the *diversity* you want and value (diversity of background, interests, knowledge, and experience)
5   Minimize *turnover*, especially among productive people who have the talent you need
6   Clarify the *goals* and the paths to achieving them
7   Establish reasonable (doable) *time frames* and *deadlines* for accomplishing specific goals
8   Structure the *process* and tasks toward goal accomplishment
9   Determine how much *control* you need and want and opportunities to be a facilitator, empowering others to act and supporting the process by providing guidance, resources, and oversight
10 Recognize the sources and extent of your *power* to determine objectives, make decisions and assignments, and obtain and allocate resources

Exercise 3: Group Interaction Patterns

Announce that you are going to hold a meeting about your social venture and attract some interested people. Hold a brainstorming session about the topic and what you might do to build and support the venture. After the meeting (and after subsequent meetings), reflect on patterns of behavior that emerged. Address the questions we asked in the group exercise earlier in this chapter.

1   Did a pattern of interaction emerge that influenced who spoke when and for how long?
2   Were some people more dominant than others?
3   Did the group members reveal their perspectives at the start of the discussion? If not, would doing so have helped the discussion?
4   What challenges did the leader face in arriving at a mission statement all group members could accept?
5   Did you structure the group process?
6   Did the group spend time planning how it would proceed?
7   Did group members feel free to express their views?

Exercise 4: Planning Leadership

As you think ahead to leading your social venture, how can you be participative, fact-centered, and change-oriented at different stages of the group process as you bring people together and get your venture underway? Use the chart below to jot down some ideas about how you can target your own leadership behavior to improve the group's productivity.

Leadership Planning Chart

Stage of Group Development	Participative Leadership Opportunities	Fact-Centered Leadership Opportunities	Change-Oriented Leadership Opportunities
Inception: Time for envisioning and engaging			
Formulation: Time for strategizing and engineering			
Sustaining: Time for taking action, assessing			

Exercise 5: Building a Winning Team

At the conclusion of Chapters 3 and 4, we encouraged you to think about the skills and competencies you would need for yourself and your team to accomplish the goals of your social venture idea. Having a set of job descriptions that outline roles is important, whether you plan to build a for-profit or not-for-profit enterprise. The following questions, adapted from Cascio's classic work (1987, p. 195) on job analysis, provide a basis for you to begin developing job descriptions. Since this is an evolving process in that jobs change as the roles develop, you probably cannot anticipate every role or committee chair you will need. Still, thinking about the roles for volunteers, employees, or partners is a useful way to plan ahead to structure your venture and recruit people.

For each possible position, consider the following questions:

1 What is the job title?
   • Why have you chosen this title?
   • What related titles held by prospective employees may readily substitute for this job title?
   • Is there anyone who is highly qualified for this position?
2 Summarize the job
   • What are the primary duties associated with this job or function?
   • Why is this function or job important?
3 Relation to others on the team
   • Who reports to this individual and to whom does the individual report?
4 What specific skills are needed to be this incumbent's supervisor?
   • Does the applicant possess these skills?
   • If the supervisor leaves his or/her position, what is the succession plan?
5 What competencies does the individual need? That is, what does the individual have to know how to do?
   • What knowledge, traits, licenses and/or other attributes must the supervisor also possess?
6 How, if at all, will the incumbent be compensated for his/her time?

*Exercise 6: Recognition of Global Forces Affecting the Social
Venture (adapted from Ball, McCulloch, Geringer, Minor, &
McNett, 2008)*

As a team, determine how your social venture is affected by the following global market forces:

1   Political: The global community is becoming more unified. How do specific political considerations such as trade agreements between states and countries affect your organization?

2   Technological: How does the development of such technology as the Internet affect your venture?

3   Market: Who are your global customers? Rank the order of the top three countries you would conduct business in and/or service consumers with your venture.

4   Cost: What are the costs associated with doing business in each of these three countries?

5   Competitive: Who are your top three competitors in each of these three countries? What are their strengths and weaknesses?

6 Overcoming Barriers and Facilitating Social Entrepreneurship

In this chapter, you will learn how to do the following:

1 Assume the role of leader and human resource manager for a social entrepreneurship endeavor, whether it is part of a corporate social responsibility (CSR) initiative or a community-based social action
2 Recognize the potential value of professional consultants as sources of knowledge and facilitation
3 Apply diagnostic questions and methods to assess organizational capacity and needs for improvement
4 Design training programs and workshops on social entrepreneurship
5 Use a host of online resources to overcome barriers and improve operations

Introduction

Social welfare organizations emphasize fairness, generosity, support, and the well-being of others (Chhokar, Brodbeck, & House, 2007). These characteristics may reflect their goals, but do they operate this way? Are members and volunteers mutually supportive and respectful? Are they concerned about one another's welfare? Do they tolerate mistakes? Are they open to new ideas, feedback for improvement, and learning new patterns of interaction? Do they brainstorm effectively as a group? Developing a humane, mission-driven organizational culture that also controls costs and facilitates high performance is not easy and often requires help. Moreover, social entrepreneurship often encounters barriers. These include lack of moneys, nay-sayers and doubters who do not believe in the cause, or (in the case of CSR) executives who feel that social responsibility detracts from mainstream corporate goals. In addition, as leaders, social entrepreneurs need to be human resource managers in that they require the support of others (recruits, contributors, service providers) to achieve their goals. As we suggested in the last chapter, managing volunteers is not easy. The human resource (HR) profession offers information, guidance, and expertise that can support social entrepreneurship. Volunteer leaders can hire HR professionals or they can learn to apply human resource interventions themselves to improve participants' motivation, interrelationships, and productivity.

Learning Social Entrepreneurship Competencies

In Chapter 3, we examined competencies for leading an effective social venture. Social entrepreneurs have powerful ideas to improve people's lives, and they start initiatives to implement their ideas. In the process, they apply business and management skills to for-profit or not-for-profit social enterprises. In addition, as entrepreneurs, they are "transformative forces"—"people with new ideas to address major problems who are relentless in the pursuit of their visions, people who simply will not take 'no' for an answer, who will not give up until they have spread their ideas as far as they possibly can" (Bornstein, 2004, p. 1). Social entrepreneurs have vision, the will to build something that will grow and endure, and leadership ability to operationalize their vision, find suitable partners, engage volunteers, and deal with inevitable setbacks (Thompson *et al.*, 2000). They envision a future state in a currently uncertain environment, give the vision direction and purpose, and identify and harness the support of other key people (Sykes, 1999). As transformational leaders, they are a source of charisma, inspirational motivation, intellectual stimulation, and consideration of individuals (Bass, 1998).

Generally, entrepreneurs use their traits and personality to formulate objectives and maintain a can-do attitude that in turn brings about venture growth. Their goals, self-efficacy, and vision are likely to have a positive effect on the success of their venture (Baum & Locke, 2004). Training and experience can be sources of self-efficacy, the feeling that "I can be effective in accomplishing my goals." Envisioning, goal setting, and communication skills can be learned. Having the ability to generate resources requires inspiring challenging visions, developing challenging yet realistic goals, and reinforcing ones self-efficacy. Traits such as tenacity affect behavior. Practice and feedback build skills. Tenacious social entrepreneurs are likely to develop organizing competencies because they work harder and longer than those with less tenacity, especially if they have successful role models or high quality training (cf. Baum & Locke).

As transformational leaders, employees engaging in CSR in their organization must communicate a vision that inspires others to join the effort, recognize their potential value to the enterprise, and instill confidence. The social entrepreneur's personality, positive traits, motivation, and transformation abilities are the major antecedents of an expressed vision for an enterprise. The social entrepreneur ignites the spark that generates others' involvement and support. That is, the social entrepreneur's insight, intention, persistence, and resilience are likely to be important to jump-starting the effort. Social entrepreneurs are likely to express concepts that resonate with others' ideas, interests, and emotions and are viewed as significant to society and the corporation. Social entrepreneurs who are sensitive to the environment, open to new ideas, and perceive their strengths and weaknesses accurately are likely to have accurate perceptions of the social need, a clear understanding of methods to address the need, and a realistic view of the availability of resources.

Support From Human Resource Professionals

HR professionals may be corporate leaders and staff members, professional consultants, or pro bono volunteers. Clients may be employees or managers in public corporations advocating for social action, "watchdog" non-government organizations or foundations, or community-based volunteer groups. The initiatives may be controversial and engage a host of stakeholders with differing opinions (e.g., pressing for human rights in a prison system with administrators, guards, or prisoners; lobbying legislators by engaging in civil disobedience). HR managers may be social entrepreneurs themselves, trying to further a cause in which they believe. HR professionals offer expertise in such areas as selection, reward systems, performance management, goal-setting, feedback, coaching, training, process consultation, group learning, and organization development. Also, HR professionals facilitate interpersonal communication, group dynamics, consensus building, negotiation, and conflict resolution.

The Link Between Human Resource Development and CSR

Corporate leaders increase the value of the company's reputation and profits by supporting the communities in which their companies operate (Committee Encouraging Corporate Philanthropy, 2008; Prohalad & Porter, 2003). Such efforts may include supporting health, education, economic development, and environmental conditions. The so-called fourth sector of the economy, or "B corporations," mixes profit and not-for-profit endeavors and tries to do good while making a profit or dedicating profits for societal benefit (Strom, 2007). Examples such as those described in Chapter 1 are companies that donate a portion of profits to fight illness, support education, and/or reduce poverty, promote the safety and healthful use of its products and services, and protect the environment. A social benefit directly related to the mission of human resource development (HRD) is providing gainful employment and career opportunities for economically disadvantaged members of the community.

HRD professionals help organizations establish a record of involvement in communities by developing employees' core competencies associated with social entrepreneurship (Fenwick & Bierema, 2008; Wilcox, 2006; Zappalà, 2004). A qualitative study of HRD managers in eight large North American firms showed explicit commitment to corporate social responsibility (Fenwick & Bierema, 2008). HRD engagement tended to focus on areas of employee learning and promotion, employee ownership of development, and employee safety and respect. However, the HRD managers studied were only marginally involved or interested in the firms' CSR activities.

HRD theory that initiates and sustains organizational transformation can be extended to structures, processes, and methods that enable CSR (Torraco, 2004). HRD professionals can help organizations develop employees' social entrepreneurship skills so that CSR activities will be more successful. HRD professionals may be social entrepreneurs themselves in support of sustaining continuous development, promoting inclusion, equitable access, and employability (Wilcox, 2006; Woodall & Douglas, 2000). They advocate for the recruitment, development, and retention of a diverse, vibrant workforce and promulgate equity and access to the range of developmental opportunities necessary for full participation in society (Hatcher, 2002; Margolis & Walsh, 2003). So they should understand their own and others' motivation and competencies for social entrepreneurship.

Human resource professionals' work with social entrepreneurs may differ from their work with other organizational clients in several respects. Social entrepreneurs may be speaking for others who can't speak for themselves. Social entrepreneurship initiatives are likely to rest in a strong sense of social entrepreneurs' values and perceptions about what is right and wrong. Others may disagree. Indeed, the purpose of the social entrepreneurship is likely to be to convince decision makers who hold resources that this is a worthwhile cause, achieve a negotiated solution to a problem, and/or overcome barriers to meet the needs of beneficiaries. The client may be the social entrepreneur who requested advice and consultation from the HR manager. However, the HR professional may need to work with a wider array of stakeholders, perhaps redefining the client-consulting relationship to be effective. In addition, the HR manager may become the social entrepreneur (e.g., hired—or volunteering—to represent the interests of juvenile offenders, children in foster homes, the homeless, or any number of other causes). The HR manager may also be involved in facilitating interactions between conflicting parties or linking corporate resources and initiatives to community welfare projects.

HR professionals have the knowledge and understanding of human behavior and organizational practices (strategy, culture, leadership) that can be of value to social entrepreneurs, just as they benefit other management initiatives. However, to do this, HR managers need an in-depth understanding of how social entrepreneurship emerges and develops in corporate and community contexts. This includes individual characteristics, situations, and interpersonal processes that motivate and direct social entrepreneurship. HR managers can provide an understanding of social entrepreneurs' motivation, commitment, skills, knowledge, strategies, and persistence with the aim of training people to be more effective social entrepreneurs and facilitating their success. HR managers can address entrepreneurship processes to understand how other individuals and/or groups respond to social entrepreneurs. These stakeholders may be direct beneficiaries or decision makers (e.g., legislators, social agency executives and case managers, voters, and/or consumers) who control resources, make decisions, or deliver care on behalf of beneficiaries. Stakeholders may also be supporters and volunteers who aid social entrepreneurship initiatives and opponents or doubters who constrain social entrepreneurship. HR managers can help understand social entrepreneurship strategies (applications of social influence, power and control, and commitment processes) and identify critical individual characteristics that define and shape social entrepreneurship efforts. HR managers can examine how social entrepreneurs gain insight into themselves and others and develop realistic goals and formulate ways to achieve them. Also, they can recognize the spin-off effects of entrepreneurship (e.g., teambuilding and positive public relations from corporate social responsibility initiatives).

Companies have banded together to provide consulting services and research in support of CSR. For instance, Business for Social Responsibility (http://www.bsr.org), founded in 1992, works with a global network of more than 250 member companies to develop sustainable business strategies and solutions through consulting, research, and cross-sector collaboration. This membership organization has six offices in Asia, Europe, and North America, with experts in environment, human rights, economic development, and transparency and accountability "to guide global companies toward creating a just and sustainable world."

Another example is the Resource Mentoring Project of the University of Maryland-Baltimore School of Social Work. The program "is dedicated to empowering community and faith based organizations, through a mentoring process, to build their organizational capacity in an effort to gain and maintain organizational health" (http://www.ssw.umaryland.edu/rmp/). They offer local agencies support for board development, business systems, fund raising, grant writing, HR and organization structure consulting, information technology consulting, organizational assessments, help in writing statements of mission, vision, and values, program marketing, staff training and development, and strategic planning. Other university-based programs may provide similar services.

Organization Assessment

Applied psychology offers methods for measuring needs, attitudes, and perceptions of individuals and groups and facilitating delicate interpersonal processes on behalf of the social entrepreneur as principal client and, more broadly, the community of stakeholders. Organizational psychologists have tools and methods that can assist social entrepreneurs and their opponents. As consultants, they can help social entrepreneurs assess conflicting interests and perspectives, understand how their own and others' beliefs about people influence their entrepreneurship strategies, listen to opposing viewpoints and differences in opinion about ways to accomplish goals, and reflect on how others react to their strategies and behaviors. They can increase social entrepreneurs' sensitivities to the broader systems that impinge on accomplishing entrepreneurship goals, how to involve stakeholders (supporters, opponents, and observers) recognizing their personal contact with the beneficiaries and potential impact on the issues, and possibly how to develop and implement systemic processes that meet multiple, initially conflicting interests.

Table 6.1 presents a set of diagnostic questions for assessing social entrepreneurship processes. It derives from the foregoing discussion of social entrepreneurs' prosocial motivation, entrepreneurial skills, situational conditions, and beliefs about people, strategies, process, and outcomes. Organizational consultants and HR professionals can use this as an initial review of a social venture and the contributions of the principal social entrepreneur(s). The survey can be completed by

Table 6.1 Diagnostic Questions for Assessing Social Entrepreneurship Processes

I.   Issue or Need for the Social Entrepreneurship Initiative [to provide insight about likely stakeholders, sources of information about related initiatives, geographic locus of the problem (local, global), social entrepreneurs' contact with the intended beneficiaries, and potential for impact]

1.   Purpose of the social venture
     a.   Health promotion (funding for research, behavior/prevention, support for people in need—those with mental and/or physical illnesses)
     b.   Safety (consumer safety, product safety, preventing harm from abusive behavior such as drunk driving)
     c.   Poverty and economic development
     d.   Environmental protection
     e.   Other_____
2.   Severity of the issue or problem the organization is addressing?
3.   Geographic scope of the issue or problem addressed by the social entrepreneurship effort (local, global)?
4.   Are the beneficiaries known to the organizers and supporters by name?
5.   What is the immediacy of the problem? Is this is a long-term problem that doesn't have to be dealt with immediately, or is this a crisis that must be dealt with immediately?

II. Social entrepreneurs' characteristics [to understand the extent to which the social entrepreneurs demonstrate prosocial characteristics, altruism, voice, social entrepreneurship, and beliefs about how to influence people; provides a basis for understanding how social entrepreneurs formulate strategies and initiate actions]
     Prosocial
     a. Treat others fairly and equitably
     b. Stand up for the rights of others
     c. Give others a chance to voice their opinions
     d. Want to help others
     e. Believe he or she can be effective helping others
     Altruism
     a. Give up something for the benefit of others
     b. Put others' interests ahead of one's own
     c. Stand up for the disenfranchised
     d. Champion the cause of people who can't speak for themselves
     e. Speak out when someone is treated unfairly
     Voice:
     a. Stand up for what they believe is right
     b. Pursue a cause doggedly (not give up easily in pursuing a cause)
     c. Put their reputation on the line for a cause
     d. Not afraid to be viewed as outspoken
     e. State their opinions forcefully even when others disagree
     f. Express a clear opinion on a controversial topic
     Social entrepreneurship:
     a. Initiate actions
     b. Form organizations structures
     c. Delegate
     d. Try to bring about change
     e. Not take "no" for an answer

(continued ...)

Table 6.1 continued

Beliefs about how to influence people
a.   Believe that people don't change their opinions easily
b.   Believe that people respond rationally when presented with the facts
c.   Believe that people respond only when they perceive an impending loss or gain
d.   Believe that people are motivated to improve their self-worth

III.   Situation [to understand why the situation prompted the social entrepreneurs to initiate action and the extent to which social entrepreneurs and supporters are likely to be involved and feel engaged]
6.   Do the social entrepreneur and supporters have direct contact with the intended beneficiaries?
7.   Do the social entrepreneur and supporters believe they can have a substantive impact in helping the beneficiaries?
8.   To what extent are resources (e.g., money, facilities, medication) available?
9.   How well known is this social entrepreneurship effort?
10.   Who are the stakeholders? Do stakeholders see the social entrepreneur as believable, trusted, respected, and worthy of support?
11.   To what extent are there barriers to accomplishing the social entrepreneurship effort's goals? Are there adversaries or stakeholders who have different opinions?

IV.   Strategy-Methods for Achieving Goals [to understand the social entrepreneurs' actions, involve other stakeholders some of whom may be adversaries, determine the need for entrepreneurship training and facilitation directed at all parties, not just the initial client, and/or become a social entrepreneur for compromise, negotiated solutions, and conflict resolution]
12.   What is the purpose of the entrepreneurship? …prevent a problem? … help others overcome hardship? …achieve something of positive value (e.g., happiness, beauty, improved quality of life, higher education or economic achievement)? …change attitudes/perceptions of beneficiaries, supporters, and/or public (i.e., change awareness and feelings about an issue)? …elicit action from supporters (volunteer, donate, vote, make a specific decision)? …change beneficiaries' behavior (for example, cause them to do something differently to prevent disease and maintain wellness)?
13.   To what extent are goals specific, measurable, actionable (clear actions to be taken), realistic, and time-bound (clear time frame for accomplishing goals)?
14.   To what extent is the goal (or are the goals) achievable?
15.   To what extent does the organization…
a.   Focus on information and rational arguments, for example, (research results-data-facts, demonstration-role models, rationale statement of pros and cons, and information about values, probabilities, and immediacy of outcomes)?
b.   Focus on emotional issues and appeals about gains that elicit sympathy (e.g., feeding hungry children, rescuing stranded people) or warnings of crisis or dire consequences?
c.   Depend on the strength of the leader's personality (charisma), vision, and inspiration?

V. Outcomes [to understand successes and failures to date and determine need for interventions]

16. How successful has the entrepreneurship effort been up to this point?
17. What were the outcomes of the entrepreneurship effort *during the last year*? To what extent were...
    a. Favorable impression generated?
    b. Behaviors of supporters and beneficiaries changed?
    c. Support increased (members increased, training provided, resources raised)?
    d. New alliances/relationships established?
    e. Measures of results collected and reported, indicating degree of success?
    f. Specific goals or targets met?
    g. Short-term goals achieved?
    h. Long-term goals achieved, new goals set?
    i. Entrepreneurship effort is sustainable (the effort will continue, it is not faltering)?

the social entrepreneur and stakeholders to pinpoint areas for further exploration and intervention, whether it be further needs analysis, data collection, coaching, process reflection, entrepreneurship training, stakeholder analysis, negotiation, outcomes evaluation, and the like or, more likely, a combination of interventions.

Social entrepreneurs who do not take the time to conduct systematic needs analyses may address the wrong problem and discover that their efforts have been wasted. Organizational consultants and HR professionals can help social entrepreneurs measure the extent of a social need. They can educate social entrepreneurs in measurement techniques and the value of data analysis. They can facilitate brainstorming potential solutions and exploring their feasibility. They can design demonstration and pilot programs with control groups and pre- and post-measures to evaluate a social program and then use the results to improve the program while providing ammunition for the entrepreneurship effort. They can measure the attitudes and reactions of multiple stakeholders (decision makers, observers, potential and actual contributors-volunteers) using multiple subjective and objective criteria when possible. They can establish accountability mechanisms and systems to reward accomplishments and communicate successes and learn from failures and overcome barriers.

Social entrepreneurs, as a client population, are likely to be, or represent, people who are oppressed, disenfranchised, or marginalized. The HR professional and other consultants who work with one social entrepreneur would be working with only part of the total system. A role of HR professionals may be to train social entrepreneurs to increase their chances of achieving their preferred solutions. As such, HR professionals may be viewed as aligning themselves with the social entrepreneurs in a win-lose conflict (or potentially a win-win negotiation) with some other group or subsystem of a community or organization. Consultants are, therefore, enhancing the chances of the client–social entrepreneur possibly at the expense of others. An alternative strategy would be to provide similar training and consultation, perhaps simultaneously, to other stakeholders with whom the social entrepreneurs are to engage. Another strategy would be to work with professional mediator-arbitrators to convene all involved parties in a joint problem-solving effort. This would ensure a more balanced, unbiased initiative. The effort may start with assessing the broader situation and convincing the initial client that the consultation needs to be expanded.

The notion of support for social entrepreneurship raises areas for investigation to enable those who are the beneficiaries to engage more effectively with the social entrepreneurs or to become social entrepreneurs themselves for their own benefit. One area for investigation is whether there are differences between social entrepreneurs and entrepreneurship processes in CSR compared to social entrepreneurs in their communities. Corporate executives and managers as social entrepreneurs have resources and time before being held accountable to shareholders. They can act for the mutual benefit of the organization and social needs (e.g., building a new factory with renewable materials and energy conservation measures; gaining goodwill by providing the company's products or services for free to indigent communities). However, they may face barriers, such as executives and shareholders who see such efforts as decreasing immediate profits for uncertain long-term benefit to the organization. The link between contributing to social welfare and corporate benefit may not be clear, and some stakeholders may insist that such a link be evident and strong for the organization to be involved. The HR leader can raise these conflicts, help the social entrepreneur understand the multiple perspectives, facilitate avenues for internal social entrepreneurs to express their views, examine alternative influence strategies, and identify ways to bridge differing opinions about corporate civic engagement. Community social entrepreneurs initiate action on their own or with like-minded partners to address a problem. They may face barriers such as vocal opponents, lack of resources, and lack of power base or position for communicating the message. HR professionals can offer training in effective social entrepreneurship methods, ways to influence decision makers and affect public policy, and ways to cross boundaries of multiple vested interests. Moreover, the HR professional in the public arena can become a social entrepreneur for systemic growth and development, bringing conflicting sides together to achieve compromise and resolve conflicts for social good.

Corporate Social Responsibility Scale

A question for executives and HR professionals is the extent to which their organization is concerned about, and acts to promote, CSR. You can use the following scale to rate a company. Respond to each item using a 5-point scale where 1 = not at all, 2 = very little, 3 = somewhat, 4 = very much, and 5 = absolutely.

1   The company adheres to a clear set of values.
2   The company either provides free services to those in need or is a significant charitable giver. _____
3   The product/service that the company is marketing has at least a potentially significant potential impact on the community and/or society. _____
4   The company minimizes negative environmental impacts from its operations (e.g., avoids waste, pollution, and unnecessary energy consumption). _____
5   The company has a board of directors that objectively and judiciously monitors the ethical behavior of the firm._____
6   The company proactively provides reasonable accommodations to its disabled workers. _____
7   The company encourages diversity._____
8   The company allows for—and even encourages—internal whistle-blowing activities from workers who witness unsound ethical practices within the corporation. _____

A score above 32 (a rating of 4 or 5 on each item) would be high. The items could be extended to include how the organization treats its employees (e.g., provides health benefits, makes fair personnel decisions, evaluates and provides constructive feedback on performance, develops and advances people to higher levels of responsibility). Feel free to rewrite the items or add others that you feel better reflect CSR and apply them to the companies you want to assess. Ask your friends or coworkers to respond to the survey for the same company or companies and compare your perceptions.

Who should receive social entrepreneurship training? Local governments can sponsor workshops to train community social entrepreneurs on all sides of an issue. As such, the HR professional does not enhance the competencies of one side of an issue while limiting those on the other side but rather provides opportunities to strengthen community relationships or organizational learning and culture. Some social entrepreneurship issues do not have opponents as much as they lack an opportunity for expression and influence. HR professionals can provide training that will help social entrepreneurs recognize that their views of the issue (their contact with beneficiaries and perceptions of possible impact) do not necessarily match those views held by other stakeholders. Also, social entrepreneurs may think that one strategy may be beneficial because of the assumptions they hold about how others form attitudes and make decisions. The HR manager can provide training and facilitation to help social entrepreneurs to understand alternative perceptions of situational pressures for action and ways people are more likely to respond positively.

Summary

HR professionals have a potentially important role in facilitating social entrepreneurship, whether working for organizations in the area of CSR or assisting community members engaged in social entrepreneurship. Contact with those in need and the perceived ability to make a difference (have a significant impact on resolving the problem or redressing the need) are likely to stimulate social entrepreneurship and suggest needed actions. Social entrepreneurs' beliefs about how to influence stakeholders are also likely to affect the social entrepreneurship strategies they adopt (Chapter 4). These in turn suggest roles for HR professionals to facilitate social entrepreneurship. HR professionals can help understand motivation, assess situational conditions, shape strategies, and facilitate processes. They can apply measurement and research tools to diagnose and evaluate social entrepreneurship efforts. As such, the HR profession can be a partner in local and global efforts that repair the world through individual initiative and interpersonal processes.

Situational Conditions That Motivate Social Entrepreneurship

Social entrepreneurs' transformational strategies begin with assessing the external environment. The environment is likely to be turbulent and complex, if only because social causes are thorny societal problems for which there are usually no easy solutions or sources of support. Consider the following nine environmental elements (Ball *et al.*, 2008):

1   Competitive: What types and how many competitors does your organization have?
2   Distributive: What agencies and international services are available to assist your organization/consumers of your organization?
3   Economic: How do variables such as labor cost and labor supply affect your venture?
4   Socioeconomic: How does the economic condition of each of your market segments influence your product or service?
5   Financial: How do factors such as inflation, taxes, and interest rates affect your organization?
6   Legal: How do local, national, and/or international laws affect (or potentially affect) your organization?
7   Physical: How do geographical elements such as climate and natural resources affect your organization?
8   Political: How does local, national, and/or international legislation affect your organization?
9   Sociocultural: How do factors such as the esthetics, religious beliefs, education, languages, family values, and other attitudes and beliefs of your consumer and/or surrounding community affect your organization?

Like the corporate entrepreneur who actively searches for opportunities and recognizes patterns that represent opportunities (Baron, 2006), the social entrepreneur promoting corporate civic responsibility needs to assess opportunities and the risks of not taking action (e.g., people continue to suffer; the need will go unmet). Motivation to make a positive (prosocial) difference in other people's lives through CSR depends in part on the structure of the corporate context, particularly the extent to which the situation (e.g., job or role) allows the individual to have an impact on beneficiaries (Grant, 2007). The situation may include opportunities to increase the growth, fulfillment, and development of others and to further the corporation's goals (Groenland, 1990; Ryan & Deci, 2001).

Grant (2007) outlined four situational dimensions that affect an endeavor meant to improve social welfare: (1) magnitude (degree and duration of the potential effects), (2) scope (number and breadth of people potentially affected), (3) frequency (how often a positive impact can be achieved), and (4) focus (chances to prevent harm or promote gains to others). Another situational condition that affects prosocial motivation, in addition to potential impact, is contact with beneficiaries. Contact is a function of five dimensions: frequency of contact, duration, physical proximity (geographic and interpersonal space), depth (degree of mutual expression of cognitions, emotions, and identities), and breadth (range of different groups of beneficiaries) (Grant, 2007). Opportunities to impact others will affect perceived impact on beneficiaries (i.e., awareness of how they can affect others), and contact will increase effective commitment and perceived impact, which in turn affect motivation to exert effort, persist, and develop competence, self-worth, and self-determination to make a prosocial difference (Grant, 2007). This suggests that situations may spark social entrepreneurship. Also, social entrepreneurs can structure situations so that potential volunteers and supporters have a sense that their actions affect others positively and by creating opportunities for contact with beneficiaries.

Opportunities and threats in the environment influence the vision, reflecting the need that is to be addressed by the CSR initiative and the challenges that must be overcome. Crises induce action. Opportunities do as well. Opportunities may be openings for overcoming crisis (e.g., providing goods and services of the corporation to help victims of a natural disaster). Strong situational conditions suggest what type of help is needed and how it can be provided. However, this doesn't guarantee that people will act in a productive way. Some situations are so complex that the needed resources and actions may be underestimated, goals may be unrealistic, or operations may be mishandled. (Global warming is an example. The issue has been brewing for 20 years or more and there is still uncertainty and controversy about the source and nature of the problem, its severity, and what corporations and governments can do about it.)

Table 6.2 summarizes conditions that may facilitate social entrepreneurship and conditions that may discourage or be barriers to social entrepreneurship.

Here are some recommendations to turn a discouraging situation into a supportive one (from London, 2008, pp. 323–324):

- *Get the word out*: Educate employees about CSR, how the organization is contributing, and how they can help. Provide education and opportunities for participation about specific issues and initiatives, whether they are corporate-wide donation campaigns and team efforts (the United Way, Habitat for Humanity), individual employees' volunteering in the community (one employee starting a soup kitchen for the homeless in a local community), or corporate investments in environmental sustainability in the community (a recycling initiative).
- *Link to bottom-line objectives*: Clarify the tie between social entrepreneurship and the corporation's success. Don't assume

Table 6.2 Conditions That Facilitate and Discourage Social Entrepreneurship

Situational Conditions	Conditions that Facilitate Social Entrepreneurship	Conditions that Discourage Social Entrepreneurship
Contact with the beneficiary	Personal beneficiary (the social entrepreneur or someone close: identifiable by name), visible need	Impersonal (e.g., send money to a village in Africa) or general common good (e.g., global warming)
Time frame for action	Short-term, immediate outcomes; help needed now (e.g., to assist flood victims)	Long-term outcomes, outcomes will occur sometime in the future (e.g., save energy, promote green construction)
Clarity of goals and action	Clear goals and high agreement about what to do	Ambiguous goals and low agreement about what to do
Goal and action difficulty	Low—desired outcomes require minimal effort and resources	High—desired outcomes require considerable effort and resources
Cost and value	Action is low cost, high value	Action is high cost and low immediate value (but presumably high long-term value)
Relationship between effort and effect	High—direct impact; high relationship between effort, action, and goal accomplishment (e.g., seeking volunteers to drive cancer patients to chemotherapy appointments)	Low—low impact; low relationship between effort, action, and goal accomplishment (e.g., raising money for cancer research, which eventually affects medical treatment and outcomes)
Support	Clear alliances and coalitions with shared goals, volunteers readily available	Few shared interests
Social encouragement (peer pressure and reinforcement)	High	Low
Adversaries, nay-sayers, and doubters (controversy and potential polarization)	Low	High

that stakeholders will see the relationship. Explain how the effort helps to attract more customers or talented employees, for instance.

- *Recognize accomplishments*: Celebrate (reinforce) achievements to build organizational commitment and loyalty and honor those who contributed most.

- *Highlight spin-off benefits*: Show how CSR can increase employee pride and loyalty, enhance teambuilding, improve communication between departments, and generate goodwill that benefits sales and attracts and retains valued employees.

- *Invest corporate resources*: Provide support for individuals who want to be involved in corporate social entrepreneurship efforts or start their own. Consider starting a community service support center that would offer materials, advice from fellow employees who are social entrepreneurs, and money (e.g., small grants, micro-loans, or contributions from company-wide fund raising efforts with employees determining how to distribute the proceeds).

- *Encourage employee participation*: Identify people who have a proclivity to work on and lead social entrepreneurship efforts. Ask for volunteers. Assess their skills and development needs (e.g., design an assessment center or online, self-administered assessment tools) to evaluate social entrepreneurship skills such as communication ability, political sensitivity, and knowledge of change management. Involve executives in CSR projects to increase the projects' visibility and importance. These can become developmental assignments for high-potential managers. Don't make these assignments for soon-to-be-downsized executives or people who are being forced to retire.

Now, here are some ways to overcome these barriers and respond to nay-sayers and doubters:

- *Provide convincing data or other information*: This may be information about the numbers of people affected; the costs to the individual, the company, or society; testimonies from those affected or helped or in other ways demonstrating the seriousness of the problem or issue and the positive impact that is possible.

- *Join forces with others who have like minds or shared interests*: There is power in numbers, especially if others are opinion leaders, people who are respected and have resources.

- *Negotiate with opposing forces*: People who object strongly may be amenable to small trial efforts or experiments to demonstrate the value of the initiative. If the goal is seeking volunteers for a community initiative, the social entrepreneur may start in one department or business unit to see how people react. In general, small, local efforts may be more palatable to the organization than grandiose ambitions. Small efforts can get employees involved and demonstrate impact. Note that the social programs of Henry Schein Inc. are targeted initiatives (See p. 97). Over the years, specific efforts have become part of a corporate strategy for social entrepreneurship in relation to the health care mission of the business.

• *Use behavioral tactics (e.g., demonstrations, ad campaigns, petitions)*: Today, there are many methods to gain attention including online blogs, Youtube, and television sound bites. Corporate leaders can use such technology within their organizations to build momentum and enthusiasm for a social issue.

• *Learn social entrepreneurship skills*: Leaders can learn and practice social entrepreneurship skills. One step in that direction is understanding the social entrepreneurship process. Here are some steps that can be taken to educate leaders in social entrepreneurship. Leaders can observe successful social entrepreneurs, such as Stanley and Eddie Bergman and the others we described in Chapter 4. Consider examples of social entrepreneurs for local and global initiatives. Also, look for examples of social entrepreneurs who have a personal objective (i.e., to help specific individuals) and those that benefit others in general or in communities far removed. Examples might reflect a variety of topics and goals, such areas as social welfare (poverty, education, wellness, health care), the environment, politics, and religion. Include goals such as raising money, delivering services, building awareness, preventing negative outcomes, and influencing others' votes and resource allocation decisions. Understand how these social entrepreneurs carried out the basic elements of social entrepreneurship including issue identification, solution formulation, taking action, and evaluating and refining the effort. Think about the problems these social entrepreneurs faced and what could have been done (or still could be done) differently. Consider the skills and knowledge that social entrepreneurs need to be effective. These include communication skills (e.g., ways to formulate a clear message and how to use media effectively), how to elicit support (e.g., recruiting volunteers and raising money), political and cultural sensitivity, knowledge of change management (unfreezing seemingly intransigent attitudes), forming alliances and coalitions and seeking compromise, and resolving conflicts and negotiating agreements.

• *Practice social entrepreneurship*: Leaders can practice and fine-tune their social entrepreneurship efforts. Try the following: Write a mission statement. Are your goals clear? Collect to determine the nature and scope of the problem(s). Set short-term goals that target specific outcomes, (e.g., increase recycling in the organization by 5 percent within the next year). What actions will you take? Determine who controls policies and brainstorm ways to approach policy makers (e.g., a letter-writing campaign, forums for speaking, anticipating questions and practicing answers). What transformational and transactional leadership steps will you take to recruit, motivate, and direct volunteers? Consider how you can evaluate and report outcomes, celebrate your successes, and learn from failures.

Support for Training

HR development experts can help design training programs on social entrepreneurship and community service to be delivered to employees in organizations and students and community members in schools and libraries. For instance, Sharma (1996) designed a training guide to support social advocacy in Africa. The training included methods for issue identification, solution formulation and selection, awareness building, policy action, and evaluation. These can be useful to social entrepreneurs in a variety of contexts. HR professionals can go beyond providing such basic training in the process of advocacy to study, inform, and facilitate strategies and policies in support of CSR and social entrepreneurship. HR professionals can be organization development facilitators for social entrepreneurship enterprises within the community. HR professionals can also consult for executives who are engaged in CSR efforts, such as volunteer initiatives that enhance company loyalty and teamwork while raising money for causes. In the process, also, HR professionals can help new and experienced social entrepreneurs to learn from their experiences.

Social entrepreneurship competencies include methods for affecting corporate policies, building constituency awareness, recruiting volunteers, garnering and allocating corporate and non-corporate resources, and delivering services. Other social entrepreneurship competencies are impression management, interpersonal influence, organizational change, and communication—all important for transformational leadership (Ratts, D'Andrea, & Arredondo, 2004). Hof *et al.* (2006) developed and evaluated a daylong training program to acquaint mental health professionals, university faculty, and students with social entrepreneurship competencies. They received instruction about such competencies and how to develop a social entrepreneurship plan, brainstormed how to implement the competencies in their work environment, and then generated a plan to accomplish a needed initiative. Post-training interviews indicated that the primary barrier to implementing social entrepreneurship was time, not unwillingness or lack of priority. Another barrier was social entrepreneurship activity's not being clearly defined or supported as part of their job descriptions. Resistance to social entrepreneurship on the part of other employees was consistently identified as a participant concern, and the authors suggested emphasizing methods to cope with resistance in training programs.

Would-be social entrepreneurs need to understand the alternative forms of social welfare initiatives and ways of working with people to engender support, garner resources, and assess outcomes, especially working within a corporation to promote its societal responsibilities. HR development programs link social entrepreneurship to community service, corporate civic responsibility, service learning, leadership development, and career opportunities They incorporate social entrepreneurship and integrate organizational behavior, individual and organizational learning, and the entrepreneurship concepts.

Executive Retraining Program

In December, 2008, Harvard started a student fellows program, The Harvard Advanced Leadership Initiative, for successful executives and entrepreneurs seeking a second career in a new stage of life (Lohr, 2008). The program included course work, tutorial, and field trips. In their fifties and sixties, the first 14 fellows were a high-achieving group, including a former astronaut, a senior official at the U.S. Agency for International Development, a physician-entrepreneur from Texas, and a former health minister from Venezuela. The yearlong program was aimed at helping them learn how to be successful social entrepreneurs and leaders of nonprofit organizations that focus on social problems. The initiative was part of a larger effort to help the upcoming flood of retiring baby boomers (more than 75 million people born from 1946 to 1964) find productive next careers and at the same time fill a top-tier leadership gap in the nonprofit sector. This could be a model of social entrepreneurship and second-career education programs at universities and community colleges around the world.

There is a wealth of training, information, and monetary resources available on social entrepreneurship. Some initiatives offer training to help other would-be social entrepreneurs. For example, The Institute for Sustainable Communities merged with the Advocacy Institute to offer free materials and information on how to craft an advocacy campaign, empower the coalition, speak to inspire, ensure long-run success, and build an effective team (see http://www.iscvt.org/what_ we_do/advocacy_and_leadership_center/). Ashoka offers grants and fellowship programs (http://www.ashoka.org), Miracle Corners of the World runs an annual week-long training session for youth around the world to help them become social entrepreneurs (http://www. miraclecorner.org).

The Skoll Foundation is a research and education center that "promotes the entrepreneurial pursuit of social impact through the thoughtful adaptation of business expertise." Jeff Skoll, a founding executive of eBay.com, created the foundation in 1999 in Palo Alto, California. Skoll provides information, grants, and awards to benefit communities around the world by investing in, connecting, and celebrating social entrepreneurs (www.skollfoundation.org). For instance, one grant program offers a $1 million award paid out over 3 years. The blog, www.socialedge.org, was established by the Skoll Foundation to host discussions about social entrepreneurs' barriers and achievements. Social entrepreneurs, nonprofit professionals, philanthropists, and others in the social sector use the site to network, learn, inspire one another, and share resources.

Initiatives may be university-based. Duke's Fuqua School of Business operates the Center for the Advancement of Social Entrepreneurship (CASE). The Center offers degree programs, internships, and educational materials (www.caseatduke.org). In partnership with the Skoll Foundation, CASE is studying the educational needs and key players in the field of social entrepreneurship. The Center's goal is to be the leading disseminator of practical social entrepreneurship knowledge and training.

Tables 6.3 provides more information about these and other online resources.

Conclusion

Social entrepreneurship deserves attention from professionals in HR and allied fields, such as organizational psychology and training. Here we considered characteristics of the employee as social entrepreneur in conjunction with situational pressures and opportunities as drivers for the emergence of CSR initiatives. The social entrepreneur

Table 6.3 Examples of Programs and Resources that Support the Development of Social Entrepreneurship

---

- Ashoka: Innovators for the Public, was established by Bill Drayton in 1981 (Ashoka, 2007). This is a global association of leading social entrepreneurs. Ashoka provides stipends, professional support, and access to a global network of peers in more than 60 countries. They "develop models for collaboration and design infrastructure needed to advance the field of social entrepreneurship."
- Skoll Foundation was established in 1999 by Jeff Skoll, the first president of eBay, to pursue his "…vision of a world where all people, regardless of geography, background or economic status, enjoy and employ the full range of their talents and abilities" (Skoll Foundation, 2007). The foundation offers the Skoll Awards for Social Entrepreneurship, 3-year awards to support programs that have already demonstrated some success in areas such as tolerance and human rights, health, environment, sustainability, economic and social equity, institutional responsibility, and peace and security, institutional responsibility, and peace and security. The Skoll Foundation supports a networking and information Web site for social entrepreneurs called Social Edge (2007). It includes blogs, discussion boards, feature articles, and resources.
- Schwab Foundation for Social Entrepreneurship (2008) identifies and highlights accomplishments of social entrepreneurs at the regional and global levels to stimulate productive linkages between them and help them learn from and leverage each other's successes. They partner with companies and social investors seeking to support social entrepreneurs around the world.
- Social Work Community Outreach Service (SWCOS, 2007) at the University of Maryland, Baltimore. It includes the Grassroots Nonprofit Resource Mentoring Project, mentioned earlier in this chapter, which provides assessment and development service to support community social justices and welfare efforts (SWCOS, 2007).
- Institute for Sustainable Communities (http://tools.iscvt.org/) develops training and provides financial, educational, and consulting support to social efforts around the world. They have focused on such issues as anticorruption, environmental protection, disability rights, information access, and a host of local community initiatives. Training materials are readily available. The Institute's Center for Social Entrepreneurship, Leadership, and Organization Development training offers development programs on such topics as fundamentals of social entrepreneurship, strategic planning for advocates, strategic project management, message strategy, leadership, building effective coalitions, monitoring and evaluation, and the social entrepreneurship issue life cycle.
- University Network for Social Entrepreneurship (2007) develops social entrepreneurship as a vocation and a field of intellectual endeavor and carries principles of social entrepreneurship for corporate civic responsibility and social entrepreneurship into other disciplines and sectors. They are a resource clearinghouse and an action-oriented discussion forum.
- Oxford's Saïd Business School offers courses that introduce students to social entrepreneurship in the international context, innovation in social entrepreneurship, institutional design and development in social entrepreneurship, and related electives (Oxford, 2007).

(continued …)

Table 6.3 continued

- New York University's Stern School of Business sponsors the Stewart Satter Program in Advocacy. This program fosters social ventures creation by teaching advocacy skills and thinking, providing students with opportunities to practice these skills, sponsoring research on advocacy, and creating a community of students, scholars, and industry leaders devoted to improving the social sector (http://w4.stern.nyu.edu/berkley/social.cfm?doc_id=1868).
- Duke University's Fuqua School of Business, the Center for the Advancement of Social Entrepreneurship (CASE): "A research and education center that promotes the entrepreneurial pursuit of social impact through the thoughtful adaptation of business expertise."
- Service Nation: A campaign for America: "The ServiceNation Movement is a national grassroots campaign that launched immediately following the ServiceNation Summit in New York City. It rallies the voices of ordinary Americans behind the idea that citizen service can strengthen our democracy, and help solve our most persistent social challenges and crises."
- The ServiceNation Organizing Committee is composed of large state and national organizations and associations committed to expanding service opportunities in their communities. http://www.bethechangeinc.org/servicenation

Sources to help write grant proposals:

- http://wise.fau.edu/~rcnyhan/images/grants.html: This site provides the reader with a number of grant writing links. These links provide guides, tutorials, and other free information. The site is useful for grant writers and educators.
- http://www.npguides.org/guide/index.html: This site provides grant writing tools for nonprofit organizations. The site provides advice on how to write preliminary proposals, full proposals, and sample proposals. Information pertaining to full proposals includes the components of a grant proposal, the cover letter, the cover sheet, and the budget. The site stresses the need for planning and strategy when writing and proposing a grant as a nonprofit.
- http://foundationcenter.org/getstarted/tutorials/shortcourse/components. html: This site features a proposal writing short course for the viewer. Other features include a section to learn about foundations and fund raising, proposal writing, nonprofit management, and tools and resources. There is also a section on research studies including regional, national, and international trends. Also included are sections for international visitors, children and youth, and people with disabilities.
- http://www.grants.gov/: This site is a source for finding and applying for financial grants from the United States government. This site does not allocate funds, but the site does include a key word search for grants that is fairly comprehensive.
- http://www.grantwritersonline.com/components-of-a-grant-proposal-1.html: Although this is a corporate site, it does include timely free information including an in-depth outline of the components of a grant proposal. The site also includes tips on writing a grant and a number of sample grant proposals.

needs to attract stakeholders who have their own motivation for getting involved. Having common interests is critical to creating a vision that leads to realistic goals and implementation strategies that in turn influence process and outcomes. Ongoing assessment is needed to identify directions for future learning and growth. Social entrepreneurs' altruistic motivation, readiness to learn, and transformational leadership abilities contribute to a clear, engaging, and realistic vision. Characteristics of the situation and stakeholders need to be measured (e.g., strength of pressures and opportunities). Perceptions of the vision can be assessed to determine the extent to which it is clear, realistic, and motivating. The nature of the goals and strategies can be evaluated.

Our analysis of determinants of social entrepreneurship and the development of CSR initiatives suggests directions for assessing social entrepreneurship at different stages of development. Would-be social entrepreneurs can learn to analyze the initiative they create or propose from the standpoint of the intended beneficiaries and the corporation. Indeed, corporate executives and shareholders are likely to require such analyses. Training in social entrepreneurship competencies can provide employees with experience in formulating CSR plans, conducting needs analyses, assessing opportunities for resources and service delivery, and reflecting on personal career options and opportunities, goals, and values.

Overall, HR professionals and organizational psychologists can contribute to social entrepreneurship in the following ways:

- Understand the motivation driving social entrepreneurship (prosocial characteristics, altruism, and entrepreneurial skills); recognize that multiple motives may be involved and that disagreements among volunteers may be the result of hidden agendas.
- Evaluate situational factors that affect social entrepreneurship motivation; determine whether social entrepreneurs perceive the needs correctly and are communicating them clearly to others (potential volunteers, contributors, and decision makers).
- Understand how social entrepreneurs' beliefs about people influence the strategies they adopt: whether social entrepreneurs believe that people respond to information and data, are more sensitive to possible losses than gains, react rationally to contingencies between effort and valued outcomes, respond to social pressure, are motivated to join coalitions of like-minded people, and/or respond to negotiations to maximize mutual gain.

- Provide training for employees and community members in areas such as needs assessment, entrepreneurial skills, change management, communications, transformational and transactional leadership, impression management, social influence, commitment enhancement, networking and coalition building, negotiation, conflict resolution, and outcomes evaluation.
- Facilitate social entrepreneurship processes (problem definition, information collection and interpretation, determination of resource requirements, goal setting, identification of decision makers and other stakeholders, information dissemination, selection and placement of volunteers, performance management in a volunteer context, and results measurement and feedback).
- Coach social entrepreneurs on skill development, feedback about others' reactions to them and the social entrepreneurship initiative, HR issues such as staffing and performance management of volunteers, and succession planning and transition (e.g., help the founding social entrepreneur to turn over leadership to ensure a sustainable organization).

Questions for Reflection And Discussion

1   Think of the social venture you would like to establish. What are the corporate values that stimulate and characterize the initiative?
2   Use the questions in Tables 6.1 and 6.2 to evaluate your social venture. What organizational factors might be barriers to accomplishing your goals?
3   What situational factors will help and hurt as you get your social venture under way?
4   What types of training do you feel you need to be an effective social entrepreneur? Investigate some online sources for learning social advocacy and social venture management.
5   How can the HR function help you in recruitment, development, and evaluation of volunteers?
6   What do you need to know about the situation before establishing your social venture? What situational and organizational conditions can you change to improve your chances of success?

Social Venture Exercises

Exercise 1: Describe the Following Conditions and Whether They Support or Hinder Your Efforts. (For each, indicate what you can do to create conditions that will help your venture.)

1 Contact with the beneficiary
2 Time frame for action
3 Clarity of goals and action
4 Goal and action difficulty
5 Cost and value
6 Relationship between effort and effect
7 Support
8 Social encouragement (peer pressure and reinforcement)
9 Adversaries, nay-sayers, and doubters (controversy and potential polarization)

Exercise 2

Exercises in other chapters asked you to consider the motivation (Chapter 2), competencies (Chapter 3), and job descriptions (Chapter 5) needed for each role or position that you will need on your staff or committee. As you recruit people, you assess their interests, motivation, and capabilities. No doubt, you will want to interview them, perhaps asking several colleagues to interview them as well together or separately. Here are some interview questions that could help. Adapt them to your social venture.

1 What motivates you to get involved?
2 Have you ever been involved in a similar effort before (e.g., volunteering or in other ways contributing to such an initiative)? If so, describe what you did and how you helped.
3 What skills and competencies do you bring to the table? Describe how they would be particularly valuable here?
4 What would you like to do?
5 Describe a situation in which you disagreed with a colleague? How did you handle it?
6 Describe a situation in which you developed and implemented a new idea.
7 Describe a situation in which you were a member of a team.

Exercise 3: Brainstorming Experience

The following are suggested brainstorming topics you can use to train the volunteers you recruit for your social venture. This can be a teambuilding exercise and a way to practice brainstorming ideas.

Instructions: The following are suggested topics. Select several and ask the group to brainstorm answers to the questions related to each topic. In brainstorming, be nonevaluative. Have team members indicate their ideas and ask fellow team members to expand on them. However, at this stage, avoid evaluating the ideas by talking about what is good or bad or what might work or cannot work.

1   Alternative energy
   a.   How can solar and/or wind power be generated in an efficient, profitable, affordable, and aesthetically pleasing manner?
   b.   How can the tides be used to provide energy without disrupting beach goers and boaters?
   c.   Develop a financial strategy for attracting more homeowners to invest in solar power in your region.

2   Corporate social performance
   a.   Design a plan that rewards and empowers ethically responsible businesses in your region.
   b.   Design criteria to be used for evaluating the level of ethical behavior of regional companies.

3   Diversity and multiculturalism
   a.   Design a center that provides opportunities for minorities in your area with the opportunity to either improve their employment prospects or their ability to start their own businesses.
   b.   Design an event that would take place in your region that would integrate the business interests of members of different cultures.
   c.   Design a strategy that will allow consulting groups specializing in the promotion of multicultural literature for high schools and junior high schools in your area to flourish.

4   Education and literacy
   a.   Design a strategy that will enable high school students to assist other, less fortunate high school students through a distance-learning initiative.
   b.   Design a center that will allow students with learning disabilities to be mainstreamed with other students in a manner that is mutually advantageous to both the learning-disabled and non-learning-disabled students.
   c.   Develop a "creativity center" for children.

5   Entrepreneurial opportunities for persons with disabilities

    a.   How can the persons with disabilities be provided with additional employment opportunities in your region?

    b.   How can persons with disabilities be provided with opportunities to start and grow their own businesses in your region?

    c.   Develop an innovation that would assist members of the disabled community.

6   Environmental studies

    a.   Design a cost-efficient plan for lowering carbon dioxide emissions.

    b.   Develop a plan for restoring a "brown field."

    c.   Create a marketing plan that solicits funds for the start-up of a profitable, efficient recycling plant that utilizes sustainable energy in its operations.

7   Funding the social venture

    a.   Develop a micro-finance plan designed to provide necessary funding for the social entrepreneurial venture of your choice.

    b.   How can a college seeking to become socially entrepreneurial gain funding?

    c.   Develop a plan to gain investments from local chambers of commerce to finance a recycling plan that is run through sustainable energy.

8   Health and bioethics

    a.   Develop a cost-efficient health care plan that ensures that all children are covered by health care.

    b.   Develop a strategy that will allow a hospital in your region to operate in a more caring, cost-efficient manner.

    c.   Develop a strategy that will further encourage and facilitate the pledging of organ donors.

9   Human rights and social services

    a.   Develop an outpatient system that enables individuals with psychiatric conditions in your region to develop the ability to gain employment and live autonomously.

    b.   Design a diversity training system that is inclusive of people from all demographics in your region.

    c.   Develop a back-to-work program that harnesses the talents of ex-convicts toward profitable, socially responsive enterprises and/or employment.

10   Nutrition

    a.   Design a lunch program, complete with recipes, that will enable school children of varying ages to eat nutritious, cost-efficient, and tasty meals.

    b.   Develop an online plan for providing tasty, nutritious, cost-efficient meals to the elderly.

    c.   Develop a plan that will convert the desire for "junk food" into a desire for "jazzy nutritious food."

11   Responsible architecture

    a.   Design a marketing plan for a sustainable development company that you envision.

    b.   Devise an improvement for a presently existing sustainable development company.

    c.   Write a compelling letter to the editor outlining all the virtues and arguments for sustainable housing and building structures (preferably to be published in a local paper).

12   The digital divide

    a.   Develop a cost-efficient strategy for ensuring that all member s of your region have access to information technology.

    b.   Design a strategy for recycling old computers from businesses in your region to be used by the less fortunate.

    c.   Design a strategy for recycling old computers from homeowners in your region to be used by the less fortunate.

7 Evaluating Success

Measures of Social Performance

In this chapter, you will learn how to do the following:

1 Conduct a needs assessment
2 Examine the effectiveness of the structure and process of a social venture
3 Measure social performance
4 Design applied research to determine the outcomes of social action
5 Feed back assessment results to improve the quality of your operation
6 Establish a tracking system for continuous improvement

Introduction

There are four components to assessment: (1) identifying needs prior to taking action, (2) examining the structure and process of operations, (3) evaluating outcomes (attitudinal and factual), and (4) closing the loop to use the assessment results to improve operations and performance. This chapter covers these four components.

Social needs must be assessed and reexamined as changes occur, presumably as outcomes become more successful. In the case of nonprofit social entrepreneurship efforts, officers and executives should periodically review how well they are working together and with volunteers and paid staff to determine ways they can be more effective. A quarterly, semi-annual, or at least annual review is an opportunity to reflect on relationships between people and organizations, analyze barriers and problems, and make changes for improvement. Outcomes analysis takes several forms, depending on the goals of the initiative. Measures may include numbers of volunteers recruited, money raised, people who participated, decision(s) affected, attitudes changed, and/or numbers and types of beneficiaries helped. Evaluation is not an event but a process that entails involvement of identifying what should be measured how and how often, using the results, and making changes for improvement.

Needs Assessment

Social action often begins with the spark of an idea to address a need. Suppose you encounter a homeless person begging on a street corner or witness poverty or health problems while touring a developing country. You may be motivated to help. However you need to determine the extent of the problem, explore probable causes, and examine what others are doing to address the problem. Some data about needs are objective facts and figures. Other data are subjective, such as opinions, perspectives, and viewpoints from individuals affected directly or from experts, funding sources, and other stakeholders. Consider the following sources of information:

- *Government and institutional sources (census, police reports, social service agency reports, hospital reports)*: For instance, county or town health and human service agencies may have statistics about the homeless; census reports may tell about immigration trends; police reports may indicate levels of hate crimes as an indication of bias and discrimination; and town real estate records would indicate numbers of home foreclosures.
- *Original data from focus groups, one-to-one interviews, or surveys about the nature of the problem*: For instance, families affected by childhood mental or physical illness can be interviewed; physicians can be asked to complete an online survey; hospital administrators and social agencies case workers can be interviewed on the telephone or in person; and other service providers can be interviewed about their experiences (e.g., clergy and professional staff of local houses of worship). As an example, before a local nonprofit agency invested money in building a community center in a region, a consultant was hired to interview community members and opinion leaders about the need.
- *Observations and artifacts:*. For instance, evidence of homelessness in a community may be obtained by observing people picking through garbage cans or requesting food at a soup kitchen.
- *Cyberspace-virtual sources*: The nature of secondary research has been transformed over the last few decades by the emergence of Internet searches. There are two basic forms of searches: there is the generic, wherein one just types a subject into a search engine

such as Yahoo or Google, and there is the subscriber search engines, which are open for a fee to select users.

Process Review

Once a social action process is initiated, review the process to determine its efficiency. Examine information such as the following:

- *Cost of operations*: Where is the money going? Often personnel costs are the largest part of a social action initiative. Volunteers lower the cost but need to be managed and monitored.
- *Performance evaluation*: Ed Koch, former mayor of New York, is famous for asking, "How am I doing?" Volunteers and staff are unlikely to ask this question in any systematic way. All workers— paid and unpaid alike—should have clear goals and tasks. In other words, they need to know what they have to do and what is expected from them. Then their performance should be reviewed against these goals. Did they carry out the tasks as expected? Did they achieve the desired outcomes? If not, why not? To what extent were the outcomes (favorable or unfavorable) due to their efforts and performance or were other, uncontrollable factors at work?

  Paid staff members expect to be evaluated. Volunteers do not, and can easily be insulted if their performance is critiqued by the president of the organization or other leaders. If the volunteers are not meeting their commitments, they will be of little value. Poorly performing volunteers may actually create unnecessary work, incur added costs, or forego opportunities. As such, they need to be reviewed, given feedback, and coached about how they can improve their performance. If they are not willing to listen, the leader may need to reassign them or ask them to step aside from their post or assignment. This is another area wherein a consultant can help. The consultant can review operations, collect opinions from fellow workers/volunteers and beneficiaries, provide feedback to individual contributors and the group as a whole, lead a coaching session for improvement, and suggest changing assignment and structures. The consultant can help identify volunteers' interests and skills to determine where they might be more productive and satisfied.
- *Feedback*: Feedback is valuable for shaping, tracking, and reevaluating goals. Table 7.1 lists factors that influence the value of feedback. Table 7.2 describes how feedback can support adaptive, generative, and transformative learning in a group, depending on

Table 7.1 Factors Influencing Feedback

Components	Group Level	Individual Level
Source	Objective, subjective outsider, subjective insider	Public or private
Purpose	Task, member needs, group as a system; formative, summative	Commitment to the group focus
Clarity	Obviousness and objectiveness Timing Simple or complex	Multiple and conflicting goals Allocation of resources
Favorability	Status quo or change	Positive or negative
Demands/goals	Task importance Time availability Goal clarity and difficulty	Task importance Time availability Goal clarity and difficulty
Accountability for performance	Severity of the consequences of a performance gap	Personal responsibility for performance; consequences for the individual
Feedback and learning culture	Experience and reinforcement for seeking, accepting, and using feedback; mastery and performance learning	Experience and reinforcement for seeking, accepting, and using feedback; mastery and performance learning
Learning mode	Adaptive Generative Transformative	Adaptive Generative Transformative
Perceptions of feedback	Unified mental model of what ought to be Interpersonal congruence	Self perceptions Identification to the group
Processing feedback	Open discussion Disagreements are voiced and resolved	Automatic versus mindful
Outcomes	Readiness to learn (e.g., more open to new ideas)	Commitment to the group Accepting accountability for performance and learning Belief in capacity to learn

Source: Reprinted from London and Sessa (2006, p. 9). Used with permission.

Table 7.2 Interventions to Improve Use of Feedback for Adaptive, Generative, and Transformative Learning

Learning and Change	What is Happening	Interventions to Improve Use of Feedback Depending on Group Need		
		Start-Up	Work	Review
Adaptive	Reacting automatically to stimuli to make minor changes. Feedback is based on reinforcement	Encourage self-disclosure so that members get to know each other and what their capabilities are	Focus on positive reinforcement towards accomplishing the task	Review changes
Generative	Proactively and intentionally acquiring and using new behaviors, skills, and knowledge Feedback is group developed and performance based	Focus on plans for learning and assessment	Focus on strengths, assigned tasks—seek new ways of interacting; info and reflection on other models (best practices); feedback to compare to outcome goals	Comparison to benchmarks Learning when to learn generatively and when it is not needed
Transformative	Group is involved in recreating itself Feedback is critical for reflection with relevant parties in a safe environment	Opening boundaries and stimulating group confidence	Regularly debriefing work, extracting learning, and extracting learning about learning	Reflection on past, current state, and future potential Stopping the transformation and returning to a new equilibrium

Source: Reprinted from London and Sessa (2006 p. 18). Used with permission.

what is happening and what the group needs at the time (e.g., during start-up, as the work is proceeding, and once the work is completed).

Quality Improvement Processes

Process review can take the form of a structured examination of work processes to identify problems, their sources, and methods for improvement. Corporations and institutions such as hospitals have implemented such quality improvement processes, sometimes called continuous quality improvement (CQI), total quality management, or six sigma (Masaaki, 1997; Pande, Newman, & Cavanaugh, 2000; Revere, Black, & Huq, 2004). Six sigma entails defining the problem, measuring current performance, analyzing root causes of the problem and steps in the process that do not add value, making improvement, and maintaining the gains by handing over responsibility to the people in charge of the process every day and tracking to monitor the process (Harry & Schroeder, 2000). CQI, a similar process, was developed by Bell Telephone Laboratories in the 1920s and popularized by Edward Deming in Japan after World War II (Masaaki, 1997). CQI involves analyzing the current process through detailed data collection, making improvements, studying their effects, and implementing changes. It entails being proactive, having an idea of what you want to accomplish, prioritizing, having a win-win attitude, understanding, then clearly conveying the issues, finding and taking advantage of synergies, and sharpening your focus for ongoing monitoring. These are Stephen Covey's seven habits of highly effective people (Covey, 1989, 2004).

A CQI effort is conducted by a quality improvement team. The steps can be applied to analyze a single event or an organization. People who work on the process are invited to participate on the CQI team. Team members may be paid staff, volunteers, funders, and even beneficiaries. A facilitator who is an expert in the process, including measurement and data collection, can train the team members. Once they understand the process, they can participate in future quality improvement efforts following the same steps. CQI includes the following steps:

1   Discussing how well the program is working and identifying any problems
2   Measuring frequency of problems
3   Focusing on most frequent or costly problem(s)
4   Determining possible causes
5   Brainstorming ideas for improvement
6   Creating one or more actions—interventions for improvement

7 Repeating earlier measures to determine chance

8 Instituting a process for maintaining improvements—keeping the intervention going and continuously tracking to ensure gains are sustained

9 Implementing change more widely (throughout the organization, in other communities, etc.)

Table 7.3 shows how these steps can be applied to analyze a single event or a social venture.

Outcomes Evaluation

Needs assessment and outcome evaluation are much the same thing. Of course, needs assessment begins before taking action. Outcomes evaluation measures goal accomplishment and change immediately after an action and, potentially, long term. For instance, a program for employees to tutor high school students in an economically disadvantaged area could collect data on students' participation (e.g., lower school absenteeism), grades, staying out of trouble (decrease in involvement in crime or, at least, decrease in bad behavior in school), and attitudes of parents and the tutors themselves. Longer-term outcomes would be graduation rates, scores on standardized tests, including college entrance exams, college admission and attendance, and the like.

This suggests that there are multiple elements of success in any program. Both costs and benefits can be established. Similarly, there are multiple stakeholders (beneficiaries and families, fund raisers, decision makers, community members, etc.). Other elements of success may refer to operations (e.g., dollars raised, from whom, how, and at what cost), services delivered (e.g., to use the preceding example, numbers of tutoring sessions held during what time period), attitudes changed (e.g., volunteer tutors may learn as much about themselves and their community as the students), and decisions affected (the school system and employees' company recognizing that the program should be continued, supported financially, and grown).

Consider how surveys can be used to collect data on participants' attitudes. After each tutoring session, students and tutors can be asked to complete an online survey, perhaps before they leave for the evening, using the school's computers to log into an online survey site that asks about how the session went. (For the student: Did you learn something you didn't know before? Was the tutor clear in explaining concepts? For the tutor: Was the student cooperative? Did the student pay attention? Did the student grasp the concepts

Table 7.3 Examples of Quality Improvement Processes

Elements of the Quality Improvement Process	Example 1: Start Annual Corporate-Sponsored "Walk for Beauty" Breast Cancer Awareness Program	Example 2: County Demonstration Farm: A Consortium of 4H, the State University Office of Community Extension, and the County and Supported by a Board of Community Members Who Help with Farm Activities, Tours, and Raising Private Money to Support the Farm)
Goal	Raise awareness of regular examinations; raise money for research; involve employees and community members; demonstrate company's civic responsibility	Run tours for school children and families, provide facilities and land for 4H Club activities, be a test site for organic and sustainable farming
CQI—feedback review team formed	Leaders of initiative in the company meet with representatives of local hospital	Director of the farm formed a CQI team to find ways to improve operations. Team members represented each of the partners in the farm and a representative of the volunteer board
Discuss and identify problems	First walk included employees but few community members, inadequate PR; co-sponsors needed	The CQI team effort was a direct result of decreasing visits, decreasing interest in 4H, higher costs of operations, and decreasing funding from the county and State
Measure frequency and degree of problem	Attendance and money raised fell below expected level; little post-event PR Interviews conducted with participants and potential co-sponsors showed poor planning (inadequate information about time and location for the event and what participants would do) PR found to be a problem with other community efforts; breast cancer awareness programs in other communities have similar problems; people who participated see similar problems	Examine data on use (club activity, school visits, attendance at weekend programs, and attendance at holiday events such as the annual Halloween hay rides and "haunted farm" exhibit). Fewer volunteers were willing to spend time on the farm, and private contributions have decreased

Focus on most frequent or costly problem(s)	Low attendance, lack of PR	School's declare use of the farm and decreasing funds were the most pressing problems
Determine possible causes	Insufficient planning and involvement of co-sponsors	The team held several focus groups with school teachers and administrators who previously had sent bus loads of children to the farm. They cited lack of funds but, more important, decreasing value of the farm to elementary school curricula. Maybe a focus on global issues would help. Also, they suggested working with older students (e.g., in high school and college) to develop more sophisticated programs that would attract interest and grant funding
Brainstorm ideas for improvement	Plan earlier, recruit more corporate sponsors, involve local media earlier, place PR about the last event to generate community interest	Offer programs for high school and college students on sustainable farming; be a lab for the local university; form a consortium of farmers and groceries to coordinate forums on organic and sustainable farming, develop a global village to show children farming in poor villages of Africa, Asia, and South America (perhaps become a branch farm of Heifer International)
Create one or more actions/ interventions for improvement	Next year, start planning 6 months early, invite other corporate co-sponsors to a meeting	The team decided to investigate and plan a global village in conjunction with school and university representatives and the community volunteer board, which would help raise the money, physically build the village, and eventually help run tours and programs. The effort took considerably more time than expected, especially to gain permission from the county to expand the scope of the farm. Once the project was announced, the organizers generated interest by sending

(continued …)

Table 7.3 continued

Repeat earlier measures to determine chance	Measure attendance, money raised, and participants' satisfaction with the event, rates of exams in the community, survey of community member knowledge and awareness about breast cancer	press releases that in turn resulted in interviews in the local papers and on the local television station. Sufficient funds were raised from private contributions to begin construction. The first global village demonstration site (a typical Peruvian farmhouse and barn) was built 2 years later. Additional "living" exhibits were built during the next year
		Visits to the farm began to increase by 25% a year. Funds raised increased. The number and variety of school programs tripled
Institute a process for maintaining improvements—keeping the intervention going, and continuously tracking to ensure gains are sustained	Planning committee established for maintaining the program, link between corporations, local chamber of commerce, and hospital	The director established a research committee to track use, conduct patron surveys, and run focus groups with school teachers. The global village continued to grow and become a centerpiece for the farm
Implementing change more widely (throughout the organization, in other communities, etc.)	Communicate program to other towns, and in professional meetings	The director commissioned a new CQI team annually to examine different facets of operations and seek other ways for continued improvement. Additional projects were less dramatic than the global village, but saved money and improved efficiency (e.g., partnering with local farms to purchase propane gas and fertilizer as a consortium)

you reviewed?) This can help identify areas for improvement on the spot and make improvements. (For example, tutors can be invited to coaching sessions to give them ideas about how best to communicate and reinforce learning.)

Corporate Social Performance

"Assessing social performance and impact is one of the greatest challenges for practitioners and researchers in social entrepreneurship... Many consider it very difficult, if not impossible, to quantify socioeconomic, environmental and social effects" (Mair & Martí, 2006, p. 42). Regarding CSR, we may tend to think of a company as socially responsible or not. However, performance metrics of social responsibility place companies on a continuum of weak or strong social performance along different categories.

There are multiple indicators of social performance. For instance, Shell Oil advertises that it has a triple bottom line—people, planet, and profit—to highlight the company's commitment to sustainability (Elkington, 2004; SustainAbility, 2004). CSP can be measured by company disclosures, reputation ratings, social audits, social processes, observable outcomes, and managerial social principles and values (Orlitzky, Schmidt, & Rynes, 2003). So-called KLD Indexes are often used in research on CSP. The indexes were developed by Kinder, Lyndenberg, & Domini Research and Analytics, an independent investment research and index company that helps money managers and investors integrate social and environmental factors into their investment strategies. The indexes are based on environmental, social, and governance rankings of corporate performance in each sector of the 3,000 largest U.S. equities (large-cap, mid-cap, and small-cap) (see http://www.kld.com). Companies that are high on these indexes are (1) strong stewards of the environment, (2) devoted to serving local communities and society generally, (3) committed to high labor standards for their own employees and those in their supply chain, (4) dedicated to producing high-quality and safe products, and (5) managing their company in an exemplary and ethical manner.

Another indicator of social performance is collected by *Fortune Magazine. Fortune* started its Most Admired American Companies ranking in the 1980s. It is based on a survey of executives, directors, and market analysts who are asked to rate large corporations on the following eight qualitative attributes: quality of management, quality of products or services, value as long-term investment, innovativeness, soundness of financial position, ability to attract, develop, and keep talented people, responsibility to the community and environment, and wise use of corporate assets (de Quevedo-Puente, de la Fuente-Sabaté, & Delgado-García, 2007).

Relationships Between Social and Financial Corporate Performance

Griffin and Mahon (1997) used multiple sources of social performance in a study of the chemical industry. They include two perceptual social performance measures (a KLD Index and a *Fortune* reputation survey) and two performance-based social indices (a measure of corporate philanthropy and the environmental toxic release inventory) correlated with commonly applied accounting measures. The *Fortune* and KLD indices were very similar and tracked financial performance; however, the environmental and philanthropy measures were not correlated with the firm's financial performance. This suggests that social reputation may both contribute to and result from financial performance. Collecting and communicating a company's social responsibility involvement and successes may contribute to financial performance, which makes further social investment possible. Other research found similar results (cf. Waddock & Graves, 1998).

Orlitzky *et al.* (2003) conducted a meta-analysis of 52 studies with 33,878 observations of relationships between corporate financial performance and social performance. The results indicated positive relationships between reputational ratings of social responsibility and accounting-based measures of financial performance and, to a somewhat lesser degree, between environmental responsibility and financial performance. They noted a bidirectional causality between corporate social and financial performance, similar to Griffin and Mahon's (1997) and Waddock and Graves's (1998) findings. They mutually affect each other through a "virtuous circle," such that strong financial performance provides the resources for companies to spend more on social responsibility initiatives, which in turn helps them become more financially successful. The study shows that market forces do not penalize socially responsible companies and, indeed, that executives can use their social performance as a "reputational lever" to improve stakeholder (including customer) relationships. Corporate social actions in relation to the satisfaction of its multiple stakeholders (clients, suppliers, shareholders, employees, managers, the community, and the environment) translate past performance into an expectation for future involvement and actions, transforming social responsibility initiatives into a favorable social reputation (de Quevedo-Puente, *et al.*, 2007).

The characteristics of CEOs and other managers at the upper echelons of their organizations affect the decisions they make and the practices their companies adopt (Hambrick & Mason, 1984). This happens because demographic characteristics are related to values and perceptions that influence decision making. Manner (2009a, b) found that CEOs who have a background in social performance or a degree related to applied social science are likely to generate higher levels of social performance in their companies than CEOs whose background is more technical.

Devinney (2009) argued that CSR is not obviously related to firm value. Moreover, he pointed out that vice stocks (e.g., tobacco companies such as Altria/Philip Morris) have excellent returns. Also, there are few longitudinal studies showing a causal link between a corporation's specific CSR activities and the operational outcomes that influence performance. So it may be that financial performance drives CSR or vice versa, or there could be no relationship or a negative relationship. Hence, research is needed.

Research Design

Collecting data is important, but a research design is needed to determine whether the outcomes are due to the actions you have taken to bring about social change. Multiple measures of outcome can be collected over time to see whether the intended change has occurred. Control groups (groups of individuals who do not receive an intervention) and comparison groups (groups of individuals who receive a different intervention) can be compared. The goal is to isolate variation in outcome measures to be able to say, "Yes, what we did made a difference, and it was better than other ways of delivering the service" or "Other methods were just as effective, and maybe we can be more effective in other ways." Alternatively, a result may be "What we did affected some outcomes (e.g., we changed attitudes positively) but not others (we didn't really improve outcomes)."

By way of summary, here are the elements to consider in establishing a research plan:

- *Why measure*: See effects, change, improvement; determine cost benefit.
- *Whom to measure*: Beneficiaries, service providers, funders, other stakeholders. Compare to other groups (conduct same measurements on groups that do not receive the intervention, as in the tutoring example, measures of grades and other performance

indicators of students who are similar in most if not all respects—age, gender, ethnicity, socioeconomic status).

- *What to measure*: Process (services provided to whom over what time, behaviors, decisions); outcomes: objective indicators of change relative to goals (e.g., illness eradicated, learning improved) and subjective indicators (opinions, attitudes).
- *When to measure*: Before, during, and after intervention (immediately and long term).
- *How often to measure*: Repeat measurement process with new cohorts.
- *What to look for*: Evaluate whether effects such as influence of a pretest or simply maturation influence the results.

Research Design Components

- *Time 1*: Measures from multiple groups (those for whom service is provided and comparison or control groups). Have two control groups, one in which measures are collected and one in which measures are collected later to be sure that the process of measuring does not have a reactive effect and result in change or even improvements by calling participants' attention to the issues.
- *Time 2*: Conduct program-intervention; track process measures.
- *Time 3*: Measure immediate outcomes in all groups.
- *Time 4*: Start program with new participants; include people who were previously in the control group and start a new control group.
- *Time 5*: Institute longer-term measures.

Developing a Plan to Track Outcomes

A plan is needed to collect process and outcomes data. Too often, programs are established with nebulous goals and little attention to evaluating outcomes. Evaluation is viewed as an unnecessary cost. Or service providers may believe that the benefits will be obvious or that they can't be measured objectively. Alternatively, they may believe strongly in the program and don't want hard evidence of its effectiveness, although they may not admit this. This is penny wise and pound foolish.

Moreover, outcomes assessment is not a one-time event but a continuous process, especially if the effort is ongoing. In the tutoring example, each academic year new students enter the program. New tutors get involved. Training for tutors improves. Data collection can be an ongoing process.

Tracking System

The research plan should include a tracking system to collect data over time. This might include regular surveys of beneficiaries and participants and outcomes measures at regular intervals as appropriate (e.g., annually or semi-annually).

Here's an example of a tracking system. The Acumen Fund (http://www.acumenfund.org) is a nonprofit global venture fund that uses entrepreneurial approaches to solve the problems of global poverty. The best way to create social change is to operate like a business. The Fund demonstrates that small amounts of philanthropic capital—combined with business practices for effectiveness and efficiency, innovative, market-oriented approaches, and smart money management—can go a long way to improving services that fight poverty by delivering affordable, critical goods and services in the areas of health, water, housing, and energy. The firm makes direct equity investments, debt guarantees, and pilot investments in India, East and South Africa, and Pakistan. They typically invest between $300,000 and $2 million. To track the success of their investments and to entice others to contribute to these social ventures, they obtained funding from the Skoll Foundation to develop the Portfolio Data Management System. This uses standard accounting measures to track success, see what's working well and what isn't, and hold agencies accountable: to determine the best available charity option to accomplish given goals—"For each dollar invested, how much social output will this generate over the life of the investment relative to the best available charitable option?" Analyses are based on three general factors: financial leverage (receiving principal plus interest earned), enterprise efficiencies (output expected from the investment), and technology leverage (cost per unit delivered). This cost is per unit after return is realized and how much efficiency (cost improvement) is gained from the investment. The data from different charities aimed at the same goal can be compared to determine the likely best investment. Also, charities can be tracked over time.

Here's how this works: Say, Charity A operates a food distribution system in Pakistan. Charity B operates a similar system but plans to invest in a new inventory tracking system and fleet of delivery trucks. Acumen estimates that the cost will be less expensive, providing an efficiency index:

	Charity A	Charity B
Net cost (cost minus return):	$500,000	$200,000
Total social impact:	25,000 people fed	50,000 people fed
Net cost per person:	$16	$4
Cost effectiveness multiple:		4 times as effective

The actual data required are more complex than this example, but the idea is clear: measure productivity and expect a return on investment.

Closing the Loop: A Case Study

Data that are collected and reported need to be used. This is called "closing the loop," meaning that goals are set, plans are implemented, evaluations are conducted, and results are reviewed to determine value of the program and ways to improve it over time. Here's an example: Dolly Mendoza, director, Big Brothers Big Sisters of Long Island, provided us with a description of the organization and insight into how they evaluate their accomplishments.

> Big Brothers Big Sisters of Long Island (BBBSLI) is a full member agency of our national organization, Big Brothers Big Sisters of America. It is a private nonprofit, nonsectarian organization. The primary client group is children between the ages of 7 and 16 in need of guidance, support and a positive role model in their lives. Many of the children are from single-parent families or from two parent families where special circumstances indicate the need for outside intervention. The focus of the agency is primary prevention. Our Mission is to promote positive growth and development of Long Island's children by providing families with quality mentoring, education and support services. Currently, BBBSLI also sponsors two children safety programs called PLAYING IT SAFE and PLAYING IT SMART. PLAYING IT SAFE focuses on safety issues in and out of the home for children Pre-K through Second grade. PLAYING IT SMART is geared for children Third grade into High School and deals with more mature safety themes including abduction and internet safety. Both programs include safety seminars for parents, teachers and other adults.
>
> The support services provided by Big Brothers Big Sisters of Long Island include scholarships programs, case by case financial and material assistance, family advocacy and referral, and group activities for children and families within our program.

BBBSLI recruits, screens and then, based on their assessments, carefully matches volunteers on a one-to-one basis with a child in the program. Ongoing training and support is provided for all volunteers. The volunteers are 16 years of age or older, and the children are those who can benefit from adult attention, friendship, guidance, and role modeling. Once a match is made, an agency case manager provides support to the client and mentor on a regular basis, always striving toward the development and the achievement of short-term and long-term goals tailored to each child's needs. Through this structured individualized relationship, the agency seeks to prevent the involvement of the child in the juvenile justice system. The agency also seeks to strengthen family ties and promote the constructive development of the child. A great deal of time, care, and planning goes into each match relationship. Children are also worked with on a one-to-one basis in group settings in programs set up at high schools and college.

Generally, evaluation of the Big Brothers Big Sisters Program is measured utilizing a standardized evaluation instrument developed by Big Brothers Big Sisters of America in 1997. Because community mentors, the Big Brothers Big Sisters, do the direct service work with our clients, we feel the best evaluation is one done by the volunteers themselves. Parents of children in our community-based program are also asked to participate in evaluating as well as teachers when education goals have been established. Evaluations are done after six months and at the end of one year. The children are rated on changes in 18 different areas that fall under three headings: Self-confidence, Social Competence and Caring.

Each area is rated for improvement, no change, or regression. The volunteers, parents and teachers can also state if they are unsure whether progress has been made or whether a certain area was not a program to begin with.

At BBBSLI, 90 percent of the volunteers reported that their little sister or brother was more self-confident, and more than 66 percent of the volunteers reported that their "Little" was better able to express their feelings and make decisions. More than 83 percent of the volunteers reported that their "Little" showed trust toward them, more than 58 percent reported improved relationships with peers, and 50 percent reported that their "Little" showed greater respect toward other cultures and had better relationships with their family and other adults.

Nationally these evaluation strategies utilized by Big Brothers Big Sisters of America standardized evaluation instrument include comparisons with more than 400 other Big Brothers Big Sisters agencies throughout the nation. National results have shown volunteer responses that have ranged from 33 percent to 88 percent improvement in all categories.

Several large-scale national studies have evaluated our programs. Studies have been done in recent years that show very significant positive effects of mentoring relationships. These studies, done by Public-Private Ventures, were specific to Big Brothers Big Sisters Agencies. They have become the benchmark by which all mentoring programs are measured. [Public-Private Ventures is a nonprofit, nonpartisan organization that tackles critical challenges facing low-income communities by seeking out and designing innovative programs, rigorously testing them, and promoting workable solutions (see http://www.ppv.org).]

For traditional community-based mentoring relationships, the 1995 study by Public-Private Ventures showed that a Big Brother or Big Sister makes a real difference. Children who met regularly with their 'Bigs" are:

- 46 percent less likely to start using illegal drugs,
- 27 percent less likely to start drinking,
- 52 percent less likely to skip school,
- more confident about school work, and
- have better relationships with their parents and peers.

Public-Private Ventures did another study in 1999 specifically on our school-based mentoring programs that had equally impressive results. In addition, researchers at the University of Colorado Center for the Study of Violence and Prevention analyzed nearly 5,000 violence-prevention programs across the country and identified the 10 most effective. Once again, the Big Brothers Big Sisters program was in this group.

(D. Mendoza, personal communication, 8 July, 2008)

Organizational Analysis

Table 6.1 in Chapter 6 can be used as a checklist for organizational analysis. It provides a comprehensive framework for analyzing a social enterprise. It asks about the organization's purpose, nature of the issue (e.g., severity, immediacy), the founder or leader's social entrepreneurship orientation, situation (resources, professionalism, visibility), goals, strategies, and outcomes. The form can be completed by interviewing leaders, observing them in action, and/or gleaning information about the organization from published sources. This can be used to assess single organizations or one-time efforts. It can also be used to examine whether people who are observing or participating in the organization perceive it and its leaders accurately. The last section of the form asks about outcomes: stakeholders' opinions about how successful the social entrepreneurship effort has been and impressions about outcomes during the last year, such as ratings of the extent to which a favorable impression was generated, behaviors of supporters and beneficiaries changed, support increased (members increased, training provided, resources raised), new alliances were established, measures of results were collected and reported, specific short-term targets and long-term goals were met, and the effort is sustainable (it is not faltering and moreover, it will continue and grow).

Conclusion

This chapter described directions for assessing the needs, structure, process, and outcomes of a social entrepreneurship initiative. We emphasized the importance of evaluation at every step of the way, examining needs before determining goals and forming the enterprise to carry them out; reviewing procedures and operations and seeking ways to improve quality (a continuous process, by the way); and evaluating outcomes. Social enterprises can apply sound business methods to improve their efficiency and effectiveness, and measures of costs per unit can be examined and compared to determine the cost-benefit of different charities and methods they use to deliver service.

Questions for Reflection and Discussion

1 Why is it important to have concrete measures of effectiveness of an organization's progress? How do you intend to do so?
2 What methods would you use to assess various social needs, say hunger in a city, access to health care in low-income neighborhoods, devastation from a natural disaster?
3 Reflect on the structure and process of a service organization. What elements would you examine and what data would you collect to determine the quality of its processes and outcomes?
4 What are the advantages and disadvantages of using a survey to measure team and/or organizational effectiveness?
5 Think of an organization that you were/are part of that did not measure its success: What problems did this cause?
6 What are the greatest advantages to establishing feedback mechanisms within an organization? Design one for your organization.

7   Identify the stakeholders in your organization. How can you involve the stakeholders in your organization to enhance innovation?

Social Venture Exercises

Exercise 1: Process Review

As you plan your venture, and especially as it gets under way, conduct a periodic process review. Address (1) cost of operations: Where is the money going? ...personnel, facilities, fund raising, programs, direct service? and (2) performance evaluation of yourself, your staff (paid and unpaid), partners, suppliers, and other stakeholders. Are they meeting expectations? Do they meet commitments? Do they seek the help they need? Are they responsive to constructive suggestions and feedback? Are they looking for ways to improve?

Exercise 2: Group and Individual Feedback

Consider how you collect and deliver feedback to the people with whom you work. This is a sensitive issue, especially when dealing with volunteers. Answer the following questions:

1   What are the possible sources of feedback (e.g., survey data from beneficiaries or fellow volunteers or employees, observations of activities)?
2   Why are you giving feedback: to evaluate and make a decision about the person (e.g., how much responsibility to give to the person) or to improve the individual's performance?
3   Will the feedback be clear and specific, focusing on behaviors, not personalities?
4   Will the feedback lead to a clearer understanding of demands and goals?
5   How will you hold the feedback recipient accountable for improvement in the future?
6   Can you think of ways to encourage others to seek feedback, give feedback to one another frequently and informally, and take the feedback seriously and use it to change behavior and performance?
7   Are individuals responsive to feedback and do they want to learn and develop?
8   Do they need help recognizing and processing the feedback?
9   What outcomes do you expect from giving feedback?

Exercise 3: Program Evaluations

List the data you will collect to evaluate how close you are to accomplishing goals.

Develop a research design to assess your venture's process and outcomes. Make this a longitudinal tracking system by collecting data over time to evaluate change. Are there comparison groups— other similar efforts, perhaps in other geographical regions, that you can use to compare the performance of your venture? How much improvement will you expect over time?

Exercise 4: Continuous Quality Improvement

Apply the components of a quality improvement process (Table 7.3) to your venture.

1 Discuss how well the program is working and identify any problems.
2 Collect data on the frequency of these problems.
3 Focus on most frequent or costly problem(s).
4 Determine possible causes.
5 Brainstorm ideas for improvement.
6 Create one or more actions/interventions for improvement.
7 Repeat earlier measures to determine chance.
8 Institute a process for maintaining improvements—keeping the intervention going and continuously tracking to ensure gains are sustained.
9 Implement changes more widely (throughout the organization, in other communities, etc.).

Exercise 5: Organizational Analysis

Table 6.1 in Chapter 6 provided a comprehensive framework for analyzing your venture. It asks about the organization's purpose, nature of the issue (e.g., severity, immediacy), the founder or leader's social entrepreneurship orientation, situation (resources, professionalism, visibility), goals, strategies, and outcomes. Use the form to assess your venture and your leadership of the venture. You can also use the form to examine whether people who are observing or participating in the organization perceive it and its leaders accurately.

Exercise 6: Assessment of Relevant Stakeholders

Identify and list the major stakeholders for your social entrepreneurship enterprise. These are the beneficiaries, financial contributors, volunteers, suppliers, regulators, community members, and the like. Next, rank their importance to you from highest to lowest. In doing so, provide a paragraph description for each stakeholder relating to the following:

- How the stakeholder affects your initiative and how your initiative affects the stakeholder
- The strengths, weaknesses, opportunities, and threats presented by each stakeholder related to the ability of your organization to fulfill its mission
- A statement of why the stakeholder is important in the short term (tactically) and the long term (strategically)

8   Learning Resources

In this chapter, you will learn how to do the following:

1   Identify and learn from model programs as benchmarks for excellence
2   Use online resources as sources of information and competency development
3   Start a center for community service and social entrepreneurship education
4   Review ideas for a social entrepreneurship curriculum and workshop
5   Consider the challenges of a variety of social entrepreneurship ideas
6   Practice social entrepreneurship skills by responding to cases and exercises

Introduction

In your reading of this book, we hope you have learned how to do the following:

1   Define, identify, and evaluate leadership skills and/or abilities in yourself and others
2   Identify and participate in ways to improve the local and global community around you through civic engagement, community service, and service-learning opportunities
3   Formulate and communicate a vision of goals and methods to others
4   Motivate volunteers and participate cooperatively and constructively to develop and accomplish individual and team goals
5   Evaluate the effectiveness of your actions while identifying ways to improve

6   Identify leadership and service resources that would support your personal and professional social service endeavors

Models of Excellence

Many organizations sponsor competitions and give awards and funding to social entrepreneurship ventures. Consider competitions sponsored by business schools and the BBC.

Business School Social Entrepreneurship Competition

Only a decade ago, there were virtually no business school courses or student projects on social entrepreneurship. Today, most top business schools have both (Tyson, 2008). They recognize that social entrepreneurs can prosper as they help others and that social entrepreneurs are driven by a social mission, a desire to find innovative ways to solve social problems that are not being or cannot be addressed by either the market or the public sector. Such an emphasis has emerged in the Global Social Venture Competition, which originated at the University of California at Berkeley School of Business and cosponsored by the Columbia Business School, London Business School, Indian School of Business, and Thammasat University, Thailand. Students submit proposals for the competition that project both a financial rate of return and a social rate of return. Business models that simultaneously generate sound financial returns and demonstrable social returns are enticing to socially minded business school students and investors (Tyson, 2008). Following are some examples of recent winners (http://entrepreneurship.berkeley. edu/business_competitions/gsvc.html).

EcoFaeBrick from the Prasetiva Mulya Business School, Indonesia, produces high-quality, low-price bricks by using the abundant cow dung to solve the hygiene problem created by such waste and reduce unrenewable clay. The product is manufactured with cow dung methane biogas in place of firewood. This lowers production costs and is environmentally friendly. The venture empowers rural citizens as partners and provides a sustainable solution that can be copied in other emerging countries beyond Indonesia.

Dartmouth University business students created mPedigree Logistics to provide pharmaceutical companies with robust anti-counterfeit solutions that work in emerging markets. Leveraging the power of 4 billion cell phones worldwide, consumers can check the source and quality of their drugs before use with a simple text message. This allows genuine manufacturers to avoid millions of dollars of lost market share and the potential for increasing sales with targeted information at point of purchase.

SolarCycle, from George Washington University, manufactures low-cost reflective material from used plastic bags and the interior of metalized chip bags to replace mirrors in solar collectors used in developing countries. The product helps poor urban Africans turn a local trash problem into a low cost, green, and revolutionary product for solar cooking and water pasteurization in poor rural areas. The material can purify water for an entire village for 10 years for only $350.

BrightMind Labs, from the University of Auckland, New Zealand, creates computer games that young people with psychological needs actually want to play. The immersive games can help youngsters with depression, anxiety and posttraumatic stress disorder, for instance. The first game teaches autistic children to recognize and respond to emotions.

BBC World Challenge

Starting in 2005, the British Broadcasting Corporation (BBC) has sponsored the annual World Challenge—"a global competition aimed at finding projects or small businesses from around the world that have shown enterprise and innovation at a grass roots level" (http://www. theworldchallenge.co.uk/). The competition seeks innovative projects or ideas that demonstrate an entrepreneurial spirit working for the benefit of the community while adopting a responsible approach. Grants are awarded to the winners.

A recent World Challenge Winner was Plan Bee. This Pakistani project helps female beekeepers earn additional income by selling their top-quality honey in luxury hotels.

Another project winner was Escuela Agricola (Agriculture School) in Paraguay. This self-sufficient school educates students in sustainable agriculture. For instance, students have their own compost piles and garden plots and learn to use a green protocol. All fertilizers and insecticides are made on site, and students run their own store. Graduates receive a one-time stipend to start their own farm crop for their own profit and to provide quality food for the citizens in their hometowns.

Shanti Sewa Griha, meaning "Peace, Help and Home," in Nepal is a self-sufficient commune society for leprosy victims and other social outcasts. It offers employment through tailoring, handicrafts and organic gardening.

Similar to Ashoka-sponsored projects (see Chapter 1), these examples have a global focus with ideas that can be extended beyond a single location. They empower the participants and give them opportunities for their own economic and psychological sustenance. These enterprises were started by entrepreneurs who perceived a need, created potential solutions, and implemented their ideas, usually with little resources.

Online Resources

The field of social entrepreneurship is exploding in cyberspace. Organizations such as Ashoka are paving the way for aspiring entrepreneurs interested in profiting from socially responsive products and/or services (http://www.ashoka.org). There are many consulting organizations on the Web that are more than willing to provide social entrepreneurs with assistance. We've mentioned several throughout this book. The prominent examples follow:

- The Advocacy Institute (http://www.advocacyinstitute.org/) helps people with disabilities; the website offers considerable generic material.
- The Institute for Sustainable Communities (http://www.iscvt.org/) and its partner, the Advocacy and Leadership Center (http://www.advocacy.org), provide a wide range of educational services to help people improve their advocacy and social entrepreneurship skills.
- Socialaction.com (http://www.socialaction.com/advocacy/advocacy.shtml) offers advocacy tips, guidelines for legislative visits and writing letters to legislators and editors, and additional resources such as a search engine to identify and connect with elected officials at the federal and state levels.
- Civic Ventures (http://www.civicventures.org/) is a think tank and an incubator, generating ideas and inventing programs to help society achieve the greatest return on experience.
- Triple Pundit (http://www.triplepundit.com) focuses on integrating people, planet, and profits into today's businesses. Their Web site has thousands of readers who are sustainability decision makers, consultants, entrepreneurs, corporate change agents, MBA students, and others who seek to create a better world through the power of business.
- US AID microLINKS (http://www.microlinks.org) is a knowledge-sharing set of applications and tools to improve the impact of micro-enterprises. The site provides access to information on micro-enterprises including best practices, proven approaches, examples of partners and practitioners, a library of documents,

reports and tools, and a broad array of strategies. The site includes a range of seminars, blogs, and enterprise development resources.

- Nonprofit Guides (http://www.npguides.org) offers grant writing tools for nonprofit, charitable, educational, and public organizations. The site features guidelines related to grant-writing tips, an overview of what is involved in a full proposal, sample proposals, related links and frequently asked questions.

Centers for Social Entrepreneurship Support

Social entrepreneurship is an emerging field that is constantly changing and developing. The time has come for social entrepreneurs to form strategic alliances with one another and with key social venture stakeholders in an attempt to bridge the gap between successful social entrepreneurship practices and the intellectual and financial resources and capabilities necessary to effectively fulfill these practices. Social entrepreneurs need a place wherein they can network and exchange/borrow from each others' expertise. Many social entrepreneurs, and those who would like to be, are short on expertise related to developing and implementing their mission.

The following are examples of centers that deliver service and provide education, often online, to broaden their reach by helping other social entrepreneurs.

- The Franciscan Center for Service and Advocacy at Siena College (New York) (http://www.siena.edu/fcsa): This Siena College advocacy center seeks to reach beyond the boundaries of their campus into the neighboring community, the nation, and throughout the world. This center integrates educational opportunities for its students with hands-on service for the poor and disenfranchised. By focusing on social issues, Siena College hopes to instill in its students a sense of community service and empathy toward the needs of the community.
- Children's Advocacy Institute (CAI) at the Center for Public Interest Law at the University of San Diego School of Law (http://www.caichildlaw.org). This center is staffed by experienced attorneys and advocates and is assisted by University of San Diego law school interns. In addition to training law school students, the Center works to improve the well-being of children by ensuring that they have a safe, healthy childhood. The CAI represents the rights of children in legislative matters, in the

judicial system, with administrative agencies, and with public programs.

- The University of Denver International Human Rights Center (http://www.du.edu/intl/humanrights/). This Center provides a medium for students from graduate and law programs from the University of Denver to engage in interdisciplinary advocacy research and legal representation. The focus is in the areas of indigenous rights, disability rights, and asylum and refugees. The Center offers summer internships and externships and provides assistance in establishing human rights clinics in developing countries.

- Taking it Global (http://www.tigweb.org). This is an online integration of more than 240,000 young idealistic members and hundreds of international organizations, often student-run, that support such causes as culture and identity, health and wellness, technology and innovation, and education. The Web site serves as a hub for information on global issues. The Web site encourages networking between and among the site's members.

- Students in Free Enterprise (SIFE) (http://www.sife.org). This organization sponsors annual regional, national, ad international contests among college students. Students compete both individually and as teammates for awards based on service-oriented activities undertaken by the students over the previous academic year. SIFE is partially sponsored by major companies.

- Students Partnership Worldwide (SPW) (http://www.spw.org). This organization engages and supports young people in efforts to address health, education, and environmental issues. The SPW's programs are designed to reach more than 400,000 young people every week. The mission of the SPW is "to place young people at the forefront of change and development." The SPW works in eight countries spanning sub-Saharan Africa and Southeast Asia. This organization focuses on the methodology of youth-to-youth education.

- International Medical Volunteers Association (http://www.imva.org/). This organization promotes and facilitates medical volunteer activities through education and information exchange. Most of this organization's efforts are focused in developing countries. Volunteers can include physicians, dentists, nurses, hospital administrators, and a host of other types of health care professionals. Though the International Medical Volunteers provides education, they do not send volunteers themselves.

Developing a Center for Service Learning

One way to learn about and get involved in social entrepreneurship is to help support these initiatives. We suggest developing centers for social welfare support in corporations, universities, local municipalities, and community groups. For example, colleges and universities empower students to act as social entrepreneurs through their on-campus community service centers and service learning integrated into courses in disciplines such as sociology, psychology, social welfare, marine and environmental sciences, and so on. Campus Compact is a national organization with state chapters dedicated to community service in higher education (see http://www.campuscompact.org).

Social entrepreneur support centers can be established in local communities with resources from libraries, government agencies at the town, county, and state levels, and universities or community colleges. Companies can establish similar centers to encourage employee involvement in CSR that fits community and corporate goals. In this section, we offer several ideas for such support services in the form of both physical and virtual (Web-based) centers. Consider adapting elements of these plans to form similar organizations in your company or community. Participating in ways to support social action can be as valuable as being a social entrepreneur.

Target Audience

New needs and ideas are emerging all the time. For instance, people want to fight plans for commercial enterprises, save an historic building, reclaim land for a new park, protect the environment, start an after-school program for young people, establish an arts center, open a senior daycare facility, improve access to health care, increase low-cost housing, overcome racial biases and conflicts, increase neighborhood safety, and the like.

The target audience for the center can be people of any age (high school through senior citizens) who experienced the following:

- Have ideas and motivation to effect change in their communities but don't know how to initiate and maintain action
- Have tried to start initiatives but have failed because (1) they couldn't conceptualize and communicate clearly what they wanted to do, (2) they couldn't find the resources, (3) they didn't know who controlled resource allocation decisions or, if they did, how to influence the decision makers
- Have gotten initiatives started but are floundering because they don't know how to sustain or grow the effort

- Represent different community organizations banding together to address a common problem (e.g., working for planned growth, helping people in need, such as battered women, homeless, addicted, disabled, home-bound, the aged)

Generally, the center's goal would be to build the capacity of nascent and more experienced social entrepreneurs who are working directly to address critical community issues. The workshops and consulting would enhance these social entrepreneurs' abilities to be more effective leaders, with a focus on leadership development, effectiveness, and partnership formation to bring about change.

Services

The center can offer one-to-one advising and consulting efforts for individuals and groups who have started efforts or want to. They may be people who have participated in an introductory workshop and want to get their initiative off the ground, linking with others who have similar interests or more experience and can provide advice. Social entrepreneurship and advocacy workshops can be designed and advertised in local newspapers and library flyers. The workshops would target people who think they have an idea for social change and want to get engaged but don't know where to start. Their goal(s) may be to build awareness, influence decision makers, raise funds, and/or deliver services. Customized workshops and learning circles for like constituents can be developed for specific community groups that have already coalesced and can benefit as a group from social entrepreneurship training.

Target content areas might include the following:

- *Health*: Affordable health care to those in need on a worldwide level
- *Education*: Literacy, especially in relation to education in developing countries and rural areas
- *Multiculturalism*: An understanding of different cultures throughout the world, especially in relation to underdeveloped nations
- *Sustainable development*: Eco-friendly practices throughout the globe
- *Microfinance*: Financial opportunities to nonprofits throughout the world that do not possess collateral but do possess a workable idea and infrastructure related to positive social change

The center's activities could include the following:

- Provide a guide for forming and maintaining a nonprofit organization. Many individuals and/or groups interested in advocating for a worthy cause wish to form a nonprofit but do not know where to start. The center can build a clearinghouse of available information on the Web pertaining to the formation and operation of nonprofits.
- Develop a clearinghouse of available data already existing on the Web pertaining to the development of nonprofit enterprises. Collect information about the fields of health, education, multiculturalism, sustainable development, and/or microfinance from the perspective of assisting and empowering entrepreneurs and stakeholders. So, for instance, a section on global health care could cover such issues such as HIV/AIDS, malnutrition, malaria prevention, and disability advocacy. A section on education could include efforts to help bridge the digital divide that is providing an educational gap between the "haves and the have nots" and an emphasis on such issues as literacy in underdeveloped nations. A section on a microfinance board could attempt to match aspiring entrepreneurs of nonprofits who lack initial funds and resources with investors willing to loan such organizations starting capital.
- Establish a mentoring board for social entrepreneurship. This would be a panel of experienced community members, faculty, or advanced students who are available to help aspiring and current social entrepreneurs. The mentoring board could provide information about legal requirements for forming a nonprofit, how to apply for grants related to the formation and continuation of nonprofits, guidance on how to seek out and apply for a micro-loan for a nonprofit venture, advice about organizing and operations (e.g., recruiting and retaining volunteers and raising money), and cyber workshops and videos providing training. The network would seek qualified mentor advocates in the fields of health, education, multiculturalism, sustainable development, and/or microfinance.

Staff

The center could be guided by an advisory board that includes the principal coordinators of the project and other community members and corporate executives who could be chosen from nominations of government, community, and/or corporate leaders depending on the location and focus of the center. A full-time or part-time professional could be hired as a project manager and consultant. This person would work with the advisory board members to develop materials, provide advice and consulting to community clients, and train and supervise other part-time staff who would be paid hourly (e.g., 5 to 10 hours a week) or as needed for special initiatives.

Community members and corporate employees who have experience as social entrepreneurs can volunteer to work in the center. On university campuses, courses and workshops can support student-run social entrepreneurship and advocacy organizations. Volunteers can learn to be mentors, content-area researchers, industry analysts, and/or marketers informing would-be social entrepreneurs about the services of the center. Other ways to get involved would include designing and maintaining a Web site for the center, writing a newsletter, designing and implementing social entrepreneurship training and experience-sharing workshops, building a database of contacts, and forming alliances with other sources of support.

Evaluation of the Center

The plan for the center should include an assessment process to track participants' involvement, their responses to barriers, and their success in getting their projects off the ground. Detailed records can be kept on the numbers of people seen such as clients, the nature of their requests and interests, attendance at workshops and learning circles, and consulting to ongoing groups. Data can be recorded about process (what was done to support the initiatives) and outcomes (results stemming from the advice and consultation) in terms of each effort's establishment and its impact on the community.

To show constructive progress during the year, the center's advisory board could identify three or four social welfare efforts for in-depth consulting. For these key efforts, the center's professional staff and volunteer members could attend committee meetings, work with committee leaders to plan and facilitate meetings, provide training in group development and advocacy, and generally enhance the success of implementation strategies.

Plan for Starting a Support Center

Start-up: First Three Months

- Communicate the goal and involving local stakeholders and constituencies.
- Schedule and advertise initial workshops and services.

- Hire a part-time professional staff person as a project manager and consultant to work with the center. Responsibilities could be contributing to the development of workshop materials, delivering workshops, serving as a resource and consultant to individuals and groups, and coordinating graduate student interns. If the funds are available, hire an experienced part-time professional who can hit the ground running—someone who is an expert in social entrepreneurship, community service, and the community. Consulting and advising can begin immediately.
- Revise training material.
- Create a Web site.

Ongoing Work for Next Nine Months

- Advertise and place articles in local newspapers to generate interest in and awareness of the service.
- Administer workshops, lectures, and discussion groups (staff person working with project coordinators).
- Maintain office hours (staff person and project coordinators).
- Consult as needed with local groups (e.g., weekly meetings with project committees; again, staff person and project coordinators).
- Track progress and report results.

Social Entrepreneurship Workshop Modules and Curricula

A center for social entrepreneurship or other sponsors, such as a university or community group, can sponsor workshops on getting a social entrepreneurship venture off the ground. Student groups might develop their own workshop for fellow students to promote social entrepreneurship. Presented here are learning objectives and four modules that could be offered in a single workshop or a series of workshops depending on the depth to which each module is covered.

Learning Objectives

- Integrate leadership development, community service, and service learning.
- Recognize range of social entrepreneurship enterprises (goals, organizations, and outcomes).
- Develop individual, group, and organizational perspectives on social entrepreneurship.
- Understand and apply needs analysis and outcomes assessment methods.

- Work in a team to develop and present a plan for a not-for-profit or for-profit enterprise.
- Consider how to recruit and maintain involvement of supporters and identify sources of funds and other resources.
- Recognize how projects evolve as needs change or become clearer and resources are found or lost.
- Reflect on personal value for skill development, career advancement, social benefit, and civic responsibility.

Sample Learning Modules

- Module I: What is social entrepreneurship? Provide definitions and examples. Give examples of social entrepreneurship efforts—both local and global, including those that have a personal objective (i.e., help specific individuals) and those that benefit others in general (others far removed or others in general, including oneself). Show how these examples differed in their goals and strategies. Include examples from such areas as social welfare (poverty, education, wellness, health care), the environment, politics, and religion. Include goals such as raising money, delivering services, building awareness, preventing negative outcomes, and influencing others' votes and resource allocation decisions. Show the basic elements of social entrepreneurship including issue identification, solution formulation, taking action, and evaluating and refining the effort. Draw on several examples to trace these stages of social entrepreneurship from gestation of the idea to outcomes. Also, identify any barriers to change, adversaries, and partnerships. Give examples of social entrepreneurship efforts that succeeded and those that failed. Use cases and exercises to diagnose problems and identify what could have been done differently.
- Module II: Personality characteristics affect an individual's proclivity to get involved in a social entrepreneurship effort. Include such characteristics as altruism, caring about social justice, extraversion, willingness to stand up for oneself and others, ethics, risk taking, and optimism. Personality characteristics also affect their likelihood of persisting in the face of barriers and learning from the experience. Show how characteristics such as self-esteem, self-confidence, internal control, resilience, and mastery in learning orientation are important for effective social entrepreneurship. Provide a way for individuals to assess their own readiness to get involved and persist in social entrepreneurship.

- Module III. Cover interpersonal theories that are important for social entrepreneurship: how to change attitudes and behaviors, effective communication, interpersonal influence, issue selling, building commitment, and transformational leadership. For each theory, demonstrate principles and research findings that have practical implications for effective social entrepreneurship, give examples, and develop cases to analyze and/or participatory, role-playing exercises to apply the concepts. Possible strategies include informing, threatening, rewarding, compromising, negotiating, forcing, and fighting. Include effective use of media. Provide examples from social entrepreneurship initiatives and give cases, problems, and participatory exercises for action learning.
- Module IV: What skills and knowledge do social entrepreneurs need to be effective and how can they learn them? These include communication skills (e.g., ways to formulate a clear message and how to use media effectively), how to elicit support (e.g., recruiting volunteers and raising money), political and cultural sensitivity, knowledge of change management (unfreezing seemingly intransigent attitudes), forming alliances and coalitions and seeking compromise, and resolving conflicts and negotiating agreements. For each critical skill and knowledge area, apply behavior modeling to develop modules to help people improve their social entrepreneurship skills. Behavior modeling means defining the concept and stating the principles of its effective and ineffective application, demonstrating these principles (e.g., through cases, perhaps with video or audio demonstrations, that show good practice and bad), and one or more exercises that give participants ways to practice these skills and get feedback and reinforcement).

Table 8.1 outlines a curriculum that universities or corporations can to train people to be social entrepreneurs.

Challenges of Social Entrepreneurship Ideas

Each of the following cases raises social issues and asks questions for discovering ways to deal with them. You can read the cases and answer the questions on your own using your best judgment. You can use these problems as teambuilding exercises to help your group learn to brainstorm ideas and work together better. You can also use the cases as sources of ideas for social ventures that you might want to develop as CSR or social entrepreneurship community initiatives.

Table 8.1 Social Entrepreneurship Curriculum

1. *The business plan for the social venture:* Students will learn the basic principles underlying the development of a "double bottom-line" business plan. Online modules will cover how to devise a table of contents, executive summary, mission statement, products and services plan, marketing plan, management plan, operations plan, and financial plan. The plan will reflect the basic principle of social entrepreneurship: "doing well while doing good." The students' ventures should be a product or service that is realistic, affordable, profitable, and good for society.

2. *Global health care and social entrepreneurship:* Students will explore how health issues such as HIV/AIDS and other infectious diseases, such as malaria, fresh water shortage, access to health care, poverty, and environmental health affect and are affected by social entrepreneurship efforts to meet such health challenges. Students will be required to perform an industry analysis related to the international health issue of their choice. The final project will include the students' developing a strategic plan for dealing with the international health issue of their choice.

3. *Grant writing:* Successful grant writing involves planning and preparation. It involves researching, organizing, writing, and packaging the proposal before submission. In this course, the student will learn the basic steps necessary to prepare for and write a grant for a social venture. Equal emphasis will be placed on the acquisition of for-profit and nonprofit grants for the social entrepreneur.

4. *Cause related marketing and fund raising:* In this course, students will be presented an overview of the respective advantages and disadvantages of potential funding streams of a charity or cause. Students will develop an understanding of how consumers can be persuaded to buy a product from a company based on the company's affiliation with a charity or cause. The students will first develop a SWOT (strengths, weaknesses, opportunities, and threats) analysis associated with a specific, existing cause-related marketing campaign. Students will then develop an advertising campaign that is designed to jointly benefit a company and a charity or cause. The culmination of the course will be marked by students' effectively analyzing and providing feedback for the cause-related strategies developed by fellow students.

5. *Social entrepreneurship in action:* This course will be dedicated to allowing students to explore innovative approaches to contemporary social issues through the completion of a series of social entrepreneurship scenario exercises. Topics will include education and literacy, diversity and cultural awareness, nutrition, medical issues, disease and bioethics, entrepreneurial opportunities for the d bled, the digital divide, funding sources and opportunities for the social entrepreneur, affordable housing, corporate social performance, agriculture, water, and forestry, human rights and social services, and alternative energy.

6. *Corporate social responsiveness (larger organizations):* According to the definition of corporate social responsibility (CSR), corporations should act as social entrepreneurs of broader societal goals and not merely to benefit a more restricted number of shareholders and/or stakeholders. In this course, students will examine the level of CSR in a variety of corporations

according to the following criteria: safety records, environmental records, charitable giving, diversity, and the overall value of their product or service to society. Each student will assess five companies according to these criteria for the final project, acting in simulation as a social entrepreneur who is employed within these corporations.

7. *Social entrepreneurship opportunities in Africa:* Students will be required to study the history, innovations, contemporary issues, and special challenges that confront social entrepreneurship organizations in the countries within the continent of Africa. Special emphasis will be placed on addressing such issues as harnessing the potential of international migrants, the effective use of information and communication technologies in the development of the continent, improving access to HIV/AIDS-related services, UN Millennium Development Goals, biotechnology in agriculture, strategies for poverty alleviation, and promoting intra-African trade for the sustainable development of the continent.

8. *Social entrepreneurship as a faith-based initiative:* This module will identify the potential of revenue-generating initiatives that provide faith-based and other charitable organizations with sources of additional funding. An emphasis will be placed on how post-secondary institutions involved in faith-based initiatives can partner with religious and/or other charitable organizations to improve double bottom-line investments. The course will require each student to design a marketing plan that assists an actual faith-based or charitable organization.

9. *Research seminar in social entrepreneurship:* Students will develop the research skills needed to conduct effective environmental scanning, develop recruitment of volunteer leads, and conduct market research for both regional and national social entrepreneurship organizations. The instructor will guide students as they conduct an extensive SWOT analysis related to both the topic of a social entrepreneurship and the specific, prospective social entrepreneurship organization that is of interest to the students. Students will gain a familiarity with such data bases as Hoover's, Novel, Reference USA, and Corptech. The course will conclude with the students conducting an extensive research project designed to provide a strategic plan for analyzing the chosen social entrepreneurship organization.

- Case 1: Providing better pharmaceutical medications
- Case 2: Solar power
- Case 3: Recycling
- Case 4: Distance education for students in Africa
- Case 5: Nutrition
- Case 6: Access to education
- Case 7: Multicultural disability center
- Case 8: Design your own high school

Case 1: Providing Better Pharmaceutical Medications

According to Hammond's (2006) industry analysis research of the World Health Organization (WHO):

There are 300–500 MILLION cases of lost lives due to infectious diseases. In today's world there are many re-emerging and emerging infectious diseases that need to be brought under control. This is problematic based on this assertion from Cavazos (2006), "The (pharmaceutical) industry claim of $802 million costs per drug relies on a study from an industry-funded research center at Tufts University in Boston" (Love, 2001). Tufts researchers supposedly had access to industry data to come up with their figure, but no one else is able to see the underlying data. So if you choose to believe in this number, it is simply a matter of faith.

Consider the following fundamental questions for you to answer: "How can new drugs be introduced in a manner that is affordable to perspective users?" Choose a major distributor of pharmaceuticals. Develop a venture that does the following:

- Provides a compelling argument, both on humanitarian and economic grounds, for a pharmaceutical company of your choice to be interested in providing low-cost pharmaceuticals. This argument should refer to facts related to the industry in terms of global benefits to this strategic plan.
- Includes a plan for developing a collaborative program among several pharmaceutical companies that addresses this issue in under-developed nations. Focus on one country.
- Recognizes three major objections to your plan from the perspective of a pharmaceutical company and provide solutions that address, minimize, and even eliminate the basis of these objections.
- Explains the role that the government of the foreign country you are choosing to focus on can play in assisting the pharmaceutical company in its efforts to provide low-cost pharmaceuticals. This should be done in a manner that is both economically and socially viable to the pharmaceutical company.

Your plan should refer to the following concepts:

- Description of how your strategy provides the company with an alternative plan that allows for low-cost leadership (produce goods at lowest cost) without sacrificing quality
- An explanation of the advantages of a low-cost strategy
- An explanation of how the disadvantages of a low-cost can be minimized or eliminated in your plan

- The role of host government policies of the country you have chosen

Case 2: Solar Power

Solar power has great potential for use in under-developed countries. You have just been given $10 million in seed money from "angel investors" to develop and promote solar power in the under-developed country of your choice. Here's your challenge:

- Identify the main strength (what is positive) and the primary weakness (what is a limitation) associated with the solar power industry at this time (this requires research!).
- Describe the technology you will use to develop and promote your solar power initiative.
- Present a strategy for how you will market your product to attract additional investors: How can you raise additional funds?
- Summarize why you have selected the under-developed country of your choice as the home site for this initiative.
- Determine how will you promote the cooperation and participation of the inhabitants of the country you have chosen.
- Summarize at least one opportunity (what could go right) and one threat (what could go wrong) with your efforts. How will you maximize the chance to realize this opportunity? How will you minimize or eliminate the likelihood of this threat?
- How might you gain the support of the United Nations for this endeavor?

In addressing these questions, compare and contrast other sources of energy with solar power. Describe the geographic and socio-cultural challenges associated with the respective under-developed country chosen.

Case 3: Recycling

Recycling is an inconvenience to many people in the United States and there are not enough people pitching in to help. Recycling is a big help to our environment. Some of the benefits include saving energy, preventing pollution, and conserving our natural resources. It also reduces the amount of garbage that gets brought to the landfill/dump.

We are able to recycle newspapers, magazines, catalogues, metal cans, foil wrap and trays, plastic bottles and jars, and beverage cartons and drink boxes. If the recycling industry makes people more aware of what can and cannot be recycled, profits will be increased, and the community will benefit.

The recycling industry serves two purposes, one economic and the other environmental. From an economic standpoint, recycling makes raw materials available to manufacturers and provides an alternate source to unrecycled materials; from an environmental standpoint, recycling reduces the amount of "new" raw materials that need to be produced.

There are two ways of making recycling more profitable: (1) Increase the cost of disposing of items without recycling by imposing surcharges on garbage that is not recycled, and (2) provide subsidies to those companies that choose recycled materials over non-recycled materials to use in the production of new items.

Your challenge:

1   Summarize the main challenges associated with the recycling industry.
2   Present a plan for enhancing the profitability and effectiveness of the recycling industry.
3   Do so in a manner that enhances the awareness of the benefits of recycling to consumers and makes them want to actively participate in the recycling activities of your recycling initiative.

Now let's say that you have an operating budget of $20 million to work with. Special consideration will be given to entries that take into account recycling needs that go beyond your local region. Take into account the following concepts in presenting the plans for your recycling company:

- What are your rivals offering?
- What new entrants can enter the market to compete with existing companies?
- What role does product innovation play in your strategic plan?
- How are you going to keep your prices and costs competitive?
- What are the greatest strengths (what is positive) and weaknesses (what is a limitation that exists right now) of your plan?
- Most important, what opportunities (what could go right in the future) and what threats (what could go wrong) can you identify? How will you plan for minimizing your threats while maximizing your opportunities?

Case 4: Distance Education for Students in Africa

There is a great need for access to higher education in Africa for improved scientific, engineering, and management growth and development. The need for socially responsible businesses is especially prevalent in these regions. Here's your challenge:

1 What online courses would you offer to aspiring social entrepreneurs in Africa?
2 Explain how this program will benefit the economy, and in turn the inhabitants, of African countries that participate;
3 Argue why the World Bank should support your curriculum.

Case 5: Nutrition

Suppose you are in the frozen food business and your target market is low-income populations that are malnourished. You must develop a frozen food product that is nutritious, inexpensive, low in sodium, and convenient to cook. Come up with three product ideas that are new to market and might fulfill these criteria. They might be frozen dinners, soups, appetizers, drinks, main courses, and vegetables. Now:

1 How would you promote this product? Develop an advertising campaign with a slogan and how you would package this product.
2 How would you reduce costs while maintaining quality?
3 How would you test-market your product? What test sites would you choose? How would you experiment with variations in advertising, pricing, and packaging?
4 What would be the advantages and disadvantages of a gradual introduction of your product? Would you commercialize this product gradually or in one step? Why?

Case 6: Access to Education

The problem of inequality in educational opportunities often starts before preschool. Children in under-developed regions and even in developed countries often lack the same opportunities that their more affluent counterparts have at their disposal. By kindergarten, many of these disadvantaged students are at a competitive disadvantage in terms of such subjects as basic vocabulary and reading comprehension. These disadvantages have long roots that affect adults who have grown up under-educated in a competitive world. Of great concern is that this lack of education often leads to ignorance related to basic health care issues, such as nutrition.

You have been placed on an international task force by the United Nations to examine this issue, and your recommendations will be welcome. Of particular interest is education related to basic nutrition requirements. Many of the inhabitants of these underdeveloped regions lack basic information on the subject of obesity. Contrary to common knowledge, obesity is a common, growing problem in underdeveloped regions. Ambitious solutions are needed: What solutions can you provide?

Case 7: Multicultural Disability Center

Chelsy is eager to change the world. She has built a Web site and convinced an instructor to build class assignments in international business and business policy courses to assist her organization. Chelsy's multicultural disability center (www.cdisabilitycenter.com) is the cyber-home of a new disability organization dedicated to disseminating information related to cutting-edge technology for the mobility impaired. The mission of Chelsy's multicultural disability center is to improve the lives of persons with disabilities all over the world by providing them with information and assistance related to supportive technology and medical care. When completed, this site will include blogs, related articles, product recommendations, insurance coupons, health care recommendations, support groups, and volunteer opportunities.

The emerging organization has several challenges:

- It is started by a student with limited business experience.
- It lacks substantial capital.
- It presently lacks the resources to "live up to its name" of truly being an international force.
- What can you suggest to Chelsy to help her realize her dream?

Case 8: Design Your Own High School

Suppose you are asked to design a high school that will champion innovation and creativity in an underdeveloped region of the world.

1   What programs and courses will this high school offer?
2   How you will recruit and select teachers?
3   What type of low-cost yet innovative activities will this high school offer its students?
4   How will you get others involved and build partnerships?

Case 9: Linking Corporate Social Responsibility and Environmental Sustainability

A recent call for papers for a special issue of the journal *Business & Society* challenged authors to submit articles that address the following questions (Orlitzky, Siegel & Waldman, 2009). How would you answer them?

- What does it mean for an organization to be socially responsible and environmentally sustainable in the international arena? What is the social responsibility of global business? How can large, multinational companies become more sustainable? How do definitions of corporate responsibility and sustainability differ across countries?
- What adjustments in corporate structure, governance, reporting relationships, or incentives might facilitate the integration of financial, social, and environmental domains of business activities?
- Why might socially and environmentally responsible companies perform better or worse financially than organizations that show little concern for their social and ecological environments? What are the moderating and mediating factors that affect these relationships?
- Can socially responsible organizations actually change societies? How might organizational commitments to ecological sustainability change societies or individual attitudes?
- How are corporate social responsibility and sustainability related to leadership qualities and other characteristics of top executives or systems pertaining to them (such as executive pay structures)?
- What is the best way to measure and evaluate social and environmental performance?
- What are the relationships between corporate social responsibility, environmental sustainability, firm reputation, and organizational culture/identity?

Conclusion

This book reviewed the motivation, skills, and competencies that social entrepreneurs need to be successful. The book also described steps and strategies for establishing social welfare initiatives in corporations and communities. We covered how to develop a high-performing team and deal with domineering and misplaced volunteers. In addition, we reviewed interventions for overcoming barriers, continuous learning, and evaluating process and outcomes. In this final chapter, we suggested that another way to get involved is to learn how to support social entrepreneurship. We outlined components for a support center that can be located in a community, corporation, or university.

Becoming a better social entrepreneur takes time and experience. In the exercises throughout this book, we encouraged you to (1) start a social venture, (2) reflect on your participation as a social entrepreneur or volunteer in a social venture to increase the venture's success and improve your competence as a social entrepreneur and leader, and (3) be a continuous, generative learner who seeks new knowledge and creates and implements new ideas.

Our final set of reflection questions and exercises will help you think about your own motivation, skills, and competencies, the steps and strategies you might use, and the methods you can apply to build high-performing, continuous learning teams.

Questions for Reflection and Discussion

1 Is there a need for a center to support social entrepreneurship in your community or company? If not, how can you get one started?

2 What roles would you like to have in such a center? How can you acquire the skills you would need to be an effective educator, mentor, and consultant?

3 Do you know people who have the experience needed to provide support services to help would-be social entrepreneurs?

4 Who would you have to convince to establish such a center? What resources would be needed?

5 Can you envision a Web site that would offer such services to your local community that would provide information, help, and referral but is not readily available on existing nationally or globally focused Web sites?

6 What support services would be particularly valuable given the needs in your local area?

7 How could you use the concepts in this book as a basis for training, workshops, and facilitation?

Social Venture Exercises

Exercise 1: Review

By way of review, answer the following questions:

1 What factors motivated you to select the social venture you considered developing as the example of what we asked you

to think about at the end of each chapter? What factors would motivate others to work with you on the venture? Consider the role of personal experience, altruism, and advocacy orientation as motivational factors.

2 What are the main leadership skills and/or abilities that you and your potential partners bring to the social venture?

3 In what ways will your venture help others or improve the local and global community?

4 What will you do to plan, implement, and deliver on your goals? In other words, what will be the main activities of your venture? As you engage in the goal-oriented activities, what actions will you take to encourage others to participate cooperatively and constructively in the venture?

5 How do you plan to formulate and communicate a vision to others?

6 How will you evaluate the effectiveness of your actions and identify ways to improve what you are doing?

7 What resources will you need to support the venture and your own development?

8 How do you intend to empower your partners and volunteers while you organize tasks and delegate work? How will you motivate and reward individuals and groups with whom you work on the venture?

Exercise 2: Starting a Support Center

Do you have a support center available in your area to help you in your venture? Suppose you wanted to start such a center in your community. What components would you want and how would you get it started? Refer to the proposal for a social entrepreneurship support center that we included in this chapter. What would the center do, who would support it, what other types of initiatives/ventures could it help, what staffing needs would it require, and how would it deliver its services (e.g., through one-to-one consulting, workshops and training, information sharing and referrals)?

Exercise 3: Developing Ideas for Social Ventures

Here are some ideas for social ventures. For each, think about the following points as you review each one. Draw on the concepts that we presented throughout this book.

- Sources of motivation
- The leadership skills and competencies needed for the venture
- Needed resources

- The possible strengths, weaknesses, opportunities, and threats associated with the venture
- Ways to communicate the vision to others and the emotional, cognitive, and/or behavioral call to action of the message
- How the leader can build a high-performing team as the venture evolves, delegating, empowering, and motivating participants as they work toward a common vision
- Measures for evaluating the venture's success

Social Venture Ideas

1　A young man who suffered a physical handicap from a car accident as a teen wants to start a Web site to provide training to help handicapped home-bound individuals start their own businesses. Advertisers would defray the cost of the site. Users would obtain online training in Web site design, marketing, supply-chain (from purchasing to delivery), and financing.

2　A nephrologist (kidney specialist) wants to open a dialysis center for patients who need regular treatments to clean their blood several times a week. Instead of going to a hospital center, they can go to a private, well-appointed environment staffed by nursing personnel with physicians on call. The center would have about 30 chairs, can handle 250 patients or so, and would have insurance billings of more than $3.5 million a year. The center could be run for-profit or not-for-profit.

3　A young woman who loves horses and has taken riding lessons for many years would like to start a business that trains horses for use by riding stables for therapy sessions for children who have various emotional handicaps, such as autism. Stables could purchase these horses and offer the therapy in conjunction with local physical therapists. Training the horses could be for-profit or not-for-profit.

4　A high school teacher wants to develop a service learning initiative for students who would learn about environmental and health issues in impoverished areas in Central America. Students would learn as they collect information, interview people from the area, raise money, and eventually take a trip to Nicaragua to help villagers dig wells and build clinics, schools, and homes.

5　An employee of a large corporation located at the outskirts of a major U.S. city would like to mobilize employees to raise money and deliver gifts to needy children.

6　A company that has had negative publicity from paying low wages or low benefits wants to improve its image and show that it gives back to the communities in which it operates. What can the company do?

7 A college student who commutes 20 miles each way to campus wants to start a citizens for traffic safety advocacy group. The group would identify traffic bottlenecks, unsafe intersections, roads laden with potholes, areas of congestion, and construction and road repair sites that block traffic. The group would lobby local, county, and state governments for funds to install traffic lights, schedule maintenance and construction in relation to commuter volume and safety, reroute traffic before congestion builds, and provide commuters with up-to-the-minute online traffic reports.

8 A local business owner has an idea to reduce car and bus emissions and increase visitor volume in his town by offering free loaner bicycles. Following a model that works in Copenhagen, Denmark, bicycles would be available at stands around the town for anyone who wishes to borrow one to go from one stand to another. The bicycles would be paid for by commercial ads placed on the wheel spokes. The initial cost would be raised privately, and the bicycles would be maintained by student volunteers and monitored by the town mayor's office.

Exercise 4: Team Projects for Learning Social Entrepreneurship

This group exercise draws on the steps for business planning to formulate an idea for a social entrepreneurship venture. Develop a project proposal that provides ways for others to participate actively in support of a cause and formulate implementation plans. Create a multimedia presentation. Present your project using a PowerPoint slideshow. You might also create a Web site or design a poster. You could incorporate a video in your Powerpoint from Youtube or another source to describe the need you address. Include the following (at least one slide for each of the 10 topics):

1 *Background and motivation:* What is the setting/history behind this project? What is the problem to be addressed? What are some current approaches?

2 *Goal:* Articulate your mission. Why is this cause worth promoting and/or aiding? What is the main purpose of your project? What are the defining features and benefits of this program/project?

3 *Design a logo* that readily identifies your group and its purpose.

4 *With whom will you collaborate?* ...community agencies, organizations, and the like.

5   *Work with others* to develop consensus for statements of vision (what you hope to accomplish when successful), mission (what you are working for; whose interests you are representing; what problem you are addressing), and objectives (specific decisions and resources you aim to achieve and a time table for achieving them).

6   *Establish a lobbying campaign* (internet site, blog, videos, town hall meeting, demonstrations, letter writing). Use these techniques to educate (provide information about the problem, need, or issue including the potential benefits from taking action and costs of not acting).

7   *Develop communication strategies* for different constituencies and demographic groups (community members, merchants, students, senior citizens).

8   *What are the main rewards if this project succeeds?* What are the risks?

9   *Project evaluation:* How will you assess involvement efforts and outcome? Does your project/program effectively address your cause?

10   *Reference* any documents or resources used in planning your program/project.

Be sure to cover the following:

1   Need
2   Leader's and volunteers' motivation
3   Beneficiaries
4   Stakeholders: Decision makers, volunteers, donors, community, others
5   Alliances
6   Nay-sayers and other barriers
7   Source of funds
8   Goals/vision
9   Organization (structure, leadership)
10   Methods
11   Marketing: Brand, message(s) (informational, emotional), means of communication (Web)
12   Lobbying: Modes of influence
13   Service delivery
14   Effectiveness and efficiency.

References

Adler, P. S., & Kwon, S. (2002). Social capital: Prospects for a new concept. *Academy of Management Review, 27,* 17–40.

Afako, B. (2002). Reconciliation and justice: 'Mato oput' and the Amnesty Act. http://www.c-r.org/our-work/accord/northern-uganda/reconciliation-justice.php

Alboher, M. (2009). Solving a social problem without going the nonprofit route. *New York Times Online,* March 4. http://www.nytimes.com/2009/03/05/business/smallbusiness/05sbiz.html

Alinsky, S. (1971). *Rules for radicals.* New York: Random House.

Alvord, S. H., Brown, D. L., & Letts, C. W. (2004). Social entrepreneurship and societal transformation. *Journal of Applied Behavioral Science, 40*(3), 260–282.

Ashoka (2006). http://www.ashoka.org/home/index.cfm. Accessed January 6, 2006.

Ashoka (2007). http://www.ashoka.org/ Accessed March 14, 2007.

Avner, M. (2002). *The lobbying and advocacy handbook for nonprofit organizations: Shaping public policy at the state and local level.* St. Paul, MN: Fieldstone Alliance Wilder Foundation.

Bakan, J. (2004). *The corporation: The pathological pursuit of profit and power.* New York: Free Press.

Ball, D., McCulloch, W. Jr., Geringer, J. M., Minor, M., & McNett, J. (2008). *International business: The challenge of global competition* (11th edn). New York: McGraw-Hill Irwin.

Bandura, A. (1997). *Self-efficacy: The exercise of control.* New York: Freeman.

Bandura, A. (2001). Social cognitive theory: An agentic perspective. *Annual Review of Psychology, 52,* 1–26.

Bansal, R. (2006). Ivey On … Best practices in Corporate Social Responsibility. *Ivey Business Journal Online,* March-April. http://www.Iveybusinessjournal.com

Barendsen, L., & Gardner, H. (2004). Is the social entrepreneur a new type of leader? *Leader to Leader, 34,* 43–50.

Baron, R. A. (2006). Opportunity recognition as pattern recognition: How entrepreneurs "connect the dots" to identify new business opportunities. *Academy of Management Perspectives, 20*(1), 104–119.

Barrick, M. R., & Mount M. K. (1991). The big five personality dimensions and job performance: A meta-analysis. *Personnel Psychology, 44*, 1–26.

Barringer, B., & Ireland, R. (2007). *Entrepreneurship: Successfully launching new ventures* (2nd edn). Upper Saddle River, NJ: Prentice Hall.

Bar-Tal, D. (1985–1986). Altruistic motivation to help: Definition, utility and operationalization. *Humboldt Journal of Social Relations, 13*, 2–14.

Bass, B. M. (1998). *Transformational leadership: Industry, military, and educational impact.* Mahwah, NJ: Erlbaum.

Bateman, N. (1995). *Advocacy skills for health and social care professionals.* Brookfield, VT: Ashgate Publishing.

Batson, C. D. (1987). Prosocial motivation: Is it ever truly altruistic. *Advances in Experimental Social Psychology, 20*, 65–122.

Batson, C. D., & Moran, T. (1999). Empathy-induced altruism in a prisoner's dilemma. *European Journal of Social Psychology, 29*, 909–924.

Batson, C. D., & Powell, A. A. (2003). Altruism and prosocial behavior. *Handbook of Psychology* (pp. 463–484). Hoboken, NJ: Wiley.

Batson, C. D., Dyck, J. L., Brandt, J. R., Batson, J. G., & Powell, A. L. (1988). Five studies testing two new egoistic alternatives to the empathy-altruism hypothesis. *Journal of Personality and Social Psychology, 55*(1), 52–77.

Baum, J. R., & Locke, E. A. (2004). The relationship of entrepreneurial traits, skill, and motivation to subsequent venture growth. *Journal of Applied Psychology, 89*, 587–598.

Baumeister, R. F., & Leary, M. R. (1995). The need to belong: Desire for interpersonal attachments as a fundamental human motivation. *Psychological Bulletin, 117*, 497–529.

Berson, Y., Shamir, B., Avolio, B. J., & Popper, M. (2001). The relationship between vision strength, leadership style, and context. *Leadership Quarterly, 12*, 53–73.

Besharov, M. (2008). Mission goes corporate: Understanding employee behavior in a mission-driven business. Unpublished doctoral dissertation, Harvard Business School.

Blau, P. (1994). *Structural contexts of opportunities.* Chicago, IL: University of Chicago Press.

Bolino, M. C. (1999). Citizenship and impression management: Good soldiers or good actors? *Academy of Management Review, 24*, 82–98.

Borman, W. C., & Motowidlo, S. J. (1997). Task performance and contextual performance: The meaning for personnel selection research. *Human Performance, 10*, 99–109.

Borman, W. C., Penner, L. A., Allen, T. D., & Motowidlo, S. J. (2001). Personality predictors of citizenship performance. *International Journal of Selection and Assessment, 9*, 52–69.

Bornstein, D. (2004). *How to change the world: Social entrepreneurs and the power of new ideas.* New York: Oxford University Press.

Bornstein, D. (2007). *How to change the world: Social entrepreneurs and the power of new ideas* (updated paperback edn). New York: Oxford University Press.

Boyatzis, R., Goleman, D., & Rhee, K. (2000). Clustering competence in emotional intelligence: insights from the emotional competence inventory (ECI). In R. Bar-On & J. D. A. Parker (Eds.), *Handbook of emotional intelligence* (pp. 343–362). San Francisco, CA: Jossey-Bass.

Brannen, L. (2008). The purpose-driven corporation; corporate responsibility programs are no longer just pr banter, but instead real tools for beefing up the bottom line.(Business Strategy). *Business Finance* October, *14*(10), 36. http://infotrac.galegroup.com/itweb/nysl_li_briar. Accessed October 13, 2008.

Brickson, S. L. (2007). Organizational identity orientation: The genesis of the role of the firm and distinct forms of social value. *Academy of Management Review, 32*, 864–888.

Brinckerhoff, P. C. (2000). *Social entrepreneurship: The art of mission-based venture development*. New York: Wiley.

Bruno, L. (2009). Online genie: Site connects the needy to the charitable. *USA Today*, April 24, 6A.

Carroll, A. B., & Buchholtz, A. K. (2007). *Business and society: Ethics and stakeholder management* (7th edn). Cincinnati, OH: South-Western College Publishing.

Cascio, W. F. (1987). *Applied psychology in personnel management* (3rd edn). Upper Saddle River, NJ: Prentice-Hall.

Chhokar, J. S., Brodbeck, F. C., & House, R. J. (Eds.) (2007). *Culture and leadership across the world: The GLOBE book of in-depth studies of 25 societies*. Mahwah, NJ: Erlbaum.

Cialdini, R. B., & Trost, M. R. (1998). Social influence: social norms, conformity, and compliance. *The Handbook of Social Psychology, 2*, 151–192.

Cialdini, R. B. (2001). *Influence: Science and practice* (4th edn). Boston, MA: Allyn & Bacon.

Cialdini, R. B., & Goldstein, N J. (2004). Social influence: Compliance and conformity. *Annual Review of Psychology, 55*, 591–621.

Clarkson, M. B. E. (1995). A stakeholder framework for analyzing and evaluating corporate social performance. *Academy of Management Review, 20*, 92–117.

Colvin, G. (1993/2005). *Fiscal sponsorship: Six ways to do it right*. San Francisco, CA: Study Center Press.

Committee Encouraging Corporate Philanthropy (2008). *Board of boards: The CEO's challenge—leading the company shaping society*. New York: Committee Encouraging Corporate Philanthropy. http://www.corporatephilanthropy.org/research/pubs/CECPBoardofBoards2008.pdf. Accessed July 28, 2008.

Conzemius, A., & O'Neill, J. (2005). *The power of Smart goals*. Bloomington, IN: Solution Tree.

Cook, K., & Whitmeyer, J. M. (1992). Two approaches to social structure: Exchange theory and network analysis. *Annual Review of Sociology, 18*, 109–127.

Covey, S. R. (1989, 2004). *The 7 habits of highly effective people*. New York: Free Press.

de Quevedo-Puente, E., de la Fuente-Sabaté, J. M., & Delgado-García, J. B. (2007). Corporate social performance and corporate reputation: Two interwoven perspectives. *Corporate Reputation Review, 10*, 60–72.

Decety, J., & Batson, C. D. (2007). Social neuroscience approaches to interpersonal sensitivity. *Social Neuroscience, 2*(3–4), 151–157.

Decety, J., & Ickes, W. (Eds.) (2009). *The social neuroscience of empathy*. Cambridge, MA: MIT Press.

Decety, J., & Jackson, P. L. (2006) A social-neuroscience perspective on empathy. *Current Directions in Psychological Science, 15*, 54–58.

Dees, J. G. (1998a). Enterprising nonprofits. *Harvard Business Review, 76*(1), 54–65.

Dees, J. G. (1998b). The meaning of "social entrepreneurship." Unpublished paper, Stanford University, Palo Alto, CA.

Dekker, P., & Uslaner, E. M. (2001). Introduction. In E. M. Uslaner (Ed.), *Social capital and participation in everyday life* (pp. 1–8). London: Routledge.

Devinney, T. M. (2009). Is the socially responsible corporation a myth? The good, the bad, and the ugly of corporate social responsibility. *Academy of Management Perspectives, 5*(2), 44–56.

Dizon, D. (2009). Google, Internet portals targeted by Chinese crackdown apologize. ABS-CBN News Online, January 8. http://www.abs-cbnnews.com/print/36229. Accessed April 28, 2009.

Doh, J. P., & Guay, T. R. (2006). Corporate social responsibility, public policy, and NGO activism in Europe and the United States: An institutional-stakeholder perspective. *Journal of Management Studies, 43*, 47–73.

Dovidio, J., Piliavin, J., Schroeder, D., & Penner, L. (2006). *The social psychology of prosocial behavior*. Mahwah, NJ: Lawrence Erlbaum.

Drayton, W. (2002). The citizen sector: Becoming as entrepreneurial and competitive as business. *California Management Review, 44*, 120–132.

Eisenhardt, K. M. (1989). Agency theory: An assessment and review. *Academy of Management Review, 14*, 57–74.

Elkington, J. (2004). Enter the triple bottom line. In A. Henriques & J. Richardson (Eds.), *The triple bottom line—Does it all add up?: Assessing the sustainability of business and CSR* (pp. 1–16). London: EarthScan.

Ericksen, J., & Dyer, L. (2004). Right from the start: Exploring the effects of early team events on subsequent project team development and performance. *Administrative Science Quarterly, 49*, 438–471.

Eviatar, D. (2005). A big win for human rights: Unocal's settlement with Burmese villagers may spur better corporate conduct. *The Nation*, May 9. http://www.thenation.com/doc/20050509/eviatar. Accessed April 28, 2009.

Ezell, M. (2000). *Advocacy in the human services*. Belmont, CA: Wadsworth.

Farmer, S. M., & Fedor, D. B. (1999). Volunteer participation and withdrawal. *Nonprofit Management and Leadership, 9*, 349–368.

Fehr, E., & Fischbacher, U. (2003). The nature of human altruism. *Nature, 425*, 785–791.

Fenwick. R., & Bierema, L. (2008). Corporate social responsibility: Issues for human resource development professionals. *International Journal of Training and Development, 12*, 24–35.

Freeman, R. B. (1997). Working for nothing: The supply of volunteer labor. *Journal of Labor Economics, 15*, 140–166.

Frye, J., & Ju, S. S. (1999). The Civil Rights impact of recent welfare changes. In C. M. Yu & W. L. Taylor (Eds.), *The test of our progress: The Clinton record on civil rights* (pp. 121–142). Washington, DC: Citizens' Commission on Civil Rights. http://www.ccr.org/doc/progress.pdf, and http://www.americanprogressaction.org/events/2008/09/ing/FryeJocelyn.html

Fukuyama, F. (1995). *Trust: The social virtues and the creation of prosperity*. London: Hamish Hamilton.

Glover, D. (2007). Mixing philanthropy with business. *People, land management, and ecosystem conservation*. May 24. http://c3.unu.edu/plec/plecServ/index.cfm?template=view_plecserv.cfm&message=203. Accessed April 28, 2009.

Goldstein, N. J., & Cialdini, R. B. (2007). The spyglass self: A model of vicarious self-perception. *Journal of Personality and Social Psychology, 92*, 402–417.

Goleman, D. (1995). *Emotional intelligence*. New York: Bantam Books

Goodpaster, K. E., & Mathews, J. B., Jr. (1982). Can a corporation have a conscience? *Harvard Business Review*, Jan.-Feb., 3–9.

Graafland, J., Kaptein, M., & Mazereeuw, C. (2007). Conceptions of God, normative convictions, and socially responsible business conduct: An exploratory study among executives. *Business & Society, 46*, 331–368.

Grant, A. M. (2007). Relational job design and the motivation to make a prosocial difference. *Academy of Management Review, 32*, 393–417.

Grant, A. M. (2008a). Does intrinsic motivation fuel the prosocial fire? Motivational synergy in predicting persistence, performance, and productivity. *Journal of Applied Psychology, 93*, 48–58.

Grant, A. M. (2008b). Task significance of task significance: Job performance effects, relational mechanisms and boundary conditions. *Journal of Applied Psychology, 93*, 108–124.

Grant, A. M., & Sumanth, J. J. (2009). Mission possible? The performance of prosocially motivated employees depends on manager trustworthiness. *Journal of Applied Psychology, 94*, 927–944.

Grant, A. M., Christianson, M. K., & Price, R. H. (2007). Happiness, health, or relationships? Managerial practices and employee well-being tradeoffs. *Academy of Management Perspectives, 21,* 51–63.

Grant, A. M., Dutton, J. E., & Russo, B. D. (2008). Giving commitment: Employee support programs and the prosocial sensemaking process. *Academy of Management Journal, 51,* 898–918.

Griffin, J. J., & Mahon, J. F. (1997). The corporate social performance and corporate financial performance debate. *Business & Society, 36,* 5–31.

Groenland, E. A. (1990). Structural elements of material well-being: An empirical test among people on social security. *Social Indicators Research, 22,* 367–384.

GSVC (Global Social Venture Competition) (2008). http://www.socialedge. org/features/opportunities/archive/2006/11/28/2007-global-social-venture-competition. Accessed September 1, 2008.

Hackman, J. R., & Wageman, R. (2005). A theory of team coaching. *Academy of Management Review, 30,* 269–287.

Hambrick, D. C., & Mason, P. A. (1984). Upper echelons: The organization as a reflection of its top managers. *Academy of Management Review, 9*(2), 193–106.

Hammonds, K. H. (2005). A lever long enough to move the world. *Fast Company, 90,* 60–63.

Harding, R. (2004). Social enterprise: The new economic engine. *Business Strategy Review, 15,* 39–43.

Harry, M., & Schroeder, R. (2000). *Six sigma.* New York: Doubleday.

Hatcher, T. (2002). *Ethics and HRD: A new approach to lending responsible organizations.* Cambridge, MA: Perseus Publishing.

Hisrich, R. L., Peters, M. P., & Shepard, D. A. (2005). *Entrepreneurship* (6th edn). New York: McGraw-Hill.

Hof, D. D., Scofield, T. R., & Dinsmore, J. A. (2006). Social advocacy: Assessing the impact of training on the development and implementation of advocacy plans. American Counseling Association, *Vistas,* Article 47, 211–213. http://counselingoutfitters.com/vistas/vistas06/vistas06.47.pdf. Accessed July 26, 2008.

Holland, K. (2009). Can volunteers be a lifeline for nonprofit groups? *New York Times Online,* January 24. http://www.nytimes.com/2009/01/25/jobs/25mgmt.html

Homans, G. (1961). *Social behavior.* New York: Harcourt, Brace & World.

Human Rights Watch (2004). *Blood, sweat, and fear: Workers' rights in U.S. meat and poultry plants.* New York: Human Rights Watch.

Institute for Sustainable Communities (2008). http://www. iscvt.org. Accessed July 30, 2008.

Jenkins-Smith, H., & Sabatier, P. (1994). Evaluating the advocacy coalition framework. *Journal of Public Policy, 14,* 175–203.

Kahneman, D., & Tversky, A. (1979). Prospect theory: An analysis of decision under risk. *Econometrica, 47,* 263–291.

Kamdar, D., McAllister, D. J., & Turban, D. B. (2006). "All in a day's work": How follower individual differences and justice perceptions predict OCB role definitions and behavior. *Journal of Applied Psychology, 91*(4), 841–855.

Kanter, R. M. (1999). The social sector as beta site for business innovation. *Harvard Business Review, 77*(3), 122–133.

Kaplan, T. (1997). *Crazy for democracy: Women's grassroots movements.* New York: Routledge.

Kaplan, J. M., & Warren, A. C. (2007). *Patterns of entrepreneurship* (2nd edn). Hoboken, NJ: John Wiley & Sons, Inc.

Karylowski, J. (1982). Two types of altruistic behavior: Doing good to feel good or to make the other feel good. In V. J. Derlega & J. Grzelak (Eds.), *Cooperation and helping behavior* (pp. 396–419). New York: Academic Press.

Kawasaki, G. (2004). *The art of the start: The time-tested, battle-hardened guide for anyone starting anything.* New York: Penguin.

Keller, R. (2006). Transformational leadership, initiative structure, and substitutes for leadership: A longitudinal study of research and development project team performance. *Journal of Applied Psychology, 91*, 202–210.

Kelley, H. H., & Thibaut, J. W. (1978). *Interpersonal relationships.* New York: John Wiley & Sons.

King, M. L., Jr. (1967). *Where do we go from here: Chaos or community.* Boston, MA: Beacon Press.

Kotler, P., & Lee, N. (2004). *Corporate social responsibility: Doing the most good for your company and your cause.* New York: Wiley.

Kuratko, D. F., & Hodgetts, R. M. (2004). *Entrepreneurship: Theory/practice/process* (6th edn). Mason, OH: Thomson South-Western.

Kuratko, D. F., & Hornsby, J. S. (2009). *New venture management: The entrepreneur's roadmap* [instructor's copy]. Upper Saddle River, NJ: Pearson: Prentice-Hall.

Landman, A., Ling, P. M., & Glantz, S. A. (2002). Tobacco industry youth smoking prevention programs: Protecting the industry and hurting tobacco control. *American Journal of Public Health, 92*, 917–930.

Leadbeater, C. (1997). *The rise of the social entrepreneur.* London: Demos.

Leiber, N. (2009). The most promising social entrepreneurs. *Business Week*, May 1. http://www.businessweek.com/smallbiz/content/may2009/sb2009051_730988.htm?chan=smallbiz_smallbiz+index+page_top+small+business+stories. Accessed May 5, 2009.

Lewis, K. (2003). Measuring transactive memory systems in the field: Scale development and validation. *Journal of Applied Psychology, 88*(4), 587–604.

Liao-Troth, M. A. (2001). Attitude differences between paid workers and volunteers. *Nonprofit Management & Leadership, 11*, 423–442.

Lohr, S. (2008). Starting over, with a second career goal of changing society. *New York Times*, December 13, B1, B8.

London, M. (2008). Leadership and advocacy: Dual roles for corporate social responsibility and social entrepreneurship. *Organizational Dynamics, 37,* 313–326.

London, M. (2010). Understanding social advocacy: An integrative model of motivation, strategy, and persistence in support of corporate social responsibility and social entrepreneurship. (In press, *Journal of Management Development*).

London, M., & London, M. (2007). *First time leaders of small groups.* San Francisco, CA: Jossey-Bass.

London, M., & Morfopoulos, R. G. (2009). Problem personalities in your office. ManageSmarter.com. January 26. http://www.managesmarter.com/msg/content_display/training/e3i7b57851228481ca5f839fc5d1afeb85b

London, M., & Noe, R. A. (1997). London's career motivation theory: An update on measurement and research. *Journal of Career Assessment, 51,* 61–80.

London, M., Polzer, J. T., & Omergerie, H. (2005). Interpersonal congruence, transactive memory, and feedback processes: an integrative model of group learning. *Human Resources Development Review, 4*(2), 114–135.

London, M., & Sessa, V. J. (2006). Group feedback for continuous learning. *Human Resources Development Review, 5,* 1–27.

Longenecker, J. G., Moore, C. W., Petty, J. W., & Palich, L. E. (2008). *Small business management: Launching and growing entrepreneurial ventures* (14th edn)., Mason, OH: Thomson South-Western.

Luthans, F. (2003). Positive organizational behavior POB: Implications for leadership and HR development, authentic leadership development, and motivation. In R. Steers, L. W. Porter, & G. A. Begley (Eds.), *Motivation and leadership at work.* New York: McGraw-Hill/Irwin.

Luthans, F., Avolio, B. J., Walumbwa, F. O., & Li, W. (2005). The psychological capital of Chinese workers: Exploring the relationship with performance. *Management and Organization Review, 1,* 249–271.

Mair, J., & Martí, I. (2006). Social entrepreneurship research: A source of explanation, prediction, and delight. *Journal of World Business, 41,* 36–44.

Manner, H. M. (2009a). *Human behavior and the corporate social responsibility of firm leaders. Altruism in the social sciences.* Hauppauge, NY: Nova Science Publishers.

Manner, H. M. (2009b). The impact of other regarding behavior and leader characteristics on decision making and corporate social responsibility. Troy, NY: Unpublished dissertation, Rensselaer Polytechnic Institute.

Margolis, J. D., & Walsh, J. P. (2003). Misery loves companies: Rethinking social initiatives by business. *Administrative Science Quarterly, 48,* 268–305.

Masaaki, I. (1997). *Gemba kaizen: A commonsense, low-cost approach to management.* New York: McGraw-Hill.

McAdam, D. (1988). *Freedom summer.* New York: Oxford.

McCarthy, J. D., & Zald, M. N. (1977). Resource mobilization and social movements: A partial theory. *American Journal of Sociology, 82*(6), 1212.

McCrae, R. R., & Costa, P. T. (1990). *Personality in adulthood.* New York: The Guilford Press.

McNeely, B. L., & Meglino, B. M. (1994). The role of dispositional and situational antecedents in pro-social organizational behavior: An examination of the intended beneficiaries of pro-social behavior. *Journal of Applied Psychology, 79,* 836–844.

Meyer, J. P., Becker, T. E., & Vandenberghe, C. (2004). Employee commitment and motivation: A conceptual analysis and integrative model. *Journal of Applied Psychology, 89,* 991–1007.

Michels, R. (1962). *Political parties: A sociological study of the oligarchical tendencies of modern democracy.* New York: Collier Books.

Morgeson, F. P. (2005). The external leadership of self-managing teams: Intervening in the context of novel and disruptive events. *Journal of Applied Psychology, 90,* 497–508.

Motowidlo, S. J., Borman, W. C., & Schmit, M. J. (1997). A theory of individual differences in task and contextual performance. *Human Performance, 10,* 71–83.

Naffziger, D. W., Hornsby, J. S., & Kuratko, D. F. (1994). A proposed research model of entrepreneurial motivation. *Entrepreneurship Theory and Practice,* Spring, 29–42.

Nash, J. (1950). The bargaining problem, *Econometrica, 18,* 155–162.

Olsen, P. R. (2008). The boss: Teamwork's rewards. http://www.nytimes.com/2008/02/24/jobs/24boss.html. Accessed February 24, 2008.

Organ, D. W., & Ryan, K. (1995). A meta-analytic review of attitudinal and dispositional predictors of organizational citizenship. *Personnel Psychology, 48,* 775–802.

Orlitzky, M., Schmidt, F. L., & Rynes, S. L. (2003). Corporate social and financial performance: A meta-analysis. *Organization Studies, 24,* 403–441.

Orlitzky, M., Siegel, D., & Waldman, D. (2009). Call for papers for a special issue of Business & Society: Corporate Social Responsibility and Environmental Sustainability. *Business & Society, 48,* 133–136.

Pande, P., Newman, R., & Cavanaugh, R. (2000). *The six sigma way.* New York: McGraw-Hill.

Paton, R. (2003). *Managing and measuring social enterprises.* London: Sage.

Pearce, J. L. (1983). Job attitude and motivation differences between volunteers and employees from comparable organizations. *Journal of Applied Psychology, 68,* 646–652.

Penner, L. A. (2002). Dispositional and organizational influences on sustained volunteerism: An interactionist perspective. *Journal of Social Issues, 58,* 447–467.

Penner, L. A. (2004). Volunteerism and social problems: Making things better or worse? *Journal of Social Issues, 60,* 645–666.

Penner, L. A., & Finkelstein, M. A. (1998). Dispositional and structural determinants of volunteerism. *Journal of Personality and Social Psychology, 74, 525–537.*

Penner, L. A., & Fritzche, B. A. (1993). *Measuring the prosocial personality: Four construct validity studies.* Toronto: American Psychological Association.

Penner, L. A., Dovidio, J. F., & Piliavin, J. A. (2005). Prosocial behavior: Multilevel perspectives. *Annual Review of Psychology, 56,* 1–28.

Penner, L. A., Dovidio, J. F., Piliavin, J. A., & Schroeder, D. A. (2005). Prosocial behavior: Multilevel perspectives. *Annual Review of Psychology, 56,* 365–392.

Peredo, A. M., & McLean, M. (2006). Social entrepreneurship: A critical review of the concept. *Journal of World Business, 41,* 56–65.

Perry, J. L., & Hondeghem, A. (2008). *Motivation in public management: The call of public service.* New York: Oxford University Press.

Piliavin, J. A., & Charng, H. W. (1990). Altruism: A review of recent theory and research. *Annual Review of Sociology, 16,* 27–65.

Plaks, J. E., Stroessner, S. J., Dweck, C. S., & Sherman, J. W. (2001). Person theories and attention allocation: Preferences for stereotypic versus counterstereotypic information. *Journal of Personality and Social Psychology, 80,* 876–893.

Podolny, J. M., Khurana, R., & Hill-Popper, M. (2005). Revisiting the meaning of leadership. In B. M. Staw & R. Kramer (Eds.), *Research in organizational behavior* (pp. 1–36). New York: Elsevier Science.

Polzer, J. T., Milton, L. P., & Swann, W. B. Jr. (2002). Capitalizing on diversity: Interpersonal congruence in small work groups. *Administrative Science Quarterly, 47,* 296–324.

Prohalad, C. K., & Porter, M. E. (Eds.) (2003). *Harvard Business Review on Corporate Responsibility.* Boston, MA: Harvard Business School Press.

Ratts, M., D'Andrea, M., & Arredondo, P. (2004). Social justice counseling: Fifth force in field. *Counseling Today,* 28–30. http://www.counseling.org/Content/NavigationMenu/PUBLICATIONS/COUNSELINGTODAYONLINE/JULY2004/SocialJusticeCounsel.htm. Accessed July 26, 2008.

Ravindran, N. (2009). Community outreach through corporate social responsibility. *Today's Manager,* January, 36.

Revere, L., Black, K., & Huq, A. (2004). Integrating six sigma and CQI for improving patient care, *The TQM Magazine, 16,*105–113.

Robinson, A. G., & Schroeder, D. M. (2009). Greener and cheaper: The conventional wisdom is that a company's costs rise as its environmental impact falls. Think again. *Wall Street Journal Online,* March 23, p. R4. http://online.wsj.com/article/SB 123739309941072501.html.

Rose, D. (2007). *Advocacy.* Port Melbourne: Cambridge University Press.

Rosen, R. (2000). *The world split open: How the modern women's movement changed America.* New York: Penguin.

Rosenthal, S. A., & Pittinsky, T. L. (2006). Narcissistic leadership. *The Leadership Quarterly, 17*, 617–633.

Ross, F. (1992). *Conquering Goliath: Cesar Chavez at the beginning.* Detroit, MI: Wayne State University Press.

Rushton, J. P. (1981). *Altruism, socialization, and society.* Englewood Cliffs, NJ: Prentice-Hall.

Ryan, R. M., & Deci, E. L. (2000). Self-determination theory and the facilitation of intrinsic motivation, social development, and well-being. *American Psychologist, 55*, 68–78.

Ryan, R. M., & Deci, E. L. (2001). To be happy or to be self-fulfilled: A review of research on hedonic and eudaimonic well-being. *Annual Review of Psychology, 52*, 141–166.

Saïd Business School (2007). http://www.sbs.ox.ac.uk/skoll/mba/Courses. htm. Accessed May 16, 2007.

Scheier, M. F., & Carver, C. S. (1985). Optimism, coping, and health: Assessment and implications of generalized outcome expectancies. *Health Psychology, 4*, 219–247.

Schwab Foundation for Social Entrepreneurship (2008). The social voice of innovation. http://www.schwabfound.org/whatis.htm. Accessed July 30, 2008.

Segerstrom, S. C., Taylor, S. E., Kemeny, M. E., & Fahey, J. L. (1998). Optimism is associated with mood, coping, and immune change in response to stress. *Journal of Personality and Social Psychology, 74*, 1646–1655.

Sen, R. (2003). *Stir it up: Lessons in community organizing and advocacy.* San Francisco, CA: Jossey-Bass.

Sessa, V. I., & London, M. (2006). *Continuous learning.* Mahwah, NJ: Erlbaum.

Shane, S. (2000). Prior knowledge and the discovery of entrepreneurial opportunities. *Organization Science, 11*, 448–469.

Shane, S., & Venkataram, S. (2000). The promise of entrepreneurship as a field of research. *Academy of Management Review, 25*, 217–226.

Sharma, R. R. (1996). *An introduction to advocacy: Training guide – Support for Analysis and Research in Africa (SARA) Project Advocacy.* Washington, DC: Academy for Educational Development.

Shelly, S. (2008). The power of one. *Reading Eagle, 28*(November), C1.

Seibert, S. E., Kraimer, M. L., & Crant, J. M. (2001). What do proactive people do? A longitudinal model linking proactive personality and career success. *Personnel Psychology, 54*, 845–874.

Simone, K. S., & Adler, B. B. (2008). *The rules of the road: A guide to the law of charities in the United States* (2nd edn). Washington, DC: Council on Foundations.

Sirsly, C. A. T., & Lamertz, K. (2008). When does a corporate social responsibility initiative provide a first-mover advantage? *Business & Society, 47*, 343–369.

Skoll Foundation (2007). http://www.skollfoundation.org/aboutskoll/index. asp Accessed March 14, 2007.

Slovic, P., Fischhoff, B., & Lichtenstein, S. (1977). Behavioral decision theory. *Annual Review of Psychology, 28*, 1–39.

Smith, C. A., Organ, D. W., & Near, J. P. (1983). Organizational citizenship behavior: Its nature and antecedents. *Journal of Applied Psychology, 68*, 653–663.

Snyder, C. R. (1994). *The psychology of hope: You can get to there from here.* New York: Free Press.

Snyder, C. R. (2000). The past and possible future of hope. *Journal of Social and Clinical Psychology, 19*, 11–28.

Social Edge (2007). http://www.socialedge.org. Accessed March 16, 2007.

Spreier, S. W., Fontaine, M. H., & Mallow, R. L. (2006). Leadership run amok: The destructive potential of overachievers. *Harvard Business Review, 84*(June), 72–82.

Storper, J. S. (2008). Corporate social responsibility and good corporate governance: Is there room for both? Paper presented at the Association of Corporate Counsel, San Francisco Bay Area Chapter, 2008 CLE Spring Training Day (April).

Strom, S. (2007). Make money, save the world: Businesses and nonprofits are spawning corporate hybrids. *The New York Times*, Sunday, May 6, 3–1, 8.

SustainAbility (2004). *Risk and opportunity: Best practice in non-financial reporting.* London: SustainAbility.

Social Work Community Outreach Service, University of Maryland (2007). http://www.oea.umaryland.edu/gov/community/programs/socialwork. html?id=427. Accessed on March 15, 2007.

Sykes, N. (1999). Is the organization encoded with a "DNA" which determines its development? Unpublished paper presented at The Visioneers Conference, Putteridge Bury Management Centre, April.

Terry, S. (2007). Genius at work. *Fast Company*. http://www.fastcompany. com/magazine/17/genius.html. Accessed December 18, 2007.

Thompson, J. A., & Bunderson, J. S. (2003). Violations of principle: Ideological currency in the psychological contract. *Academy of Management Review, 28*, 571–586.

Thompson, A. A. Jr., Strickland, A. J. III, & Gamble, J. E. (2005). *Crafting and executing strategy: The quest for competitive advantage* (14th edn). New York: McGraw-Hill/Irwin.

Thompson, J., Alvy, G., & Lees, A. (2000). Social entrepreneurship: A new look at the people and the potential. *Management Decision, 38*, 328–338.

Torraco, R. J. (2004). Challenges and choices for theoretical research in human resource development. *Human Resource Development Quarterly, 15*, 171–188.

Tracey, P., & Phillips, N. (2007). The distinctive challenge of educating social entrepreneurs: A postscript and rejoinder to the special issue on entrepreneurship education. *Academy of Management Learning & Education, 6:* 264–271.

Trudel, R., & Cotte, J. (2009). Does it pay to be good. *Sloan Management Review, 52,* 61–68.

Tyson, L. D'A. (2008). Good works, with a business plan. *Economic Viewpoint: Business Week.* http://www.ashoka.org/files/newsletters/news/04november/tyson.html. Accessed October 5, 2008.

University Network for Social Entrepreneurship (2007). http://www.universitynetwork.org. Accessed on May 16, 2007.

Uslaner, E. M. (2001). Volunteering and social capital: How trust and religion shape civic participation in the United States. In E. M. Uslaner (Ed.), *Social capital and participation in everyday life* (pp. 104–117). London: Routledge.

VeneKlasen, L. (1995). *Policy players: A power map for advocacy planning.* Washington, DC: InterAction.

Venkataraman, S. (1997). The distinctive domain of entrepreneurship research. In J. Katz & R. Brockhaus (Eds.), *Advances in entrepreneurship, firm emergence, and growth* (vol. 3, pp. 119–138). Greenwich, CT: JAI Press.

Waddock, S. A., & Graves, S. B. (1998). The corporate social performance-financial performance link. *Strategic Management Journal, 18,* 303–319.

Wall, E. A. (2008). Developing a coordinated corporate social responsibility program. *Marketing the law firm: Incisive media.* http://infotrac.galegroup.com/itweb/nysl_li_briar. Accessed October 10, 2008.

Wegner, D. M. (1986). Transactive memory: A contemporary analysis of the group mind. In B. Mullen & G. R. Goethals (Eds.), *Theories of group behavior* (pp. 185–208). New York: Springer-Verlag.

Wei-Skillern, J. C., Austin, J. E., Leonard, H. B., & Stevenson, H. H. (2007). *Entrepreneurship in the social sector.* Thousand Oaks, CA: Sage.

Whiting, S. W., Podsakoff, P. M., & Pierce, J. R. (2008). Effects of task performance, helping, voice, and organizational loyalty on performance appraisal ratings. *Journal of Applied Psychology, 93,* 125–139.

Wilcox, T. (2006). Human resource development as an element of corporate social responsibility. *Asia Pacific Journal of Human Resources, 44,* 184–196.

Wilson, J. (2000). Volunteering. *Annual Review of Sociology, 26,* 215–240.

Wilson, J., & Musick. M. (1997). Who cares? Toward an integrated theory of volunteer work. *American Sociological Review 62,* 694–713.

Wilson, T. D., & Gilbert, D. T. (2008). Explaining away: A model of affective adaptation. *Perspectives on Psychological Science, 3,* 370–386.

Woodall, J., & Douglas, D. (2000). Winning hearts and minds: Ethical issues in human resource development. In D. Winstanley & J. Woodall (Eds.), *Ethical issues in contemporary human resource management.* Basingstoke: Macmillan Business.

Zafirovski, M. (2005). Social exchange theory under scrutiny: A positive critique of its economic-behaviorist formulations. *Electronic Journal of Sociology*, 1–39. http://www.sociology.org/content/2005/tier2/SETheory.pdf.

Zahra, S. A., Gedajlovic, E., Neubaum, D., & Shulman, J. (in press). Typology of social entrepreneurs: Motives, search processes and ethical challenges. *Journal of Business Venturing, 24*(5), 519–532.

Zahra, S. A., Rawhouser, H. N., Bhawe, N., Neubaum, D. O., & Hayton, J. C. (2008). Globalization of social entrepreneurship opportunities. *Strategic Entrepreneurship Journal, 2*, 117–131.

Zalesny, M. D., & Ford, J. K. (1990). Extending the social information processing perspective: New links to attitudes, behaviors, and perceptions. *Organizational Behavior and Human Decision Processes, 47*, 205–246.

Zappalà, G. (2004). Corporate citizenship and human resource management: A new tool or a missed opportunity? *Asia Pacific Journal of Human Resources, 42*, 185–201.

Index